The Lieutenant Governors of British Columbia

THE
LIEUTENANT GOVERNORS
OF
BRITISH COLUMBIA

Jenny Clayton

HARBOUR
PUBLISHING

Harbour Publishing Co. Ltd.
P.O. Box 219, Madeira Park, BC, V0N 2H0
www.harbourpublishing.com

Edited by Betty Keller
Indexed by Ellen Hawman
Cover design by Setareh Ashrafologhalai
Text design by Roger Handling
Printed and bound in Canada
Front cover images: Stained glass: Dorin_S/iStock; Steven Point: Diana Nethercott/ The Canadian Press; Janet Austin: © Province of British Columbia. Reproduced with permission; Iona Campagnolo: Government House of British Columbia
Back cover images: Eric and Aldyen Hamber: Royal BC Museum and Archives, G-04600; Judith Guichon: John Ducker photo; Woodward opening session: Royal BC Museum and Archives, D-05922; David and Dorothy Lam: Government House of British Columbia Archives
Title page photo: Lieutenant Governor Robert Randolph Bruce and his party, Galiano Island, May 1929. Royal BC Museum and Archives, F-02893

Harbour Publishing acknowledges the support of the Canada Council for the Arts, which last year invested $153 million to bring the arts to Canadians throughout the country.

Nous remercions le Conseil des arts du Canada de son soutien. L'an dernier, le Conseil a investi 153 millions de dollars pour mettre de l'art dans la vie des Canadiennes et des Canadiens de tout le pays.

We also gratefully acknowledge financial support from the Government of Canada and from the Province of British Columbia through the BC Arts Council and the Book Publishing Tax Credit.

Library and Archives Canada Cataloguing in Publication

Title: The lieutenant governors of British Columbia / Jenny Clayton.
Names: Clayton, Jenny, 1977- author.
Description: Includes bibliographical references and index.
Identifiers: Canadiana (print) 20190064331 | Canadiana (ebook) 2019006434X | ISBN 9781550178647 (softcover) | ISBN 9781550178654 (HTML)
Subjects: LCSH: Lieutenant governors—British Columbia—Biography. | LCSH: Lieutenant governors—British Columbia. | LCSH: British Columbia—Biography. | LCSH: British Columbia—Politics and government.
Classification: LCC FC3805 .C53 2019 | DDC 971.10092/2—dc23

Contents

Foreword

WHEN I WAS FIRST approached to write the foreword for this book, it was only a few weeks after my installation as the thirtieth Lieutenant Governor of British Columbia. At the time, I was still absorbing the many facets of my new post and the immense responsibilities that accompany it—from serving as the Crown's direct representative in British Columbia to upholding the framework of our constitution and ensuring the stability of our provincial government.

As the weeks turned into months, I had the opportunity to travel throughout British Columbia, visiting the many communities of our province. Whether I was attending a conference on food banks in Kelowna, visiting a seniors' home on Salt Spring Island or watching a children's choir perform in Yarrow, it quickly became apparent to me that one of the most important aspects of the Lieutenant Governor's role is to shine a light on our province's greatest asset: its people.

Throughout the calendar year, the Lieutenant Governor hosts several awards programs to celebrate the accomplishments of British Columbians. Exemplary citizens are regularly invited to Government House in Victoria, the ceremonial home of all British Columbians, where they are honoured for their efforts to improve the lives of those around them. It's one of the aspects of the role that I enjoy the most.

The Lieutenant Governor is also a staunch supporter and promoter of British Columbia itself, tasked with profiling our province's rich history, multicultural society and its natural beauty—all of which it has in spades.

In short, I have the best job a proud British Columbian could ask for.

However, it's important to acknowledge that I stand on the shoulders of the twenty-nine individuals who held this post before me, and who—each in their unique way—helped to shape the province that we call home today.

Within the pages of this book, you will learn their stories. You will read about what motivated these individuals, about their lives before they were appointed Lieutenant Governor, about the historical context in which they served and about the legacies they left behind.

I applaud the author of this book, Dr. Jenny Clayton, for her diligent and meticulous work to unearth and breathe new life into the stories of these men and women, and in the process, to raise awareness of the Lieutenant Governor's roles in British Columbia.

It is a tradition that each Lieutenant Governor has the opportunity to develop programs and initiatives that address societal issues they deem to be important. For my term, I have identified three themes that I would like to focus on, which include reconciliation with Canada's Indigenous peoples, championing inclusion, diversity and gender equality, and building support for our democracy and public institutions.

Like many, I have grown increasingly concerned about the fragility of our democracy, the erosion of respect for the institutions that support it and the decline of civility in public discourse around the globe. As Lieutenant Governor, I hope to promote and encourage democratic literacy, particularly by engaging youth and the next generation of voters. I will also encourage British Columbians to participate in courteous dialogue and informed decision making that transcends partisanship.

I feel this responsibility deeply, and sincerely hope that I can use my mandate as Lieutenant Governor to make a positive contribution to our society and, ultimately, make our province a better place.

I draw inspiration every day from the exceptional individuals that I meet in every corner of British Columbia. For that, I thank you.

Thank you also to all who made this book possible, including the Province of British Columbia, the Royal BC Museum, BC Archives, Harbour Publishing and the Government House Foundation.

A particularly special thanks is due to author Jenny Clayton, as well as the former Lieutenant Governors and the friends and families of LGs past. Thanks as well to the wonderful Friends of Government House Gardens Society volunteer archivists, notably Caroline, Carmel and Elaine.

The Honourable Janet Austin, OBC
Lieutenant Governor of British Columbia

Introduction

THE IDEA FOR THIS BOOK had its origins during the term of His Honour Steven Point (2007–12), when then-Private Secretary James Hammond along with Director of Operations Jerymy Brownridge (Private Secretary since 2015) and the staff at Government House initiated a number of projects to raise awareness of the Lieutenant Governor's roles. They updated the website to outline the vice-regal, constitutional, celebratory and promotional roles and commissioned interpretive signs—for which I supplied text and images—that were installed on the grounds of Government House in the summer of 2012. That year Government House also unveiled a statue of James Douglas sculpted by Armando Barbon, and raised a totem pole, *Hosaqami*, carved by Chief Tony Hunt, on the lawn in front of the entrance. In October 2012 incoming Lieutenant Governor Judith Guichon attended a conference on the Crown in Canada in Regina; in January 2016 she hosted a similar conference in Victoria.

Meanwhile, when perusing the extensive collection of constitutional and historical books on the shelves at Government House, James Hammond noted that the most recent historical studies of BC's Lieutenant Governors were written by D.A. McGregor in 1967 and S.W. Jackman in 1972. Perhaps it was time, Hammond suggested, to update these studies with a new one exploring how the role of the Lieutenant Governor has evolved into the twenty-first century.

When Government House approached me with this book concept, I was excited to have the opportunity to build on the knowledge I had gained while writing content in 2012 for the interpretive signs. In my years of researching and teaching the history of British Columbia, I had noted that although Lieutenant Governors showed up almost everywhere, their constitutional and ceremonial actions were rarely central to the story. This book would be a chance to shine a spotlight on their life stories and explore how they had interpreted the role to which they were appointed.

A chapter on the colonial governors sets the stage for the transition to provincial status and responsible government; it is followed by biographies of the Lieutenant Governors organized into sections based on broad historical changes. Their stories show how Lieutenant Governors carried out their vice-regal and constitutional responsibilities, which remained fairly constant, while their role as federal agents was diminishing and their ceremonial and promotional roles were expanding. The book also explores their shifting identities and priorities, their changing relationships with First Nations and their ongoing legacy projects.

I

The Evolving Role of British Columbia's Lieutenant Governors

The offices of Governor General and Lieutenant Governor are constitutional fire extinguishers with a potent mixture of powers for use in great emergencies. Like real extinguishers, they appear in bright colours and are strategically located. But everyone hopes their emergency powers will never be used; the fact they are not used does not render them useless; and it is generally understood that there are severe penalties for tampering with them.

—Frank MacKinnon, *The Crown in Canada*[1]

ALTHOUGH THE POSITION of Lieutenant Governor had antecedents in the previous century in British North America, the modern position as it is known in Canada was created at Confederation. Appointed by the Governor General on the advice of the prime minister, Canadian Lieutenant Governors generally serve for a period of five years. Although they may have had political affiliations prior to their appointment, while serving in this position they must be politically neutral so that they can represent all citizens and act as an independent arbiter in times of constitutional crises.

As the personal representative of the Crown in the provinces, Lieutenant Governors play a vital role in Canada's constitutional monarchy. They hold powers similar to those of the Governor General at the federal level, but with very few exceptions in the course of conducting the routine business of government they exercise these powers only on the advice of the premier. For example, after an election, the Lieutenant Governor appoints the premier of the province—either the leader of the party that elected the most members to the Legislature or that person who can command the support of the majority of the elected members from more than one party. At the opening of a new session of the Legislature the vice-regal representative reads the throne speech, which is prepared by the governing party and reflects that party's goals. The Lieutenant Governor opens, prorogues and dissolves the Legislature, and throughout the session he or she gives royal assent to bills so that they can become law, and approves orders-in-council.

The architects of Confederation had also wanted Lieutenant Governors to be federal agents in order to give the federal government some control over provincial laws and politics. However, the power balance shifted after 1892 when a ruling of the Judicial Committee of the Privy Council declared that Lieutenant Governors were just as much representatives of the Crown as their federal counterparts. Despite this ruling, vice-regal representatives in BC continued to act on occasion on behalf of the federal government— for example, in 1903 Henri-Gustave Joly de Lotbinière worked behind the scenes to institute party government in BC—and until 1920 representatives of the Crown in BC continued to reserve occasional bills for consideration by the Governor General. Over time, however, this role as federal agent has largely disappeared.

As well as providing vice-regal representation at the provincial level, one of the primary responsibilities of the Lieutenant Governor is the stability of the provincial government, which means ensuring there is always a premier in place who enjoys the confidence of a majority of the elected members of the Legislature. In rare cases— for example, when there is no obvious majority in the Legislature— Lieutenant Governors have exercised their discretionary or reserve powers. These reserve powers, also known as royal prerogatives, give them the right to reject the advice of the premier and include the right to dismiss and appoint a premier, withhold royal assent and refuse a dissolution of the Legislature.

Since their constitutional tasks usually take place behind the scenes, vice-regal representatives in British Columbia are often better known for their ceremonial activities such as providing hospitality to members of the royal family, heads of state, ambassadors and Governors General. They also host many events at Government House, including the New Year's Day Levée, award ceremonies and functions for various branches of the uniformed services. They serve as patrons of a wide range of organizations and highlight the work of volunteers by recognizing individuals who have given of their time and efforts to make the province a better place.

Over the twentieth century, these ceremonial and promotional roles have expanded considerably. Since the 1920s Lieutenant Governors have travelled more extensively to communities throughout the province to meet British Columbians and raise awareness of social and economic initiatives. Many vice-regal representatives have invested their time and even their salaries to renovate Government House and beautify the gardens. Since 2000 they have created their own programs and awards to celebrate cultural excellence and promote literacy, creativity and environmental awareness. In the last three decades appointees have more accurately represented the diversity of BC's population. They have also acted to promote greater understanding among British Columbians from different cultural and geographic backgrounds. As historian and private secretary Christopher McCreery observes, the Lieutenant Governor serves as the constitutional head of the province while at the same time acting as its "promoter-in-chief."[2]

II

The Governors (1849–71)

IN THE FIVE DECADES between 1791 and 1840 colonial governors in British North America held broad powers. These representatives of the Crown, generally born and educated in Britain, appointed their own executive councils and legislative councils. At first they also had the power to cancel any bill passed by an elected assembly and even dismiss such an assembly. This began to change, however, in the 1840s as Great Britain moved away from the mercantile system that had favoured its colonies and adopted a policy of free trade.

With settler colonies no longer its primary source of raw materials, paying for their administration and defence became less attractive, and the mother country became more willing to allow them to manage their own affairs. Governors were advised to form a cabinet from the party that elected the majority of members and to give assent to legislation that was passed with the approval of the majority of elected representatives. By 1849 these principles were active in British North American colonies and formed a precedent at Confederation when governors were replaced by Lieutenant Governors.

Great Britain's westernmost colonies in North America were established in Indigenous territories that had been integrated into the global fur trade economy since the late eighteenth century. However, the Hudson's Bay Company had only set up Fort Victoria, its first trading post on Vancouver Island, in 1843. This was a far-sighted move, since the company would lose access to the territory south of the 49th parallel with the passage of the Oregon Treaty three years later. The HBC's next move was to propose to the British government that it would colonize the island in exchange for a monopoly on trading for furs and other resources there. Having turned to free trade, Britain was not eager to establish new colonies. Yet, because this proposal would ensure a British presence on the Pacific Coast and the company would be responsible for both administration and defence, the government signed on, though limiting the arrangement to a ten-year period.

The colony of Vancouver Island was established without consultation with culturally and linguistically diverse Indigenous people whose communities had resided on the Island for thousands of years. For Indigenous people of this region and what would become British Columbia, colonization had many deep and lasting consequences, including the loss of land, devastating population loss resulting from introduced diseases, the interruption of traditional forms of law and governance, and a subordinate status within the new colony and nation.

—⁓—

The Colonial Office had retained the right to select the governor of this new colony, and its choice for the first incumbent was Richard Blanshard (1817–94), who had been born into a merchant family in London. He was just thirty-two when appointed and had little training for the post. He had studied to be a lawyer but had not practised law, and then travelled in the West Indies for a couple of years and served with distinction in the Sikh War of 1848–49. When he accepted the post, he agreed to serve without pay, as he expected to receive compensation in the form of a thousand-acre grant in the colony.

When he arrived at the fort in March 1850, no house had been prepared for him to live in, and he stayed on board HMS *Driver* before moving into an empty storehouse to wait until his house was completed that fall. The Colonial Office had instructed him to establish a legislative council and elected assembly, but he found few local residents with the property qualifications required to vote,

Appointed as the first governor of Vancouver Island in 1849, Richard Blanshard had difficulty governing a settler population that was almost entirely employed by the Hudson's Bay Company.

Image courtesy of Royal BC Museum and Archives, A–01112.

and almost all of them were employees of the HBC and therefore partial to the company's interests.

As a newcomer to the area, Blanshard felt vulnerable to Indigenous threats and responded by punishing groups of people for the crimes of a few. When three British sailors who deserted the HBC in 1850 were killed near Fort Rupert, Blanshard placed the blame on the Tlatlasikwala (Nahwitti) people of northern Vancouver Island and travelled north by gunboat on two occasions to have two Nahwitti villages destroyed.

After his return to Fort Victoria, Blanshard became very ill, possibly from exposure to weather while travelling by canoe. He asked for permission to resign, but due to the time required for letters to go from Victoria to London and for replies to be received, he had to wait nine months for approval. Finally, in early September 1851 Blanshard left the colony and returned to England. Just two days before he left, he had his first and last meeting with the council he had appointed, which included Chief Trader John Tod, James Douglas and settler James Cooper.

The colony's second governor was James Douglas (1803–77). Born in British Guiana, he was one of the three sons of John Douglas, a Glasgow merchant, and Martha Ann Telfer, a "free coloured woman" of Guiana. When John Douglas returned to Scotland in 1812, he took the boys with him to be educated in Lanark. At sixteen, James re-crossed the Atlantic to become an apprentice with the North West Company, which was based in Montreal, and proved himself a competent employee. The company merged with the Hudson's Bay Company in March 1821, and in the spring of 1826 Douglas was sent west to assist Chief Factor William Connolly in setting up a brigade route from the upper Fraser River south to the confluence of the Okanagan and Columbia rivers. The next spring Douglas married Amelia Connolly, "according to the custom of the country." She was the daughter of William Connolly and his Cree wife Miyo Nipiy.

An incident at Stuart Lake in 1828 helps illustrate Douglas's character. After a Carrier man beat to death an HBC employee near Stuart Lake, Douglas led a group of HBC men to find the killer and avenge the murder. They found him in the local Carrier settlement and killed him without holding a trial. The Carrier chief, Kwah, was away at the time, but when he returned he led a group of men to the trading post. Douglas ordered them to leave, but one of Kwah's men grabbed Douglas and held a knife to his throat. According to some versions of the story, it was Amelia's intercession that saved Douglas's life; she persuaded Chief Kwah to tell the man to put down his knife and let Douglas go.

Soon after this incident, possibly to keep the peace between the Carrier people and the men of the fort, Douglas was transferred to Fort Vancouver on the Columbia River. From there he travelled widely, carrying out negotiations with Russian fur traders to the north and Spanish administrators to the south to establish boundaries and obtain trading rights. In 1842–43 it was Douglas's job to establish Fort Victoria in Lekwungen territory on the southern tip of Vancouver Island, and after the Oregon Treaty of 1846, he was responsible for relocating all HBC operations north of the new border. When the British government granted the HBC the right to establish a settler colony on Vancouver Island, Douglas expected to be appointed the first governor, but he was passed over in favour of Blanshard. It was only with Blanshard's failure that the government realized the value of a governor who was familiar with the land and the people.

Following the advice of the Colonial Office, Douglas purchased land from local First Nations where he thought it would be needed by settlers. These transactions indicated that Britain recognized Aboriginal title to land, and adhered to a policy of extinguishing Aboriginal title before offering the land to settlers. These sales agreements or treaties allocated reserve land to the Indigenous people at their village sites and confirmed their right to hunt on unoccupied territory and fish as they had traditionally fished. However, neither party to these treaties spoke the other's language, although interpreters may have spoken the trade language of Chinook in common. As a result, there were misunderstandings about whether the land was to be used, owned or rented by the newcomers. According to the oral history of the W'SÁNEĆ (Saanich) people north of Victoria, the treaty that Douglas made with them was not seen as a land purchase, but as a peace treaty, since it took place shortly after a W'SÁNEĆ boy had been killed near Mount Douglas (Pkols) and loggers had cut timber without permission at Cadboro Bay. As settlers occupied and cultivated more and more land, this diminished the game and traditional food sources of the Indigenous people.

The non-Indigenous population of Vancouver Island did not increase significantly, however, until a gold rush on the Fraser River in 1858 lured thousands of miners and entrepreneurs north of the 49th parallel. The HBC had known about the gold for a number of years as the company had been purchasing gold dust from the Stó:lō and Nlaka'pamux people who collected it from the Thompson and Fraser rivers, but Douglas had hoped to keep this trade quiet, fearing that having a predominantly American population enter the territory would threaten British authority. However, by the summer of 1857 the Nlaka'pamux people were attempting to keep American miners out of their territory on the Thompson River. In response to this problem and without official approval, which would have taken months to arrive by mail, in December 1857 James Douglas extended colonial control over the mainland. He also imposed a licence fee on miners and a 10 per cent tax on imported goods. When word of his actions reached the Colonial Office in March 1858, Herman Merivale, the colonial undersecretary, was favourably impressed:

> Gov. Douglas deserves in my opinion much credit for acting—as he always has done—with promptitude & intelligence in the line pointed out to him by the home Government, and making light of difficulties instead of creating them, in a position by no means clear & with very little assistance of any kind.[3]

The trickle of miners became a rush in April 1858 when the American sidewheeler *Commodore* steamed into Victoria with more than four hundred miners on board, most of them bound for Fort Yale on the Fraser River. That summer violence broke out between the miners and Stó:lō, Nlaka'pamux and Okanagan people in what became known as the "Fraser River War," and the miners, who organized themselves into armed militia, wrote to Douglas to ask him to restore order. They had already signed peace treaties with a council of Nlaka'pamux, Kenpesq't (Shuswap) and Okanagan people at Lytton before Douglas arrived on the scene with a party of Royal Engineers, but in a rather symbolic act, Douglas had the American miners swear allegiance to the Crown.

Britain formally established the Colony of British Columbia on August 2, 1858, and James Douglas was appointed governor of his second colony, although he was now required to resign his position

A long-term employee of the fur trade, James Douglas became governor of Vancouver Island in 1851 and governor of the mainland colony of British Columbia in 1858. An agent of colonialism who recognized Aboriginal title—at least for a time—and instructed surveyors to set aside reserves large enough to meet the needs of the Indigenous population, Douglas left a complex legacy that is still being debated today.

Image courtesy of Royal BC Museum and Archives, A–O1229.

with the HBC. On November 19, 1858, the new government was installed at Fort Langley. Two of Douglas's primary preoccupations would be building roads to the goldfields and establishing British law and order.

Smallpox came to Victoria on March 13, 1862, carried by a passenger on the steamship *Brother Jonathan* from San Francisco. The ensuing epidemic was catastrophic. Within days of the ship's arrival the disease was infecting residents of the city, but Indigenous residents were hit even harder as they did not have the same level of immunity as Eurasian peoples, who had lived with the disease for millennia. Governor James Douglas and Hudson's Bay Company physician Dr. John Sebastian Helmcken met with the leaders of the local Lekwungen, today known as the Songhees, and started a program of vaccination. Meanwhile, however, the disease spread to encampments of northern coastal First Nations who had come to Victoria for trade and work. Although a few citizens, particularly the missionaries, responded with compassion and assistance to the suffering, ultimately police commissioner Augustus Pemberton made the decision to force First Nations people to return to their home communities, a policy he backed up with a gunboat escort on May 11. This decision had appalling results. It is estimated that about 90 per cent of Indigenous people on the northwest coast died during this smallpox epidemic. After the disease spread inland, about twenty thousand people, or 62 per cent of the Indigenous population of what would become British Columbia, were killed by smallpox.[4]

Already by the mid-1850s Douglas had stopped extinguishing Aboriginal title through land purchases, possibly due to lack of funds. Instead, he instructed surveyors to mark out reserves on the mainland according to the wishes of the Indigenous groups, and after 1860 the Colonies initiated a pre-emption system of land settlement for newcomers. This was a multi-step process that allowed settlers access to very cheap land even before it was surveyed. As a first step, the settler claimed a quarter section (160 acres/65 hectares), lived on it and made certain "improvements" including clearing the land, building fences, growing crops, raising livestock and building a residence. At this point he could apply for a certificate of improvement. The land was then surveyed and could be purchased for an outlay of one dollar per acre. Not surprisingly, Indigenous people often contested pre-emptions on their lands. Douglas, still hoping to make a place for Indigenous people in the new settler economy, allowed them to pre-empt land as well, but after he retired and Joseph Trutch became Commissioner of Lands and Works, this right was removed. In addition, Trutch and his assistants ignored the reserve boundaries that Douglas had instructed his surveyors to mark on the mainland and systematically reduced the size of reserves.

—⚭—

When Douglas retired in 1864, he was replaced by two governors. Arthur Edward Kennedy (1809–83) was assigned to Vancouver Island and Frederick Seymour (1820–69) to the mainland colony of British Columbia. Kennedy was born in Northern Ireland, the fourth son in an elite family. After attending Trinity College in Dublin, his first career was in the British army, in which he became a captain and served two stints in British North America between 1838 and 1844. In 1847 he was hired to be the Poor Law inspector in County Clare, Ireland, and oversee relief for its destitute inhabitants during the potato famine. He became deeply sympathetic to the plight of the poor, recalling that "there were days in that western county when I came back from some scene of eviction so maddened by the sights of hunger and misery . . . that I felt disposed to take the gun from behind my door and shoot the first landlord I met."[5] In 1851 when this office was dissolved, Kennedy sought work in the colonial service and over the next decade served as governor of Sierra Leone and then of Western Australia, where he tried to clean up corruption, reduce inefficiencies and increase revenues by attracting settlement and promoting research into available resources. In his enthusiasm for reform, however, he occasionally offended local administrators or overstepped his broad constitutional rights.

New budget cuts by the Colonial Office meant that Vancouver Island and British Columbia had to pay their own employees, so when Kennedy arrived in Victoria in March 1864, he discovered the assembly had put off purchasing a residence for him. The new governor and his family stayed at the St. George's Hotel, later renting Trutch's house while he was in England. In an open letter to the *British Colonist*, Kennedy pointed out that under these circumstances, he could not be expected to do his job properly: "My desire is to come into contact with all classes of the population, and I am only sorry that the house I have engaged will not afford me from its smallness, the opportunity of meeting as many of the inhabitants as I could wish."[6] As there was some sense that the governor should reside in a house befitting his station, in February 1865 the assembly approved $50,000 to purchase land and build and furnish a house. Meanwhile, Kennedy decided to buy his own house, Cary Castle, on the site of the present Government House, and the colony then assumed the costs of renovating and furnishing it. The Kennedys hosted their first ball there on October 26 with four hundred guests.

The third governor of Vancouver Island, Arthur Edward Kennedy, bought Cary Castle as the governor's residence in 1865 so he could better fulfill the governor's social role.
Image courtesy of Royal BC Museum and Archives, A–01402.

In his two years in office Kennedy concentrated on improving the education system, and his support for a universal education system resulted in the 1865 Common School Act. He also offered the government's financial support to a company that would identify sources of minerals on Vancouver Island, ultimately funding the

"Vancouver Island Exploring Expedition" led by Dr. Robert Brown. This expedition, which set off in June 1864, found gold in Sooke, launching the brief Leech River gold rush and increasing settler knowledge of the interior of Vancouver Island from Sooke to the southern end of Buttle Lake.

Although Kennedy treated Indigenous people in a paternalistic manner, he did support fair compensation for their lands. Unfortunately, by this point the Colonial Office had stopped insisting on treaties and rejected the Crown's responsibility to provide compensation. Kennedy also blamed the alcohol trade for so-called moral vices among the Indigenous population and tried to make it easier to convict whisky traders, but this move was blocked by the assembly. At the same time, when Kennedy thought it necessary, he sent out the gunboats to control the Indigenous population; for example, when Ahousaht people killed the captain and three crew members of the trading sloop *Kingfisher*, Kennedy approved of the bombardment of nine Ahousaht villages by the fifty-gun frigate HMS *Sutlej* to punish the entire community. In the shelling of these villages, thirteen people were killed.

Like Kennedy, Frederick Seymour had served in several other British colonies before being posted to British Columbia in 1864. Born in Belfast in 1820, he was the youngest son of Henry Augustus Seymour, the natural son of the second Marquis of Hertford, and as long as the second Marquis was alive, Henry Augustus received an income, position and accommodation. However, when the third Marquis succeeded his father in 1822, Henry Augustus and his family lost these advantages and moved to Brussels. As the youngest son, Frederick was not as well educated as his older brothers, though he did have certain occupational advantages, thanks to the fact that his eldest brother, Francis, had a successful military career, held positions at Kensington Palace and had become friends with Albert, the Prince Consort. Due to a recommendation by Prince Albert, Frederick Seymour began a career in the colonial service in 1842, holding positions in Van Dieman's Land, Antigua and Nevis before being appointed Lieutenant Governor of British Honduras in 1862. This appointment ended abruptly a year later when he contracted a fever serious enough for him to return to England to regain his good health.

When Seymour was named the new governor of the mainland colony of British Columbia in January 1864, he was offered very attractive terms, especially considering British Columbia's financial situation at the time: he would receive an income of £3,000 per year and the colony would pay for a new government house to be constructed in New Westminster. Although the residents celebrated his arrival on April 20, 1864, Seymour found the townsite of New Westminster somewhat depressing:

> I had not seen even in the West Indies so melancholy a picture of disappointed hopes as New Westminster presented on my arrival. Here, however, there was a large display of energy wanting in the tropics, and thousands of trees of the largest dimension had been felled to make way for the great city expected to rise on the magnificent site selected for it. But the blight had come early. Many of the best houses were untenanted. The largest hotel was to let, decay appeared on all sides, and the stumps and logs of the fallen trees blocked up most of the streets. [New] Westminster appeared, to use the miners' expression, "played out."[7]

However, Seymour was keen to be a champion of the colony, which residents felt had been overlooked by Douglas for the benefit of the merchants and other interest groups on Vancouver Island. It was obvious to him that reliable transportation routes were essential to a colony that depended on mining for gold at interior sites, and he was committed to continuing construction of the roads Douglas had started to the Cariboo gold district. But first, just two weeks after his arrival, he had to deal with a violent conflict over a proposed alternate route to the goldfields through Bute Inlet.

In 1860 Victoria businessman Alfred Waddington had begun building a more direct route to the Cariboo from Bute Inlet up the Homathko River and through the territory of the Tsilhqot'in people to Alexandria on the Fraser River. This enterprise was based on very limited know-ledge of the area's geography and no knowledge of the Tsilhqot'in people. The road builders abused Tsilhqot'in women, and when smallpox devastated their communities in 1862, they associated these outsiders with the epidemic. Relations quickly grew tense, and in a surprise attack in April 1864, some Tsilhqot'in killed fourteen of the seventeen road builders, several white settlers, and some individuals who were providing supplies to the road crew.

The second governor of British Columbia, Frederick Seymour, shown here with his pet cat, had a long career in the colonial service. Shortly after he arrived in New Westminster, Seymour travelled north to deal with a conflict over road construction in Tsilhqot'in territory.
Image courtesy of Royal BC Museum and Archives, A–O1749.

The question of whose territory this was, who had the right to enter it, and who had the authority to punish crimes in the area was never in doubt in the minds of the colonial administrators, and although agents of colonial authority were thin on the ground, Seymour responded by sending two expeditions north to arrest the responsible Tsilhqot'in men. Seymour himself accompanied a group of fifty volunteers headed by police superintendent Chartres Brew. Finally, a Tsilhqot'in chief arranged a meeting between Seymour and Klatsassin, who had organized the massacre, but instead of this being a peace meeting, Klatsassin and seven of his followers were taken prisoner. After Judge Matthew Baillie Begbie conducted a trial in Quesnelle Forks, five of them were hanged, and another man who was sent to New Westminster for trial was also hanged. (In recent years the province of BC has recognized that steps taken by colonial authorities to end the "Chilcotin War" were duplicitous, and in October 2014 Premier Christy Clark apologized for "the wrongful hanging of the six war chiefs").[8]

While Seymour forcefully exerted colonial authority over Tsilhqot'in territory, he was also trying to establish peaceful relations with other First Nations in BC, or at least to have them respect him as he thought they had respected Douglas. In 1864 he started a tradition of inviting Indigenous people to celebrate the Queen's birthday at Government House in New Westminster. On these occasions he handed out gifts of "inexpensive" canes with silver tops and "cheap" English flags. His Indigenous guests used the opportunity to petition him to protect their land rights. For example, a petition from the Stó:lō people in 1864 extended a warm welcome to the Queen's representative but requested him to "Please ...protect our land, that it will not be small for us; many are well pleased with their reservations, and many wish that their reservations be marked out for them."[9] Over the next few years, however, Seymour's chief commissioner of Lands and Works, Joseph William Trutch, actually reduced the size of mainland reserves that had been allocated by Douglas's representatives. The Stó:lō's frustration over this reduction was evident in a petition they presented to Seymour in 1866: "The white men tell many things about taking our lands: our hearts become very sick. We wish to say to Governor Seymour: please protect our lands. Many are our children and some go to school, one of them has written this. We do not like to pay money to carry lumber and other things in our canoes on the river of our ancestors. We like to fish where our fathers fished."[10]

By the fall of 1864 British Columbia's economy was in decline. However, in spite of the expected boatloads of miners failing to appear the following spring, Seymour continued to build roads to the boom-and-bust mining districts, spending about $1,342,000 on roads to the Cariboo, improving the Dewdney Trail and building a road along the Thompson River to the Big Bend mining district. It

Frederick Seymour invited Indigenous chiefs, including those depicted in this photograph ca. 1867, to meet in New Westminster to celebrate the Queen's birthday. At these events, Indigenous leaders urged Seymour to protect their land rights, which were being eroded by Commissioner of Lands and Works Joseph Trutch.
Image courtesy of Royal BC Museum and Archives, C–O9263.

was largely the continuing expense of building this infrastructure that finally convinced the British government in 1866 to unite the two colonies on the Pacific Northwest coast. Kennedy's appointment was ended, while Seymour remained to govern a new colony consisting of Vancouver Island and mainland BC for a salary of £4,000. This union was a step back for responsible government as Vancouver Island lost its elected legislative assembly while the new combined colony kept the mainland's legislative council of appointed advisors. Then, possibly to appease the islanders, Seymour allowed the council to vote on the location of the capital, and they chose Victoria, in opposition to Seymour's personal preference.

Frederick Seymour governed the colony for three more years after the union. Despite being in failing health after 1867, he travelled widely throughout the colony, visiting settlements and dealing with disputes. In August 1867 he travelled to the Cariboo to settle a conflict between two mining companies, and a month later he was a guest at William Duncan's mission community at Metlakatla on the north coast. Under his direction, the Legislative Council inaugurated institutions and passed regulations that helped lay the foundation for a modern state in BC. These included the establishment of a public school system, improving the court system, drawing up public health regulations and regulating the mining of silver, lead, copper and coal.

In May 1869 Seymour made one last voyage north on the naval gunboat *Sparrowhawk* to try to negotiate a peaceful settlement to a conflict between the Nisga'a and Tsimshian communities. On the way back to Victoria he came down with dysentery, and on June 10, 1869, he died after the *Sparrowhawk* dropped anchor at Bella Coola. At his funeral James Douglas was one of the pallbearers. Seymour was buried in the naval cemetery in Esquimalt.

Sir Anthony Musgrave, British Columbia's last governor before Confederation, was born in 1828 in Antigua where both his father and grandfather had held government positions. After receiving a basic education there, Musgrave finished his schooling in Britain. Like Kennedy and Seymour, he was appointed to increasingly more responsible positions in British colonies, including private secretary to the governor-in-chief of the Leeward Islands, secretary of Antigua, president of Nevis and Lieutenant Governor of St. Vincent. His first position in British North America was as governor of Newfoundland from 1864 to 1869. From the beginning of his tenure there, Musgrave tried to convince the people of Newfoundland of the advantages of joining New Brunswick, Nova Scotia, Prince Edward Island, Canada East and Canada West in a union. The Colonial Office and Newfoundland's premier, Frederic Carter, supported Confederation, but the electorate was not yet convinced that joining a larger union would benefit the colony economically. As a result, Newfoundland opted out of Confederation in 1867, but Musgrave went to Ottawa anyway in the fall of that year to discuss with Governor General Monck and Prime Minister John A. Macdonald terms of union that might be tempting to Newfoundland.

When his son died in the summer of 1868, a grieving Musgrave went on leave to England.

Meanwhile, with the advent of the telegraph, the efficiency of government on the West Coast had been vastly improved. On June 14, 1869, after Government House in Victoria was apprised of Seymour's death four days earlier, Colonial Secretary Lieutenant Philip James Hankin was appointed temporary administrator. On June 15 a telegram was sent to inform the Colonial Office, and that same day Victoria received the information that the new governor would be Anthony Musgrave. This was a far cry from twenty years earlier when Richard Blanshard had to wait nine months for confirmation of his resignation.

At this juncture in history the new governor's most important mission was persuading British Columbia to join Canada in order to ensure Britain's continuing presence on the Pacific and thwart annexation efforts by the United States. Lord Granville, secretary of state for the colonies, writing to Queen Victoria in June 1869 to inform her of Seymour's death, told her, "This sad event is not a matter of regret as regards Your Majesty's service. It is important to fill his place as soon as possible with the best man, for on the future Governor will much depend whether British Columbia will join the Canadian Dominion or become Americanized."[11]

Despite Musgrave's inability to convince Newfoundland to join Confederation, the Colonial Office had chosen him to succeed Seymour, confident that he would work harder than Seymour had in nudging BC toward union with Canada. Musgrave found he had increasing agency in his role as governor since the West Coast Colonies did not have responsible government. He spent the first few weeks touring the colony, and the first few months fixing problems related to finances, the postal system and legal jurisdiction. Then, as per his instructions, he set about convincing British Columbians of the benefits of Confederation; he was aware that success would put him out of a job in BC, but it would ensure his continued employment in the colonial service.

Several prominent government appointees in BC, such as Joseph Trutch and Dr. John Sebastian Helmcken, were opposed to Confederation—in Trutch's case, because his position would be in jeopardy, and in Helmcken's case, because of BC's great distance from Canada. Musgrave assured Trutch and others that they would

Although Sir Anthony Musgrave had not succeeded in bringing Newfoundland into Confederation, as governor of British Columbia he convinced leading officials that joining Canada would be advantageous.
Image courtesy of Royal BC Museum and Archives, A–O1514.

have secure employment in the new government order and began promoting the idea of a railway connecting BC with central Canada. He worked with council members to draft terms of union, then sent Trutch, Helmcken and Robert Carrall to Ottawa to negotiate the terms. The Dominion government responded generously, offering completion of a railway to the Pacific within ten years. In gratitude for his successful work ushering BC into Confederation—and doing so behind the scenes so it appeared to be a local initiative— Musgrave was awarded a Companion of the Order of St. Michael and St. George and invited to become the province's first Lieutenant Governor, an offer he declined. He and his wife, Jeanie, who was pregnant, left the colony in July 1871. He later served as governor of Natal, Australia, Jamaica and finally Queensland, where he died in 1888.

—⚊—

The five governors of the West Coast Colonies had much more authority and responsibilities than the Lieutenant Governors who would follow them. Blanshard and Douglas promoted settlement, established a government and judicial system, and used gunboats and the threat of swift punishment to exert control over Indigenous peoples. In advance of the expected rush of miners, Douglas proclaimed British authority over the mainland, and when the miners did arrive, he tried to maintain peaceful relations between them and Indigenous people while he channelled colonial funds into constructing roads to the goldfields. The governors who followed Douglas were career colonial servants, giving them the advantage of previous administrative experience in far-flung parts of the British Empire. Arriving at the conclusion of the major gold rushes, Kennedy sought to diversify the economy by funding exploration of the interior of Vancouver Island. Seymour had a complex relationship with Indigenous residents of the mainland, embarking on an expensive mission to track down Tsilhqot'in people who had killed road builders in their territory, yet acting as a conciliator on other occasions. Musgrave's mission, which he accomplished in less than two years, was to end British Columbia's colonial status by bringing it into Confederation.

III

Ottawa's Men

FROM FEDERAL AGENTS TO INDUSTRIALISTS
(1871–1914)

BRITISH COLUMBIA'S FIRST seven Lieutenant Governors were not only representatives of the Crown but also agents of the federal government, Ottawa's men in Canada's westernmost province. All had spent part of their careers in the capital working for the federal government or had served as federal government agents elsewhere. They were first and foremost politicians and not required—as later Lieutenant Governors were—to travel the province or be accessible to a wide range of British Columbians.

Their political experience was also a far more important qualification for the job than being a wealthy or talented host. As historian John Saywell notes, "neither Macdonald nor Laurier ever considered personal wealth or social graces as factors worthy of serious consideration."[12] Prime Minister Alexander Mackenzie, known for reducing expenses, went as far as to state that Lieutenant Governorships "should have been plain, simple positions like those of the Judges, without any pretence to State show or expectation of lavish entertainment, political or social."[13] Rather, their role was constitutional and associated to some degree with power and prestige; in British Columbia they were expected to integrate the province into the new nation by laying the foundations of responsible government while instituting government along party lines and staving off secessionist sentiment due to delays in railway construction.

Some of the men appointed as Lieutenant Governors received the post as a sort of retirement gift; John A. Macdonald called it "a proper reward for a statesman who from age, ill health or other circumstances had earned retirement from political life."[14] In other instances the position was offered to a member of the Senate in order to fill his seat with someone more capable or loyal, though according to Saywell, "the office was most valuable . . . as a pasturage for unwanted federal cabinet ministers."[15]

Despite a ruling by the Judicial Committee of the Privy Council in 1892 that Lieutenant Governors should not be subordinate to Governors General, in BC Lieutenant Governors continued to act on behalf of the federal government for the next decade, and until 1920 they reserved specific bills for review by the Governor General. Once party government was in place in British Columbia, however, those appointed as Lieutenant Governors did not need to have experience working for the federal government. Rather, they were wealthy businessmen whose political experience was limited to provincial affairs, until a new set of "Ottawa's men" were appointed starting in 1941.

Joseph William Trutch (1871–76)

In 1871 British Columbia joined the new nation of Canada with terms that were very favourable to the province. They included Canada's commitment to complete a transcontinental railway within ten years, the eradication of the colony's debt, annual payments to the new province based on an inflated population estimate, control over its own lands and resources, and the continuation of its pre-Confederation Indigenous reserve land allocation policy. Furthermore, Canada agreed that British Columbia would have responsible government "when desired by the inhabitants." These terms had been negotiated by a three-person team sent to Ottawa by Governor Anthony Musgrave, and the team's spokesperson was Joseph William Trutch, whose reward, once Confederation was completed, was appointment as the province's first Lieutenant Governor.

Engineer and surveyor Joseph William Trutch trained in England and worked in the United States before arriving in British Columbia in 1859.
Image courtesy of Royal BC Museum and Archives, A–01705.

An engineer, surveyor and builder, Trutch had taken a round-about but not uncommon route to the colony in the mid-nineteenth century. Although born in Ashcott, England, in 1826, he had spent his early childhood in Jamaica, where his parents, William Trutch and Charlotte Hannah Barnes, owned land. When he was eight, the family moved back to England and he entered Mount Radford School in Exeter before being apprenticed to engineer John Rennie and working on the construction of the Great Northern and Great Western Railways. Then in 1849, attracted by the opportunities afforded by the California gold rush, he left Britain to seek work in San Francisco. Wealth, social standing and manners were, however, very important to Trutch, and he found most Californians he met were lacking in these areas. Hoping to make the right connections, he wrote to his parents, "If I could get known among the best people, I mean the capitalists, I should be sure to do well."[16] When he failed to meet "the best people" there, he moved north to the Oregon Territory where he found work surveying the townsites of St. Helens and Milton.

In Oregon Territory, Trutch met his future wife, Julia Hyde, the sister-in-law of his supervisor, surveyor general John Bower Preston. They married in 1855 and moved to Illinois, where Trutch again worked for Preston, this time on the Illinois and Michigan Canal. When news of the Fraser River gold rush arrived in 1858, Trutch saw it as an opportunity to move to a warmer climate in British territory, but rather than proceeding directly to the goldfields, he went first to London to meet with colonial officials to secure, if possible, a position ahead of relocating to the West Coast. In London he met Richard Clement Moody, the head of the Royal Engineers and chief commissioner of Lands and Works in the colony of British Columbia, and he came away with a letter of recommendation from Sir Edward Bulwer-Lytton, secretary of state for the colonies, to Governor James Douglas.

After arriving in British Columbia in June 1859, Trutch worked on a series of government surveying and road construction contracts, and in 1862 he took on the contract to build the section of the Cariboo Road from Chapmans Bar to Boston Bar. The road had to cross the Fraser in this section, and Trutch constructed the impressive Alexandra Suspension Bridge about 40 kilometre (25 mi) north of Hope; it was over 80 metres (265 ft) long and crossed

Joseph Trutch built the Alexandra Suspension Bridge north of Spuzzum in 1863 as a link in the Cariboo Road. Costing about $45,000 to construct, this 80–metre bridge earned Trutch an estimated $10,000 to $20,000 in tolls per year.
Image courtesy of Royal BC Museum and Archives, A–03926.

the canyon 27 metres (90 ft) above the water. The structure cost him $45,000 to build, so the government gave him a licence to charge a toll of $7.40 per ton of freight crossing the bridge for the next seven years, which earned him an estimated $10,000 to $20,000 per year. He also augmented his income by investing in land, especially on Vancouver Island.

In 1861 Trutch bought 10 acres (4 ha) of James Douglas's Fairfield Farm and had a small cottage built there for himself and Julia. The Trutch family soon expanded their cottage into a mansion suitable for entertaining. "Fairfield House" boasted a drawing room large enough to host balls, a library, imported wood detailing, eight fireplaces and a stained glass window. In 1864 it served as a temporary residence for Governor Kennedy, who rented it while Cary Castle was being renovated.[17]

In November 1861 Joseph Trutch was elected to the Vancouver Island House of Assembly, and when Colonel Moody and the Royal

Engineers returned to England in the spring of 1864, Governor Douglas named him the colony's new chief commissioner of Lands and Works. Although he was chosen for his undoubted skills as a surveyor and engineer, his appointment was questioned at the time because of his large landholdings and his licence to collect tolls on the Alexandra Suspension Bridge. To appease these concerns, he gave control of the bridge to his brother John.

Commissioner of Lands and Works was an influential post in which Trutch would make his mark on British Columbia, a mark that has repercussions to this day. As well as assigning public works contracts, his responsibilities included both settling newcomers on the land and allocating reserves to First Nations, a situation where his prejudices and values resulted in a generous settlement policy and minimal reserve sizes. This was a marked break from the way that Douglas had handled the issue. In the mid-1850s, after the Colonial Office had stopped providing funds to purchase land from Indigenous people in order to extinguish title, Douglas changed his tactics. Instead, when the gold rush brought a flood of new settlers to BC, he had sent surveyors out to map and reserve the lands that First Nations people requested for their own use. He also offered them the chance to pre-empt land along with settlers. Joseph Trutch, in contrast, focused entirely on opening up land for white settlers while economically marginalizing the majority Indigenous population. To do so, he denied the existence of Aboriginal title. As historian Paul Tennant notes, Trutch had to "revise the history of the colony" to support his claim that "the title of the Indians in the fee of the public lands, or any portion thereof, has never been acknowledged by Government, but, on the contrary, is distinctly denied."[18] He also ended the right of Indigenous people to pre-empt land in 1866 and reduced the size of already existing reserves. His policies were consistent with the opinions of many of British Columbia's settlers, most of whom believed that the land was practically empty and that, in any case, Indigenous people were not using it productively. In fact, the Eurasian diseases that had preceded and accompanied European settlement in BC had caused severe depopulation in Aboriginal communities, and settlers saw the land as unused because they did not understand how Indigenous people owned, managed and cultivated resources.

When Trutch took on the post of commissioner of Lands and

Works, he had automatically become a member of the Legislative Council of British Columbia, and he remained on the council after British Columbia and Vancouver Island became a single colony in 1866. By this time the enormous debts from road building and the petering out of various gold rushes were nudging the united colony toward becoming part of the larger political entity of Canada. Trutch, however, was opposed to this union because of his ties to Britain and his fear of losing his position in the colonial administration. His attitude only began to change after the appointment of Anthony Musgrave as governor. The Musgrave family soon became part of the same social circle to which the Trutch family belonged, and the two families became even closer when in 1870 Joseph's brother John Trutch married Musgrave's sister, Zoe. Musgrave also reassured Trutch that he would receive another position or at least a pension after Confederation. Dr. John Sebastian Helmcken, another member of the Legislative Council and Douglas's son-in-law, was also against union and told Musgrave, "I have been elected to oppose Confederation and I mean to do it,"[19] but Musgrave pointed out that since both Britain and Canada supported the union, it was going to happen, and he encouraged him to come up with some draft terms that would be advantageous to BC. After Helmcken presented his terms to the council, he found that Trutch had even more generous terms for BC in mind, and he wrote in his journal:

> At the next meeting or so after we adjourned to luncheon (in Government House as usual), and after lunch Trutch met me in the hall and said, "Helmcken, your idea of a waggon road and railroad are good, but on thinking the matter over, I think Confederation will be valueless without a railway to the Eastern Canada!" Trutch and I were friends! He almost took my breath away. "Heavens, Trutch, how are they to build it?—and as to operate it—well, I do not see the way." "Well," says Trutch, "but I think I do." "Well, you know more about railways than I anyhow." "Then," says Trutch, "suppose I propose that there shall be, not your little tho difficult road, but a railroad all the way to the East, will you assist me?" "Yes, Trutch, with both hands." Now in the above few words was the embryo of the Canadian Pacific R.R.[20]

After the Legislative Council had discussed and approved the terms of union the colony would propose, Musgrave appointed three representatives to negotiate the terms with the federal government—Trutch, Helmcken and Robert William Weir Carrall, a medical doctor living in Barkerville, who would represent the interests of the mainland. The three men and Trutch's wife, Julia, left Victoria on May 14, 1870, travelling by sea to San Francisco and by rail across the United States. In Ottawa, Trutch was the chief negotiator. Helmcken wrote:

> In fact, he [Trutch] was to be the front and general of the whole affair. No one indeed so capable—he being a head and shoulders above us in intellect—and pertinacity—and introduced by the Governor as such, so from the word go, we were not on equal footing and soon discovered this at Ottawa. Trutch was everything and everybody—it mattered little in reality, as we all had to stick to the Terms [that the Legislative Council had approved].[21]

Three of the terms of union—those dealing with the railway, Indigenous lands and responsible government—would have significant implications for Trutch, the Lieutenant Governors who came after him and the future of Indigenous land rights in BC. Clause 11 committed Canada to starting construction of a transcontinental railway that would "connect the seaboard of British Columbia with the railway system of Canada"; work was to begin within two years of the union and the railway was to be finished within ten years. The exact meaning of the term "seaboard of British Columbia" was debated for years between advocates of a more southerly route ending near New Westminster and residents of Vancouver Island who favoured a more northerly route that would cross over to the island and end in Victoria. As for the completion date, in an effort to make British Columbia's entry into Confederation more palatable in Ottawa, Trutch made a speech assuring federal politicians that British Columbia would not insist on the railway being finished in ten years. When reported in BC, this speech offended many British Columbians.[22] Ultimately, the Canadian Pacific Railway was not in operation until 1886, fifteen years after BC's union with Canada. In the meantime, threats by British Columbia to leave the union brought two Governors General on visits to the West Coast to reassure the population that Canada still had a firm commitment to the railway.

Clause 13 of the terms of union assigned to the federal government the "charge of the Indians" and the "management of the lands reserved for their use and benefit." However, BC safeguarded its parsimonious reserve policy by stating that "a policy as liberal as that hitherto pursued by the British Columbia Government shall be continued by the Dominion Government after the union." The irony was that this was not a liberal policy at all; treaties with First Nations on the Prairies guaranteed families up to 320 acres (130 hectares), while the colonial government of British Columbia had assigned only 10 acres (4 ha) per family. Historian Robin Fisher writes that it was "highly likely that Trutch was responsible" for clause 13 since it was compatible with the reserve policy he had shaped from 1864 to 1871 and appears to have been added once the delegates were in Ottawa.[23]

Clause 14 of the terms addressed responsible government. As Helmcken recalled, "there were apparently two great reasons for Confederation:" the debt of the colonies and the desire for responsible government that "would make government cheaper and better—get rid of what was called the iron heel of despotism!"[24] The small elected assembly that had been established on Vancouver Island in 1856 had been dissolved when that colony amalgamated with the mainland colony of BC in 1866, and the united colony had reverted to an appointed legislative council. Newcomers from the United States and from eastern British North America, where colonies had enjoyed responsible government since the mid-1840s, rankled under this return to top-down government. As well, although the established colonial elite was not in a rush to introduce more democratic forms of government, the general populace of British Columbia would hardly accept provincial status without it. Clause 14, therefore, accepted this transition but allowed for delays by stating that "the Government of the Dominion will readily consent to the introduction of responsible government when desired by the inhabitants of British Columbia."

A month after BC became a province of Canada, Trutch was sworn in as the province's first Lieutenant Governor. He had a number of qualifications for this important role: he had political experience, he had played a significant role in brokering BC's union with Canada, he had good connections, he understood what was involved in building the railway, and he was a relatively long-term resident of the colony who was "not a favourite with either the British or the Canadian faction."[25] Despite these qualifications, Prime Minister John A. Macdonald had been somewhat hesitant to appoint him and wrote to his colleague George-Étienne Cartier in June 1871:

> They say, and there is much force in the objection, that Trutch is known to have strong opinions as to the Terminus of the Pacific Railway, and that he has property the value of which will be affected by the selection. His speech also as to the Railway has caused great indignation in British Columbia, and his appointment, it is feared, might cause the first elections to go against us. This would be most disastrous.

Still, Macdonald wanted to have Trutch at work somewhere in the public service, if not as Lieutenant Governor, then "certainly as Senator or in some other public capacity."[26] For his part, Trutch would have preferred a role in building the new railway, but in the meantime he was willing to accept the vice-regal position.

One of Trutch's main tasks, and one about which he was not overly enthusiastic, was to introduce responsible government. Therefore, his first executive council was temporary and made up of appointed members, including John Foster McCreight, a Victoria lawyer and judge who was designated Attorney General. Trutch then began personally directing the organization of the province's first elections that October to make sure they would run smoothly, "establishing electoral divisions, appointing Returning Officers, and the like." He was a little nervous about the outcome, writing to Macdonald, "I think I can manage to get some decent men to take a hand in the government, although most of our representatives will be a *queer kittle cattle* I fear."[27]

As the election results demonstrated no clear party lines, Trutch chose McCreight, who won the seat for Victoria, as the province's first premier, and McCreight then recommended the two other elected members who should be on his executive council. The members of this first cabinet, all of whom had opposed responsible government, were not overly popular, especially with reform newspaper editors such as Amor de Cosmos and John Robson. And according to his fellow judge Henry Crease, BC's first premier may have been a legal expert, but he was not only "bad tempered" but also "by fits & turns extremely credulous & extremely suspicious . . . excessively obstinate in the wrong places . . . close and reserved in his daily life . . . [and] utterly ignorant of politics."[28]

Initially Trutch "resisted democratizing forces"[29] by attending every meeting of the executive council and even participating in the formulation of legislation. While prior to Confederation, the franchise had been limited to men with property, laws passed by British Columbia's first provincial administration made the government responsible to a broader range of white voters by extending the franchise to all adult white men. At the same time, however, legislators removed the vote from Chinese and Indigenous residents who at this time made up 4.3 per cent and at least 71 per cent of the population, respectively.

Even though Trutch was deeply involved in guiding the first provincial administration, he recognized that he had to allow for the establishment of responsible government, and he sought advice from Macdonald on this issue. He asked, for example, if his throne speech should express his own opinion or that of his ministers; Macdonald responded that the ministers should advise Trutch on the speech while "at the same time from your position you can exercise a legitimate influence in pressing upon them the various topics that should be mentioned or avoided."[30] He also told Trutch that it should be up to the Legislature to decide whether McCreight's administration would continue or not, and that if McCreight's ministry fell, then Trutch should either call on the leader of the Opposition or, failing that, the person who put forward the vote of non-confidence to decide on the composition of his council, which would then have to be approved (or not) by the Legislature.

In response to some observers who said that Trutch tried to influence the government more than he should, he defended himself by saying that he was easing off on the reins of power as the government got itself established. In fact, he had so little to do that he complained to Macdonald in October 1872 that he was becoming bored, and that the office of Lieutenant Governor would better suit an older man in retirement. The position, he said, had become "tedious and irksome to one at my time of life—of naturally active mind, and habituated for years past to such exciting business avocations as are characteristic of all new countries."[31]

That December, Trutch had the chance to show that he supported the principle of responsible government when McCreight resigned following a non-confidence vote. Trutch called on Amor de Cosmos, founder of the *British Colonist* newspaper in 1858 and an outspoken supporter of responsible government, to be the next premier. Historians are divided over whether responsible government was achieved by Trutch as he "accepted as premier a man . . . whom he had bitterly opposed politically"[32] or by De Cosmos, whose "monumental achievement" was to remove "the lieutenant-governor from the executive council."[33]

As BC's first Lieutenant Governor, Trutch also kept the federal government informed on BC affairs. When there were threats of a Fenian invasion in 1871, he was influential in maintaining the presence of Royal Navy vessels in Esquimalt and called for a militia to be established in BC. He also put forward names of potential first senators for BC, including Clement Francis Cornwall of Ashcroft, who would return from Ottawa to become BC's third Lieutenant Governor.

Trutch continued to suppress Indigenous rights to land in British Columbia, but found his powers limited since the terms of union had made the federal government responsible for the "management of Indians." In 1872 Macdonald appointed a superintendent of Indian Affairs for BC, Dr. Israel Wood Powell. Trutch disapproved of Macdonald's choice, writing to the prime minister that Powell should act "under the immediate direction and advice of someone of more experience here," meaning himself, and he added, "I am of the opinion, and that very strongly, that for some time to come at least the general charge and direction of all Indian affairs in BC should be vested in the Lt. Governor." Though rebuffed at this time, in 1874 Trutch tried to secure for himself the leading position on a three-person board dealing with Indian affairs in BC, but he was informed by Minister of the Interior David Laird that, "I very much doubt . . . whether the Government would be prepared to delegate to any person in British Columbia the general control and management of Indian affairs in that Province."[34]

Just a year into his term, Trutch had reminded Macdonald that he would rather work on the railway as soon as it was underway, but in 1873 Macdonald had to resign after it was revealed that he had accepted campaign funds from the promoters of a company seeking the contract to build the CPR, and his minority government fell. Following this so-called Pacific Scandal, Governor General Lord Dufferin called on Alexander Mackenzie, leader of the Liberal party, to form a government, but he was hesitant to spend money the government did not yet have to cover the enormous costs of railway building, further delaying the transcontinental connection. As a result, Trutch remained BC's Lieutenant Governor for the full five-year term, after which he and his wife retired to England, where he received the Order of St. Michael and St. George in May 1877. When Macdonald was re-elected in 1878, he did not forget Trutch, and two years later convinced him to return to British Columbia to act as a special "Dominion agent" supervising federal construction contracts in the revitalized railway program and other federal commitments. Trutch, who received a knighthood from Queen Victoria in 1889, held this position as Dominion agent until 1890, when he and his wife returned to England to live on an estate in Somerset.

Although Trutch had spent almost three decades of his career in British Columbia, he does not seem to have had strong sentimental attachments to this province. This was not the case for his wife, who asked to return to Victoria in 1895 when she was suffering from ill health. Julia Trutch died there later that year and was buried in Ross Bay Cemetery. Trutch went back to Somerset alone, where he died in 1904.

The railway, responsible government and Indigenous land allotments were the three most important elements in the terms of union that Trutch helped craft, and since the railway was delayed, it was the other two that would define his term as Lieutenant Governor. As he was never a supporter of responsible government, he was slow to ease the way for it and did so only after seeking advice from Macdonald and carrying out his recommendations. In the end it was his determination to maintain his influence over Indigenous land rights for which he would be remembered. While his land policies benefited the predominantly male settler society of BC, they placed Indigenous people, who formed the majority of BC's population at Confederation, on the economic margins for generations, both because he reduced the size of reserves and because he denied Aboriginal title, strategies that influenced provincial policy for over a century.

Albert Norton Richards (1876–81)

In 1873, two years after British Columbia joined Confederation with the promise of a railway, John A. Macdonald was forced to resign as prime minister during the Pacific Scandal. To address the frustration of British Columbians over subsequent delays in railway construction, Lord Carnarvon, secretary of state for the Colonies, came up with a compromise known as the "Carnarvon Terms," which included building a railway on Vancouver Island, completing surveys on the mainland as soon as possible, increasing the minimum expenditure on railway building in BC and completing the railway by 1898. Although the terms were satisfactory to many British Columbians, they were rejected by the Senate in 1875. This continuing controversy over the railway and its association with the unpopular Mackenzie shaped the entire term of British Columbia's second Lieutenant Governor, Albert Norton Richards.

Richards came from a family of reform-oriented lawyers and politicians in Ontario. His grandfather, William Buell, was a Connecticut-born Loyalist who moved to Montreal during the American Revolution and served with the British army. In 1784 Buell established a mill on the St. Lawrence River southwest of Montreal and supported nearby community development by subdividing his land for housing, opening a school in his home and donating land for a courthouse and to churches of several denominations. In 1790 he was elected to the House of Assembly where he often voted in opposition to the government, initiating a reform tradition that his children and grandchildren would continue. During the War of 1812 the village that had grown up around Buell's mill was renamed Brockville after the commanding British general, Sir Isaac Brock.

William Buell's sons, William and Andrew, launched a reform newspaper, the *Brockville Recorder*, in 1823. His daughter, Phoebe, and her husband, Stephen Richards, had several sons who trained as lawyers; the eldest, William Buell Richards (1815–89), had a distinguished career as a lawyer, politician and judge and in 1848 was elected to the House of Assembly as a reformer and appointed attorney general in 1851. His expertise and competence as a judge was acknowledged again in 1875 when he was appointed the first chief justice of the new Supreme Court of Canada, established by Alexander Mackenzie's Liberal government.[35]

The third son of Phoebe Buell and Stephen Richards, Albert Norton Richards, was born in 1822, studied law and in 1848 was called to the bar in Canada West. Like his older brother, he entered politics, taking a seat on the Brockville town council before being elected in 1863 to the assembly of Canada West as a Liberal for the constituency of South Leeds. That December he was appointed solicitor general and had to run in a by-election, one that was hotly contested since the Liberals held only a slim majority. He lost his seat by five votes to the Conservative candidate, a loss that led to the resignation of the Liberals and the installation of a government under John A. Macdonald and Étienne Paschal Taché.

It was a series of personal tragedies that apparently motivated Albert Norton Richards to consider relocating his family to British Columbia. His first wife, Frances Chaffey, whom he had married in 1849, died in 1853. Now a widower with four young daughters, the following year he married Ellen Chislett and became the father of several more children. But between 1860 and 1866 five of Richards's children died, a tragedy that seems to have been the impetus for him to begin searching for a healthier climate for his family, and he took a reconnaissance trip to British Columbia in 1868.

The next year Richards accepted an appointment as attorney general of the North-Western Territory and joined Lieutenant Governor William McDougall's party, which journeyed by train from Ontario to St. Paul, Minnesota, and from there another 800 kilometres (500 mi) by Red River cart, horseback, and horse and buggy to Pembina. McDougall's government was not to be, however, as a national committee of Métis, including Louis Riel, stopped the party from entering the territory from the United States, and they returned to Ottawa. Manitoba became a Canadian province the following year but with a different Attorney General.

In 1871 Richards again travelled to British Columbia where Chief Justice Begbie admitted him to practice as a barrister. A year later he was back in Brockville where he ran for election as the Liberal MP for that riding, but after three more of his children died in 1872–73, he decided to relocate his family to BC. With his wife and their two remaining children, he arrived in Victoria in January 1874, and as he was always inclined to support political and legal reform, he was soon working to lower the cost of litigation in the courts. (The Vancouver firm of Richards Buell Sutton traces its origins to Richards's practice.[36]) He was also outspoken in defending the federal Liberal government, and although this stance offended some British Columbians, in the spring of 1876 he was appointed Ottawa's legal advisor in BC.[37]

Later that same year Albert Norton Richards became BC's second Lieutenant Governor. It is likely that his loyalty to the Liberal government and his brother's competence as Canada's chief justice had done much to recommend him for the position. Certainly, the Governor General, Lord Dufferin, was optimistic that his appointment would improve relations between the Dominion and BC; in a private letter to the secretary of state for the colonies, the Earl of

Brother of the chief justice of the Supreme Court of Canada and a loyal Liberal, Albert Norton Richards became BC's second Lieutenant Governor in 1876.
Image courtesy of Royal BC Museum and Archives, A–02431.

Carnarvon, he remarked that, in the context of BC's grievances over delays in railway construction:

> One lucky thing has already happened. Trutch, the late Lieutenant Governor, has concluded his term, and he has been replaced by a new man, Richards, a brother of our Chief Justice, who will probably prove more friendly to the Dominion and more willing to promote harmony than his predecessor.[38]

Lord and Lady Dufferin made an extended trip to British Columbia in the summer and fall of 1876, the first visit of a Governor General to BC. The Senate had just rejected the Carnarvon Terms, and British Columbians were frustrated by the continued delays in railway construction and indecision over the location of the western terminus, but Dufferin was warmly welcomed by local residents, while Richards faded into the background. Following his landing at Esquimalt on August 16, 1876, Dufferin wrote:

> The new Lieutenant Governor came on board to meet me. His name is Richards, and he is the brother of the chief justice, but far inferior to him in every respect. His personal appearance and his manner are bad, and he has just been long enough in the colony where he came two or three years ago to practice as a Barrister to lose the prestige which he might have retained had he come as a stranger. His appointment is bitterly resented as a social insult, and he himself is denounced as a carpet bagger. One of the most difficult things I had to do during my stay at Victoria was to provide for proper precedence and attention being accorded to him at the social gatherings we attended together.[39]

As was common in the late nineteenth and early twentieth centuries, community groups had built several arches around Victoria to welcome the vice-regal couple. These were temporary but elaborate structures that carried messages expressing the loyalty, admiration and values of distinct interest and ethnic groups. On this occasion, the Governor General toured the city, following a route that would take him through the various arches, but he refused to pass under an arch that exclaimed: "The Carnarvon Terms or Separation." This was exactly the type of separatist sentiment that he had hoped to appease by making the long trip to the western province, so when the makers of the arch refused to change "Separation" to "Reparation," his procession altered its route. The following day, however, Dufferin was diplomatic enough to pass under the arch and wave to its builders while going shopping with Lady Dufferin. This "gracious act" brought the makers of the arch to Government House that evening "with an assurance that they meant nothing disrespectful to myself personally nor disloyal to the Queen by anything they had done."[40] Dufferin's visit, reported the *British Colonist*, had helped to make Vancouver Islanders feel more connected to the Dominion, confident that the Governor General had taken the time to "appreciate the indefinable but powerful influence which we call local sentiment."[41]

Around the time that Richards began his term as Lieutenant Governor, his daughter from his first marriage, Frances Elswood Richards, embarked on a career as an artist. In 1877 twenty-five-year-old Frances enrolled in the Academie Julian in Paris, and when she returned to Canada, she became acting head of the Ottawa School of Art, opened in 1880 under the patronage of the Marquis of Lorne and his wife, Princess Louise. After painting a portrait of

This arch was built on the Point Ellice Bridge connecting Victoria and Esquimalt to welcome Governor General Lord Dufferin and Lady Dufferin in August 1867. Another, less welcoming arch threatened that British Columbia would separate from Canada if railway surveying and construction did not proceed at a reasonable pace.

Image courtesy of Royal BC Museum and Archives, A–O2727.

her uncle, William Buell Richards, she was also commissioned to paint portraits of Lady Macdonald and other influential Canadians. Frances Richards also met writer Oscar Wilde when he stopped in Ottawa in May 1881 as part of his North American speaking tour. They met up again in Paris and London, and the portrait she painted of him in December 1887 appears to have been the inspiration for his novel *The Portrait of Dorian Gray*. As Wilde explained later to the *Pall Mall Gazette*:

> Allow me to clear up the mystery: In December 1887, I gave a sitting to a Canadian artist who was staying with some friends of hers and mine in South Kensington. When the sitting was over, and I had looked at the portrait, I said in jest, "What a tragic thing it is. This portrait will never grow older and I shall. If only it was the other way!" The moment I had said this, it occurred to me what a capital plot the idea would make for a story.[42]

Albert Norton Richards did not succeed in becoming a popular Lieutenant Governor. When he received an expression of loyalty from the residents of Yale, he responded that he was sure that the majority of British Columbians were loyal Canadians and would not wish to separate from Canada over delays in railway construction. This formal response elicited criticism in the press, especially from those most firmly committed to the Carnarvon Terms. After June 1878 when George Anthony Walkem became the new BC premier, life became even more difficult for Richards as he now had to work with Conservative governments on both the provincial and federal levels.

When his term ended in July 1881, Richards went back to Ontario. However, the West Coast still held a strong appeal for him, and he returned with his family three years later to take up the post of police magistrate in Victoria and practice as a lawyer. Although on one occasion in 1886 he reportedly "threw his wig and walked out of court objecting to Judge Begbie's interruptions,"[43] Richards was one of Begbie's pallbearers when he died in 1894. Richards himself died three years later at the age of seventy-four.

Although he came from a well-connected family, Albert Norton Richards played only a minor role in nation-building. In the beginning he had raised hopes, at least according to Lord Dufferin, that as Lieutenant Governor he could bring about some form of conciliation between a province threatening to separate and the nation of which it had so recently become a part, but on closer association, Dufferin—and the people of BC—had found Richards disappointing.

Clement Francis Cornwall (1881–87)

When the Cornwall brothers—Clement Francis, aged twenty-six, and Henry Pennant, aged twenty-four—arrived in Victoria in June 1862, smallpox was spreading north from Victoria like wildfire through the Indigenous communities of the coast and up into the interior of the colony. This and previous epidemics of introduced diseases resulted in severe loss of life. Newcomers like the Cornwall brothers, however, were mostly unaware of "the demographic catastrophe" taking place around them, imagining instead that they had "fallen into paradise in the form of a beautiful, empty land, there for the taking."[44]

Compared to most of the gold seekers who arrived at this time, the brothers had two distinct advantages: education and money. Both had studied at Cambridge, and Clement had articled in law. In addition, they had access to capital through their father, a rector in Gloucestershire, who was chaplain to Queen Victoria. The brothers spent only a week in Victoria before heading for New Westminster and following the Harrison–Lillooet route into the Interior. But at Lillooet, rather than follow the gold seekers into the Interior, they began looking for agricultural land to pasture cattle. They followed the Fraser River to Pavilion, went south to Hat Creek, then east to the junction of Hat Creek and the Bonaparte River and finally settled near the point where Gavins Creek joins the Thompson River. They pre-empted two 160-acre (65-ha) sections of land adjacent to each other and recorded their claims in July 1862.[45] The pre-emption policy at that time allowed the settler to pay a small registration fee to live on the land while building a dwelling, constructing fences and putting in crops, after which he could acquire a certificate of improvement and pay for the land at the price of one dollar per acre. He was also allowed to buy adjoining land at the same rate. For those with little capital the process of making improvements was time-consuming and back-breaking, but Cornwall senior sent his sons $3,840 in November 1862 and an additional $4,800 in July 1863, enabling them to hire construction workers, Indigenous agricultural

Clement Francis Cornwall and his brother Henry Pennant Cornwall built Ashcroft House with hand–sawn lumber in 1863 to accommodate travellers along the Cariboo Road. It proved to be a profitable enterprise.
Image courtesy of Royal BC Museum and Archives, F–03027.

labourers and a Chinese cook, readying them to purchase their land within the first year. Early crops included barley, clover, oats and timothy grass, and root vegetables such as carrots and turnips. Over the years they purchased more land and their estate grew to 6,452 acres (2,580 ha).[46]

The location of the Cornwall farm, adjacent to the Cariboo Road, proved advantageous. After finding that miners and packers were happy to pay them to take care of their horses and mules for the winter, the brothers expanded their business by building a road-house, which they named Ashcroft House. It was a great success, providing shelter for "judges, prostitutes, dance-hall girls, professional gamblers, miners, English nobility, politicians, clergy," and Indigenous travellers.[47]

Their next project was the construction of a water-powered mill, one of the first in the colony. This complex enterprise required the brothers to apply for water rights on Ashcroft Creek and construct extensive infrastructure. The water wheel and a sawmill were completed in 1863, and a flour mill added the next year.

In June 1864 the brothers purchased their first thirty-three head of cattle, and the next year, after they brought in another three hundred head from Oregon, they wrote to Governor Seymour requesting a lease of 15,000 acres (6,000 ha) in the Hat Creek Valley for pasture. This attempt to reserve such a large landholding angered packers and cattle drovers who wanted to be able to pasture their own animals en route. As the *Cariboo Sentinel* complained in August 1865:

> Three or four men can, if this holds good, monopolise the whole country, and packers will have to cross the Rocky Mountains to get a square meal for their mules, besides cattle dealers will be held in check on the 49th parallel instead of coming into the country with their stock.[48]

Although the Cornwalls were unsuccessful in their bid for such a large lease, they were granted a more modest 6,000 acres (2,400 ha) in the Hat Creek Valley for grazing.

In addition to operating a large and successful ranch, the Cornwall brothers brought elite British sports to the British Columbia Interior. After building a racetrack in 1865, they established a series of horse races, including the Yale Steeple Chase, the Lytton Steeple Chase and the Ashcroft Derby. These popular events increased the ranch's income, bringing in as much as $1,500 in just two days of racing.[49] As they had also been fond of fox-hunting in Britain, they initiated a similar sport in BC, substituting coyotes as the prey. Coyotes had long held a significant status in the local Nlaka'pamux territory where Coyote was a "trickster-transformer" and provided fur, skins and meat. However, the neighbouring settlers with their fences, cattle and ploughed fields viewed coyotes as pests and had no objections when the Cornwalls made getting rid of them a leisure activity. After the hounds they had ordered arrived from England in 1868, the grasslands became the brothers' coyote-hunting playground, and Clement Cornwall now felt like "the whole country was one's own, it was beautifully grassed throughout, 'coyotes' were sufficiently numerous, and there was nothing to interfere with hunting."[50] This activity helped the brothers maintain their upper-class identity, and they invited their elite visitors to join them in the hunt.

Having established community connections through their roadhouse and horse racing, in 1864 Clement Francis Cornwall drew on his background in law to enter the political sphere by accepting an appointment as Justice of the Peace and standing for election to the Legislative Council to represent Hope, Yale and Lytton. (His brother Henry became the local Indian Agent.) Clement took a break from politics in 1866, but four years later he joined the Legislative Assembly that would approve the terms of union.

On June 8, 1871, Clement Cornwall married Charlotte Pemberton, a marriage that connected him to a network of colonial surveyors. Charlotte's cousin, Joseph Despard Pemberton, had surveyed the townsite of Victoria and mapped the southeastern coastline of Vancouver Island. Charlotte's sister, Mary Letitia Pemberton, was married to surveyor Benjamin William Pearse. Both men had served as Surveyors General of the Vancouver Island colony, Pemberton from 1859 to 1864, and Pearse from 1864 to 1866.[51] Having accumulated land and sold it during the gold rush, the two surveyors faced accusations from some quarters that they had "profited from their control of crown sales."[52]

Shortly after they were married, Clement and Charlotte moved to Ottawa as Cornwall was one of the first three British Columbians appointed to the Senate. In 1879 he appeared before the House Select Committee on Chinese Labour and Immigration, chaired by Victoria MP Amor de Cosmos, and reported that, from his observations, Chinese in British Columbia were industrious, honest and clean. As a landowner, however, he was opposed to Chinese residents owning land themselves, and he was not sure whether they should have the vote. On his ranch, he told the committee, he preferred to hire white men or local Indigenous workers, but he acknowledged that Chinese residents were "wonderfully good gardeners," since they provided Victorians with vegetables in all seasons.[53]

In the summer of 1881 Clement Cornwall retired from the Senate in order to serve as BC's Lieutenant Governor, but he returned to a province that was demonstrating increasing frustration with Ottawa over the promised transcontinental railway that had failed to materialize. Although the BC Legislature had accepted the terms Lord Carnarvon had proposed in 1874 for an extension of the railway completion date, Ottawa had not, and early in 1876 the BC Legislature had supported a motion to secede from Canada. Then, less than a year after Cornwall returned to BC, Premier George Walkem lost the support of voters over poor budgeting for the completion of the Esquimalt dry dock, and resigned in June 1882. Cornwall invited Robert Beaven to form the next government, but Beaven did not have the support of the majority of members, who stated in an open letter that they would prefer William Smithe as premier. Meanwhile, Beaven, determined to remain in power, stubbornly delayed calling a session of the Legislature.

To calm down the wave of separatist feelings in this distant province, Canada's fourth Governor General, the Marquis of Lorne, and his wife, Princess Louise, visited the province that fall. This was only the second time that a Governor General had visited BC, and it was the first visit by a British princess; Louise Caroline Alberta, born in

After serving as a senator in Ottawa from 1871 to 1881, Clement Francis Cornwall (middle back) moved to Victoria with his wife, Charlotte Pemberton (left), and their children. The man in the top hat at left may be outgoing Lieutenant Governor Albert Norton Richards.

Image courtesy of Royal BC Museum and Archives, A–O1192.

1848, was the fourth daughter of Queen Victoria and Prince Albert. Visitors flocked to Victoria to see the Queen's daughter, and once again several community and ethnic organizations built arches to welcome the vice-regal couple. They stayed for almost three months, and while she painted pictures of Victoria and Government House, he travelled up the Fraser and Thompson Rivers to the Okanagan to investigate the region's economic potential. As all his activities were reported in eastern Canada's newspapers, the Governor General's sincere interest helped promote British Columbia, and his secretary, Sir Francis De Winton, was able to write to Prime Minister Macdonald that "The visit of His. Ex. & Princess to BC was well worth the money for you won't have any trouble either there or from the home govt. for the next three years."[54] Once the Governor General left BC, the assembly finally met on January 25, 1883, and Beaven's administration was immediately defeated. William Smithe became the next premier, holding the position until he died in office in March 1887.

In September 1885 the next Governor General, the Marquis of Lansdowne, travelled to British Columbia on the Canadian Pacific Railway before it was quite finished. To bridge the 76-kilometre (47-mi) gap in the rails near Revelstoke, Lansdowne travelled on horseback. He was slated to drive the last spike, but his presence was suddenly required in Ottawa after the federal government announced its decision on the politically dangerous question of the fate of Louis Riel. The honour of hammering in the last spike of the Canadian Pacific Railway at Craigellachie on November 7, 1885, went instead to Donald Alexander Smith (later Lord Strathcona). Riel was hanged a week later, on November 16, 1885, in Regina.

Seven years earlier, John A. Macdonald had returned to the office of prime minister, having run successfully as an MP in both Marquette, Manitoba, and Victoria, BC. He chose to represent Victoria—though he had never been there. His first visit to the West Coast took place in the summer of 1886, when he and his wife Agnes travelled across the country by rail. Agnes famously sat on the train's cowcatcher to gain a better view of the scenery. On August 13 at Shawnigan Lake, Macdonald drove the last spike for the Esquimalt and Nanaimo (E&N) Railway, constructed by a consortium led by Robert Dunsmuir.

Clement Cornwall's term as Lieutenant Governor came to an

end on February 8, 1887, and the following October he represented the federal government on a joint federal-provincial commission investigating First Nations complaints over land allocations on the Northwest Coast. In January of that year, a delegation of north coast leaders had met with Premier Smithe in Victoria to formally request a treaty. Despite the fact that treaties had been concluded on the Canadian Prairies a decade earlier, Smithe stated that such a request was "simply misguided." Instead, he had claimed that "The land all belongs to the Queen . . . A reserve is given to each tribe, and they are not required to pay for it."[55] Despite Smithe's dismissive attitude, a commission was established, and Cornwall and Robert Planta (representing the province) met with the Tsimshian and Nisga'a communities in Port Simpson and on the Naas River "for the purpose of hearing the expression of their views, wishes, and complaints, if any."[56] They were advised "to discountenance, should it arise, any claim of Indian title to Provincial lands."[57] The commission took five days to meet with witnesses, who spoke about the importance of treaties, self-government and access to land to harvest the resources they needed. When the commissioners claimed that the British North America Act and the Terms of Union gave the Canadian government control over Aboriginal people, Nisga'a leaders reacted with incredulity. The final report of the commission acknowledged that the Nisga'a and Tsimshian might need larger reserves, but it dismissed the idea of title. The commissioners also recommended that Canadian government authorities should establish more control over Northwest Coast people, since "to leave them longer to pursue their course unaided, uninstructed, as to the objects and purport of the law, and uncontrolled by the civil power, would be fatal to any probability of future peace."[58]

At the conclusion of his work on the commission, Cornwall returned with his family to Ashcroft where he sat on the county court bench from 1889 to 1906. He died in 1910 at the age of seventy-four. A well-educated English immigrant with family funding, Cornwall had promoted British law, culture and sport in the BC interior, but like his predecessor, Joseph Trutch, he had helped construct BC as a province where Aboriginal title did not exist, a perception that the province would cling to for the next century.

Hugh Nelson (1887–92)

Hugh Nelson was born in 1830 in Larne, Northern Ireland, the son of a linen factory owner, Robert Nelson, and his wife, Frances Quinn. In 1854 Nelson left home for California where he worked for four years before coming to Vancouver Island. By 1861 he was secretary of the Yale Steam Navigation Company. The next year he built a large warehouse in Yale and partnered with Cariboo miner George W. Dietz to purchase the Pioneer Fraser River Express Company, which took passengers and freight from Victoria to Yale and Lillooet; they renamed it the British Columbia and Victoria Express. Its primary value lay in the fact that it formed the central link between two other express operations: Wells Fargo, which connected California to Victoria, and the Cariboo Express, owned by Francis Jones Barnard, which provided connections from Yale and

Co-owned by Hugh Nelson and George Dietz, the British Columbia and Victoria Express carried freight and passengers from Victoria to Yale and Lillooet, linking the Wells Fargo and Cariboo Express operations. The New Westminster branch of their business is shown here.

Image courtesy of Royal BC Museum and BC Archives, E–07739.

Lillooet to the Cariboo. For a time Dietz and Nelson partnered with Barnard on a government contract to deliver the mail to the Cariboo, but in 1867 they sold out to Barnard.

A year earlier Dietz and Nelson had invested in Sewell Prescott Moody's water-powered sawmill on the north shore of Burrard Inlet. Moody, who had purchased it in 1864, was exporting lumber to points around the Pacific Ocean and to Great Britain, but with access to Nelson and Dietz's capital, he could expand the operation, and in 1868 he replaced the water-powered equipment with a new steam mill. By 1870 the company was known as Moody, Dietz and Nelson.

Meanwhile, Nelson had become a keen supporter of responsible government and joined the Confederation League, and in September 1868 he attended the Yale Convention, a meeting of delegates from around BC who favoured Confederation with Canada. The objective of the convention was to demonstrate that there was widespread support for an immediate union that included responsible government. Calling the colonial government a despotism that would "weaken the attachment of the people to the Crown and British connection," the delegates set out a number of terms under which BC should be united with Canada. Some of these points influenced the final terms of union, among them that Canada take on BC's debt and provide an annual payment to the new province to help pay for its government, that BC retain control over all "Crown Lands, Mines, Minerals," and that within three years of the union Canada should start building a wagon road to connect with BC.[59]

In 1870 Nelson was elected to the Legislative Council of British Columbia, and he also represented New Westminster in the House of Commons from 1871 to 1873, but during the Pacific Scandal he resigned in support of John A. Macdonald. He did not run in the election of 1874, and Moody and his associates supported another candidate, who lost the election. The editor of the *Mainland Guardian*, J.K. Suter, was relieved as he had frequently criticized Moody, Dietz and Nelson for their greedy use of resources:

> Some lumbermen of Burrard Inlet, not satisfied with the wealth they are allowed to make in the country while denuding it of its finest timber, have assumed to dictate to the people of the City and District how they should conduct their affairs and

have endeavoured to monopolise every apparently profitable undertaking in the lower Fraser. In fact, so puffed up with the idea of their own importance had these men and their agents become that they absolutely boasted that they would send whom they pleased to represent us in parliament.[60]

After the election Nelson happened to meet Suter and physically assaulted him, resulting in charges; to Suter's disgust, Nelson was discharged with a fine of just $2.50 and costs.

The sawmill at Moodyville burned down on December 22, 1873, but it was soon rebuilt, powered this time by the steam engine from the decommissioned HMS *Sparrowhawk*, the vessel that had taken Governor Seymour on his last voyage to the north coast four years earlier. Housed in a building about 90 metres (300 ft) long, this engine drove a network of "shafts, bands, and wheels" to power about thirty saws. The rebuilt mill employed over a hundred men and cut about 18,000 metres (60,000 ft) of lumber daily.[61]

In November 1875, Sewell Prescott Moody was lost at sea. He had been on his way to San Francisco on the SS *Pacific* when it collided with the sailing ship *Orpheus* off Cape Flattery and sank with the loss of all but two of the passengers. A piece of wreckage later washed ashore at Beacon Hill with the message: "S.P. Moody. All Lost."[62] After Moody's death, Hugh Nelson became manager of the company, which he renamed the Moodyville Sawmill Company.

When John A. Macdonald became prime minister again in 1878, he did not forget the support Nelson had given him during the Pacific Scandal, and a year later he appointed Nelson to the Senate. It is not clear how much time Nelson actually spent in Ottawa in the first years of his term as senator, since he was also managing the mill. In February 1882 he was in Moodyville when the town installed the first electric light system in British Columbia. Keen to see the effect, the Victoria mayor, Noah Shakespeare, and councillors journeyed to Moodyville. When they arrived after midnight "they repaired to the residence of Senator Nelson, who turned out of his warm bed and ordered the lights to be put into operation for their benefit. The demonstration was only partially successful because the man who was operating the machine was doing so for the first time."[63]

In 1882 Nelson resigned as manager of the Moodyville Sawmill

Company, after which he seems to have spent more time in Ottawa, where on September 17, 1885, he married Emily Gardiner Stanton, the daughter of Revenue Department clerk Isaac Brock Stanton.

On February 8, 1887, Nelson returned to BC with his wife to take up the post of Lieutenant Governor. Unfortunately, Cary Castle had fallen into disrepair, and the *Colonist* newspaper reported that it "offered a fantastic view but little comfort."[64] In the winter of

An Irish immigrant who operated transportation and sawmilling companies on the mainland, Hugh Nelson served as a senator in Ottawa before returning to British Columbia as Lieutenant Governor in 1887.

Image courtesy of Royal BC Museum and Archives, A–01848.

1887–88, wind whistled through cracks in the walls and rain dripped through leaks in the roof. The castle had recently been connected to the city water system, however, so a new heating system had been installed with hot water radiators, which allowed for the installation of a heated conservatory while the Nelsons were in residence. Yet, when one of the thirty-four chimneys caught fire in December 1889, city firemen, responding quickly to a telephone message, had to use a bucket brigade to put out the fire because there was not a strong enough flow for them to use their hoses.

Despite the deteriorating condition of Cary Castle, Hugh and Emily Nelson hosted many large events, increasing the public profile of the office of Lieutenant Governor in a way that the unpopular Albert Norton Richards and family-oriented Clement Cornwall had not. The Nelsons enjoyed entertaining. They hosted their first ball on November 2, 1887, and the following September Emily Nelson held a garden party and ball for Lady Macdonald. She also hosted "at homes," a typical form of socializing at the time where the lady of the house would advertise in the newspaper that she would be "at home" on a certain day so that her friends could visit her for tea and gossip. For the chatelaine of Government House, however, such events occurred on a much grander scale; in September 1889 she hosted an "at home" that welcomed 450 guests including naval officers, with music supplied by the band of HMS *Swiftsure*.

In the fall of 1889 then-Governor General, Lord Stanley, and his wife stayed with the Nelsons, and the following May the Duke and Duchess of Connaught visited on their way back to England from India. Prince Arthur, the Duke of Connaught, was the son of Queen Victoria and would become Canada's Governor General in 1911. Their visit coincided with the completion of the Royal Jubilee Hospital, named to honour the fiftieth anniversary of the Queen's ascension to the throne. Emily Nelson had laid the cornerstone on April 23, 1889, on top of a copper time capsule holding coins, material related to the construction of the building and some newspapers of the day. The most expensive hospital in Canada, by the turn of the twentieth century the Royal Jubilee, with its operating rooms, laboratory and new x-ray machine, provided patient care that was at the forefront of what medical science had to offer.

Hugh Nelson completed his term as Lieutenant Governor on November 1, 1892, and in December he and his wife travelled to

The Nelsons entertained many guests during their time in Victoria, including the Duke and Duchess of Connaught, seen here in their carriage at the opening of the Royal Jubilee Hospital in May 1890.
Image courtesy of Royal BC Museum and Archives, A–02847.

London. Four months later he died of Bright's disease while staying with his sister in Clapham. He was sixty-three. His widow, Emily, returned to Canada where she lived in Toronto until her death in August 1924.

According to the *Colonist*, Nelson had made a good impression, having "performed the duties of his office without making a single enemy or without incurring the slightest ill will. He has been kind and courteous to all who have had the occasion to do public business with him."[65] However, his biographer, Zane H. Lewis, wrote that "Nelson's life is difficult to assess. As a businessman he was always in partnership with others, so that his role in the various companies cannot easily be determined. His career as an elected politician was short; he was a supporter of union with Canada and sought the extension of the Canadian Pacific Railway to the Pacific Coast, but it cannot be claimed that he was instrumental in achieving these goals."[66]

Edgar Dewdney (1892–97)

British Columbia's fifth Lieutenant Governor, Edgar Dewdney, was born in Bideford, Devonshire, in 1835, two years before Victoria ascended the throne, and he studied civil engineering in Cardiff, Wales. Then, after hearing news of the Fraser River gold rush in British Columbia, he contacted Colonial Secretary Edward Bulwer-Lytton, hoping to receive an appointment in the colony. Instead, Lytton provided the young man with a letter of introduction to Governor James Douglas, and he began the long journey by ship across the Atlantic, by rail over the Panama isthmus and by ship up the Pacific coast, arriving in Victoria in March 1859. Douglas directed him to Colonel Richard Clement Moody, head of the Royal Engineers, and Moody gave Dewdney a job with his survey and clearing crew on the site of the new capital of the mainland colony of British Columbia, New Westminster. When that job ended, he harvested hay on Sea Island, surveyed townsites, sold town lots and prospected for gold.

Moody next hired Dewdney and another young civil engineer and surveyor, Walter Moberly, to manage a construction gang on the Hope–Similkameen mule trail, but they quit when he did not provide adequate funding. In 1861 Douglas gave Dewdney and Moberly a contract to build a wagon road from Hope to a gold strike east of the Similkameen, but by the time they had built 40 kilometres (25 mi) of road, the gold rush had ended and Douglas cancelled the project. Fortunately, in 1862 Dewdney received a contract to build the 35-kilometre (22-mi) section of the Cariboo Road from Lytton to Cook and Kimball's Ferry (later Spences Bridge), after which he spent two summers working as a surveyor at William's Creek, near Barkerville.

Edgar Dewdney met his future wife while travelling on the steamer from New Westminster to Hope. Jane Shaw Moir was on her way to settle in Hope with her mother, Jane, sister Susan, and stepfather Thomas Glennie. Susan Moir, who later married rancher John Fall Allison and settled in the Similkameen Valley, wrote a detailed memoir of life in British Columbia in the 1860s and 1870s. In it she tells how Dewdney took both Moir sisters horseback riding along the Hope–Similkameen road but always rode beside Jane, so Susan "had to struggle along the best way [she] could, sometimes losing the trail in the brush, but the horse, better used to it, always found it again."[67] On March 25, 1864, Edgar Dewdney and Jane Moir were married in the Anglican church in Hope. Following the wedding and a lunch at the Hudson's Bay Company store, the bride and groom left on Captain Irving's sternwheeler *Reliance* to make their home in New Westminster.

Appointed governor of British Columbia in the spring of 1864, Frederick Seymour carried on Douglas's project of building access routes to the colony's resources. This policy provided Dewdney with regular employment as a road surveyor and builder, and in 1864 he was given a contract to clear a 1.2-metre (4-ft)-wide pack trail just north of the border from Hope to a gold strike on Wild Horse Creek in the East Kootenay region in order to protect BC merchants from losing business to their American counterparts. Dewdney hired Royal Engineers, Indigenous packers and Chinese and white miners to build the 576-kilometre (360-mi) trail, which was completed within a year at a cost of $74,000 and became known as the Dewdney Trail. However, like all the other boom-and-bust gold rush settlements in BC, Wild Horse Creek was soon played out, and traffic was never as heavy as anticipated.

In 1868, after the two colonies were united, Dewdney was elected to the Legislative Council on behalf of the District of Kootenay. He had not intended to run and claimed the voters nominated and returned him without his knowledge while he was busy at a property he owned at Soda Creek. As a result, he did not attend the first council session, which ran from December 1868 to March 1869, but he was present for the next one, which opened in February 1870, even though attending meant a six-day journey from Soda Creek. The main issue of that session was Confederation, which Dewdney supported despite opposing responsible government. He stated that in his travels on the mainland he had "yet to meet the first individual who has expressed his desire for Responsible Government." Rather, his constituents only wanted "money to keep their trails in order and a resident magistrate to administer and carry out the laws."[68]

In the summer of 1872, while Dewdney was fulfilling a surveying contract for the CPR near Yale, he ran successfully in the federal election as a Conservative for Yale. Shortly after the election he was also offered the post of Surveyor General of British Columbia. Since he could only hold one of these positions, he chose to remain an MP, partly because, if he resigned, the region would not have a representative in the next parliamentary session.

Dewdney was very impressed with Prime Minister John A. Macdonald and described him as a "strong and singularly gifted man," whom "every man and woman in the country was always anxious to hear."[69] A year after Dewdney was elected, however, the Pacific Scandal brought down Macdonald's government. Under the Liberal government of Alexander Mackenzie that followed, railway surveys continued, and Dewdney and Amor de Cosmos, the Liberal MP for Victoria, maintained a lively rivalry over the selection of the route: De Cosmos supported the Bute Inlet route that would terminate in Victoria, while Dewdney favoured the Fraser River route with its terminus at Burrard Inlet. When Governor General Lord Dufferin visited British Columbia in August 1876, Dewdney helped organize his trip into the Interior to consider the potential routes first-hand. Not surprisingly, Dufferin was persuaded that the one through the Fraser Valley was more practical, and in December 1877 Mackenzie announced this was the one the railway would follow.

Meanwhile, on the southern Prairies between 1871 and 1877 the federal government had negotiated seven treaties with First Nations to acquire rights to land needed for the transcontinental railway and the settlement of Euro-Canadian farmers. However, another problem had now arisen: bison, the primary food source for the Indigenous people of the Prairies, had become virtually extinct due to overhunting, and some Indigenous groups were now expressing their willingness to sign treaties in exchange for the equipment and education needed to become farmers. Treaty 6, signed in 1876, had also promised food in times of famine.

In 1879 John A. Macdonald, whose Conservatives had been returned to power a year earlier on a platform that included the completion of the railway and settling Euro-Canadian farmers on the Prairies, created the position of Indian Commissioner for the North-West Territories to oversee the administration of the treaties there. Dewdney was not his first choice for the job, but he was the one who accepted. As Indian Commissioner, his duties included establishing supply farms, distributing food and setting up farming agencies to teach Indigenous people to farm. But he did not like living on the Prairies, and a short time after he took on the job, he asked Macdonald to appoint him to the Senate instead. Macdonald replied with an increase in salary from $3,200 to $5,200, then named him Lieutenant Governor of the North-West Territories as well, making "Dewdney a virtual autocrat in the North-West."[70]

Dewdney met with First Nations leaders near the Cypress Hills to hear their grievances, most of which related to the terms of the treaties, and while realizing the treaty terms were not exactly fair, he used the promise of food to ensure compliance, offering gifts or relief to those who were cooperative and withholding them from those who were not. Despite the government's early assurances that Indigenous people could choose where their reserves would be located, when they requested reserves close to each other in the Cypress Hills, Dewdney turned them down, fearing that a concentration of reserves would give them more power and independence. Consequently, in the spring of 1882 when the Cree chief Big Bear and his followers joined about 2,000 Plains people already located there, Dewdney's response was to undermine the authority of Big Bear and other major chiefs by offering recognition to "any adult male Cree as chief of a new band if that man could induce 100 or more persons to accept him as leader."[71] Dewdney also refused to give any aid to Big Bear until he gave in and signed a treaty that involved taking a reserve to the north; Big Bear finally signed in December 1882. Dewdney then delivered gifts of food, clothing and tobacco to the other chiefs in the area, after which the North West Mounted Police forced them all to settle on dispersed reserves.

As Lieutenant Governor of the North-West Territories, Dewdney held more power than provincial Lieutenant Governors because the districts in the North-West were not eligible for elected representatives until they acquired a population of one thousand white adults, so the first electoral district was not formed until 1881. Meanwhile, the federal government paid for the expenses of running the Territories' government, and Dewdney decided how to spend that money and whom to appoint to the civil service. As a result, new settlers often complained about his hold on power and their lack of political representation.

One of Dewdney's first decisions after his appointment as Lieutenant Governor had been to select, with the collaboration of CPR general manager William Cornelius Van Horne, the site for the new capital of the North-West Territories; they named the site Regina. It soon became public knowledge, however, that Dewdney had earlier purchased a section of land adjacent to the new capital and therefore benefited financially from this choice. He also invested in land in Winnipeg and Port Moody, making a tidy profit when the arrival of the railway increased the value of land in these settlements.

The early 1880s was a period of severe hardship for Indigenous people on the southern Canadian Prairies, and the suffering was made worse by federal government policy and the way it

Edgar Dewdney's policies as Lieutenant Governor and Indian Commissioner enlarged the pockets of contractors, but contributed to famine conditions for Indigenous groups following the extinction of the bison on the Canadian Prairies. The sign in the background reads, *Starved by a "Christian" Gov't.*
Grip Magazine, April 1888.

was administered by Dewdney and others. About three thousand Indigenous people died of starvation, malnutrition and associated diseases. These appalling post-treaty conditions resulted in an Indigenous resistance movement, which, along with a parallel Métis resistance, failed when the federal government sent three thousand troops to the North-West Territories via the new railway in 1884–85.

Although Dewdney appears to have been unconcerned with the survival of Indigenous cultures, he was interested in wildlife preservation. In 1887, fearing that farming settlements enabled by the construction of a railway (of which he was a shareholder) about 80 kilometre (50 mi) northwest of Regina would eliminate the habitat of birds that nested at Last Mountain Lake, he wrote to the Minister of the Interior to recommend that the area be closed to settlement and protected as a wildfowl sanctuary. It became the only federal sanctuary for birds created before the passage of the Migratory Birds Convention Act in 1917, and in the late twentieth century Last Mountain Lake was host to over 280 species of migrating birds.[72]

After the resistance of 1884–85 Dewdney was once more eager to leave the Prairies and return to British Columbia, and he asked Macdonald to appoint him Lieutenant Governor there. Instead, that position went to Hugh Nelson, and Macdonald offered Dewdney the position of Minister of the Interior and Superintendent General of Indian Affairs. As this post required Dewdney to be an elected member of Parliament, in September 1888 he ran in a by-election in Assiniboia East and won, after which he and his wife moved to Ottawa where he became a member of the federal cabinet. By this time Dewdney was so trusted by Macdonald that, before the latter died in June 1891, he named Dewdney an executor of his will.

After Macdonald's death Dewdney remained in Prime Minister John Abbott's cabinet for another year before he was at last granted the position of Lieutenant Governor of British Columbia. After being sworn in to his new position on November 1, 1892, by Judge Matthew Baillie Begbie, Dewdney and his wife moved to Cary Castle. Shortly after settling in, they were visited by Macdonald's widow, Agnes, who described Cary Castle as "quite charming— such an English-looking place—and a dear old house, just the place Mrs. Dewdney will enjoy with a capital big garden and orchard—a pretty conservatory and above all a first rate poultry yard."[73]

According to Dewdney's biographer, Brian Titley, "the lieu-tenant-governorship involved few responsibilities and numerous social events, and Dewdney enjoyed it immensely."[74] Daily life for his chatelaine was relatively relaxed as well, and reserve commissioner Peter O'Reilly wrote that "She is to be seen every morning in the town, about 9 o'clock, shopping, marketing is more correct. He drives about a good deal in a sort of tea cart and is generally accompanied by [niece] Louisa Allison—the coachman wears a light drab fashionable livery and cockade. Changed time for Ned, you will say."[75]

Lord and Lady Aberdeen, then-Governor General and his wife, visited the Dewdneys twice in Victoria. Lord Aberdeen had purchased the Coldstream Ranch near Vernon in 1891 and he and his wife became pioneer orchardists in the Okanagan. Ishbel Maria Marjoribanks, Lady Aberdeen, was a social reformer and maternal feminist who was president of the International Council of Women and the National Council of Women of Canada, and in 1897 she

The wife of the Governor General of Canada, Ishbel Hamilton–Gordon, or Lady Aberdeen, was a leading maternal feminist who helped found the National Council of Women of Canada. Taken during one of the Aberdeens' visits to Government House, this photograph shows Lord Aberdeen standing second from left with his daughter and son. To his left are Lady Aberdeen and Edgar Dewdney; Jane Dewdney stands to the right at the front.
Image courtesy of Royal BC Museum and Archives, A–O1071.

founded the Victorian Order of Nurses for Canada. She appreciated the "roomy & comfortable" Government House with its lawn tennis courts and croquet ground, noting that it was "well worth coming across the continent to get here."[76] When she attended the inaugural meeting of the local Women's Council in Victoria in November 1894, she was surprised to see the Lieutenant Governor and his wife there. She had thought they were "supposed to be opposed to it," but "both spoke & were very cordial."[77]

While Dewdney had minimal responsibilities in British Columbia, he also had much less power than when he had been Lieutenant Governor of the North-West Territories, yet he did not give his automatic assent to all bills passed by the BC Legislature. In 1897 when MLAs passed a bill called the Alien Labour Act that restricted the employment of Japanese and Chinese workers, Dewdney, aware that Canada was bound by treaties between Great Britain and Japan, pointed out that Ottawa would very likely overturn the bill, and he withheld consent. His decision was later supported by the federal justice minister.

Since his constitutional responsibilities were light, Dewdney continued to travel and manage his business interests, and in the summer of 1893 he and Jane went on a coastal cruise to Alaska. Later Lieutenant Governors would travel on naval vessels to visit coastal communities in an official capacity, but this trip was a private holiday, and Dewdney's journal entries show that he was entranced by the scenery, while critical of Indigenous ways of life.[78] In July 1896 he travelled to England where he spoke to the press about British Columbia's "partnership" with Canada, suggesting that he saw BC as more than just a province in a federation. However, Titley suggests that the real purpose of his visit was to find investors for a copper mine near Princeton in which he had invested.

During Dewdney's tenure, the province celebrated Queen Victoria's diamond jubilee. For Victoria, a city named after the queen, this was a major event, and the celebrations included a parade, rifle competition, regatta and band concert as well as a church service at Beacon Hill attended by thousands, including Dewdney in his official uniform.[79]

With no children of their own, Edgar and Jane Dewdney often provided a home for their nieces and nephews when they were studying in Victoria. However, Gold Commissioner Peter O'Reilly was critical of the Dewdneys for prioritizing their extended family rather than holding the grand events that were expected from the vice-regal representative. A year after they moved into Cary Castle, the Dewdneys had a house full of older and younger relatives, but, wrote O'Reilly, "already there are murmurs of discontent at the absence of entertainments at Gov't. House; there have been two or three small dances—but *no Ball!*"[80]

When the Dewdneys left Government House at the end of his term on November 18, 1897, they moved to a home they had built on Rockland Avenue, but he was still keenly interested in mining activities, and when the gold rush began in the Yukon, he became a director of the Klondyke Mining, Trading and Transport Company. In January 1898 he went to Wrangel to oversee construction of a warehouse and wharf. In 1900 Dewdney ran again for the federal Conservative party, this time in New Westminster, but Laurier and the Liberals were by then very popular and he did not win the seat.

Jane Dewdney died in January 1906, and three years later while Edgar Dewdney was spending a few months in England, he met and married his second wife, Blanche Kemeys-Tynte, and returned with her to Victoria. When the Conservatives returned to power in 1911, Dewdney, hoping for a secure retirement, sought an appointment to the Senate or a pension. His new wife wrote to Prime Minister Borden to say that Dewdney's recent ill health "was entirely brought on by financial worry he has never even been *comfortably* off and of late years when he ought at his age to have been able to retire and to take life easily he has had to do what he could to earn a living."[81] His biographer, Brian Titley, has observed that "Edgar Dewdney's abiding ambition was to achieve a 'competency.' That meant having sufficient resources to live a life of comfortable independence."[82]

Edgar Dewdney died on August 8, 1916, in Victoria; his widow outlived him by two decades. At his death he possessed approximately $35,000 in properties and investments in British Columbia and another $45,000 outside the province. Historian S.W. Jackman concludes that "he did not enrich himself, in part because he was not sharp enough and in part because when he had money he spent it."[83]

Dewdney's work as a trailblazer and Lieutenant Governor were important to British Columbia but it was his career in the North-West that had a more significant impact on Canadian history. Dewdney's loyalty to Macdonald had earned him well-paid positions of power. Well aware of the problems of starvation and malnutrition on the Plains following the disappearance of the bison, he used food as a tool to pressure Plains people to agree to a treaty and disperse to separate reserves. This conditional rationing of aid, which failed to meet treaties' legal promises, exacerbated the suffering on the plains and precipitated the North West Resistance.

Thomas Robert McInnes (1897–1900)

The only Lieutenant Governor to be fired from the job, Thomas Robert McInnes has gone down in BC history as an ineffectual representative of the Crown, or at least one who overstepped his constitutional authority. In his defence, however, it must be said that the end of the nineteenth century was a very fluid time in BC politics, and as historian John T. Saywell writes, "McInnes found extant a political situation that would have taxed the ingenuity, patience, and resourcefulness of the greatest of statesmen."[84]

Thomas Robert McInnes was born on November 5, 1840, in Lake Ainslie, Nova Scotia, to parents who had emigrated from Scotland. After training as a teacher, he pursued a university education at Harvard before studying medicine at the Rush Medical College in Chicago. His first work experience was treating soldiers of the Union Army in the American Civil War. After the war ended, McInnes settled in Dresden, Ontario, where he set up his medical practice in a store owned by George Webster. After Webster died, McInnes married his widow, Martha, and the couple had two sons, Thomas Robert Edward McInnes, born in 1867, and William Wallace Burns McInnes, born in 1871.

Dr. McInnes was elected reeve of Dresden in 1874, but later that same year he moved his family to the West Coast where they settled in New Westminster. His brother, physician Loftus R. McInnes, had already moved there, and in 1884 third brother, John Hamilton McInnes, left a career as a sailor to pre-empt land in Brownsville, just across the Fraser River from New Westminster, in what is now Surrey.

Dr. Thomas McInnes worked first as a surgeon and physician at the Royal Columbian Hospital, and in 1878 also became the part-time medical superintendent of the Provincial Hospital for the Insane, which had opened in New Westminster earlier that year to accept the thirty-six patients suffering from mental illnesses who had been living in the crowded Royal Hospital in Victoria. A report submitted to the Provincial Secretary in 1883, however, suggested that the management and structure of the asylum were deficient in many ways: not only was the building gloomy and overcrowded but the employees were unmotivated and uncooperative. As the report called for a resident physician-superintendent who would have "entire control over the medical, moral, and dietetic treatment of the patients,"[85] McInnes resigned his post there.

While engaged in his medical career, McInnes also held a number of elected offices. He was mayor of New Westminster from 1876 to 1878, and in March 1878 (after he took on the administration of the asylum) he won a seat in the House of Commons in a by-election and kept it in a general election that September. Although elected as an independent, he tended to support John A. Macdonald, and having studied and worked in the United States, he also supported reciprocity. McInnes became very engaged in his work as an MP, serving on committees to investigate Chinese labour, agriculture, immigration and colonization, banking and commerce, railways, canals and telegraph lines. In December 1881 Macdonald appointed him to the Senate to represent the district of Ashcroft. However, his support for Macdonald faded when it became evident that the land McInnes had purchased in Port Moody would decrease in value due to the extension of the CPR to a new terminus at Coal Harbour (now Vancouver).

In 1897 Liberal Prime Minister Wilfrid Laurier named Thomas McInnes Lieutenant Governor of British Columbia. For Laurier, this posting accomplished two purposes: it removed a Conservative-leaning opponent from the Senate and created a space there for a committed western Liberal, William Templeman, owner and editor of the *Victoria Daily Times*.[86] Although McInnes and his family had spent much of their time in Ottawa while he was an MP and then a senator, in 1890 they had moved their home base from New Westminster to Victoria where they had purchased the Presbyterian manse on Michigan Street. The new Lieutenant Governor chose his elder son, thirty-year-old Thomas Robert Edward McInnes, as his private secretary, a move that historian S.W. Jackman described as "perhaps not overly wise."[87] The younger McInnes, his wife Laura, and their young son Loftus moved into Cary Castle along with Thomas and Martha. The McInnes family's adherence to temperance principles of no smoking or drinking—likely an element of their Presbyterian culture—also set the tone for more sober social occasions at Government House.

One of Thomas McInnes's first ceremonial functions as Lieutenant Governor occurred on February 10, 1898, when he opened the new Parliament Buildings in Victoria with a golden key. This official opening coincided with the start of the fourth session of the seventh Parliament, and almost four thousand people vied for the 650 seats available for spectators. Five years earlier the twenty-five-year-old English architect Francis Mawson Rattenbury had won the competition to design the new Legislature, promising to keep the cost under $550,000, but the completed buildings had come to a total of $923,882.30. Thus, while the new buildings brought prestige to Victoria and created a boom in the construction trades, they drew criticism for an extravagant use of public funds. In the provincial election campaign of July 1898, the newspapers reminded readers that Premier John Turner had "squandered" funds on a "luxurious marble palace," and when the votes were counted, Turner could only count on the support of seventeen out of thirty-eight members. Representatives of mainland ridings were especially vocal in calling for the dismissal of this prominent Victoria merchant. Faced with his first constitutional challenge, McInnes dismissed Turner on August 8. As Turner was still trying to convince various members to support him, he challenged McInnes's decision, but McInnes was not willing to give Turner any more time and instead invited Robert Beaven, who had just lost his seat in the election, to form a government. After four days spent trying to rally support, Beaven had to admit that he could not do so. McInnes next turned to cattle rancher Charles A. Semlin, but since Semlin could only count on the support of eight members, he asked the leaders of two other factions, Joseph Martin and Francis Carter-Cotton, to serve in his cabinet. The precarious government they formed lasted only until February 1900.

Meanwhile, on May 18, 1899, Cary Castle, the residence of BC's Lieutenant Governors since 1865, had burned down. This was not altogether unexpected since the building was a known firetrap: "It was no surprise to the firemen to receive a call to Government House," stated one newspaper report. "They have been there before, not once, but no less than seven times; but on each previous occasion

When Cary Castle burned down on May 18, 1899, Thomas Robert McInnes was only able to save his uniform. Here, employees and onlookers gather on the lawn after the fire.
Image courtesy of Royal BC Museum and Archives, A–05819.

the fire had been discovered before it had made such headway as that of yesterday morning." Private secretary T.R.E. McInnes heard the fire crackling as he was on his way to breakfast and sounded the alarm.

> [After running] the gauntlet of falling embers, [the] Lieutenant–Governor and his family and staff immediately set about saving what they could, but already most of the upper portion of the building was enveloped in flames, and it was only possible to save the furniture in the rooms on the main floor. With the exception of his uniform, which was thrown out when the alarm was first given, the Lieutenant–Governor and his family lost all their personal effects, including clothing, jewels and private papers.[88]

McInnes and his family moved to a temporary home on Moss Street, an Italianate villa built a decade earlier that now forms part of the Art Gallery of Greater Victoria. As he left office in 1900, McInnes never had the opportunity to live in the new Government House, which was designed by Rattenbury and Samuel Maclure and completed in 1903.

In June and July 1899 McInnes paid a visit to Atlin in northern BC to see "the last gold rush." Speaking at a banquet there in his honour, he commented on the beauty of the region before explaining that he had been drawn there out of curiosity rather than as a representative of the Crown. This was backed up on July 22 by the *Atlin Claim*, which assured its readers that McInnes had not come there "at the instigation of any minister, nor in a public capacity, but simply as a citizen." But it seems McInnes was really there to appease the residents as he claimed that he "would do anything in his power to rectify any mistakes that had been made," a reference to a reform law passed in the BC Legislature that had been intended to restrict the rights of Chinese miners but had inadvertently done the same to American miners. The latter were numerous in Atlin, as reflected in the toasts raised at McInnes's banquet, first to the Queen, then to the President

In the summer of 1899, soon after fire had destroyed Cary Castle, McInnes (left) travelled to Atlin, BC, to witness the gold rush. This trip earned him some disapproval in Victoria for neglecting his political duties.
Image courtesy of Royal BC Museum and Archives, A-06706.

of the United States and finally to the Governor General of Canada. Twenty-nine-year-old MLA Richard McBride, who was on his second trip to Atlin, also spoke at that banquet, stating that he "was now in a better position to judge the wants of the district and would do what he could to have any mistakes rectified."[89]

Meanwhile, back in Victoria the press was criticizing McInnes for being away from the capital for so long while there was a "crisis in cabinet."[90] In fact, that crisis would grow until it resulted in the government of Premier Charles Semlin being defeated in the House in February. Charging Semlin with "incompetence and financial irresponsibility," McInnes asked him to resign, and he appointed MLA Joe Martin in his place. But Martin was not a popular choice, and when McInnes arrived to prorogue the Legislature on February 28, 1900, all the members except Martin walked out. In the election that followed that June, Martin carried out an energetic and convincing campaign, with his supporters gaining more seats than Semlin's allies, while Semlin himself was defeated. But Martin still did not have the confidence of the majority of elected members, so he recommended James Dunsmuir as the next premier, and the Lieutenant Governor followed his advice. One of the first things the new government did, however, was ask Prime Minister Laurier to dismiss McInnes, so on June 20, 1900, McInnes became the only British Columbia Lieutenant Governor to be dismissed from office. Laurier then replaced him with Sir Henri Joly de Lotbinière, a seasoned Liberal politician and constitutional expert from Quebec with a reputation for honesty and integrity.

When he found himself out of public office, McInnes set off to explore Australia and New Zealand. On his return to BC he and his family moved to Vancouver, where in 1902 he changed his political orientation once more and became honorary president of the socialist Provincial Progressive Party. In 1903 he ran as an independent in a federal by-election for Burrard and came in third. As Jackman observes, "McInnes had the interesting career of having in the course of time alienated Conservatives, Liberals and finally Socialists as well."[91]

Thomas Robert McInnes died on March 19, 1904, aged sixty-four, while his widow Martha, who was eleven years older, outlived him by a quarter century.

Sir Henri-Gustave Joly de Lotbinière (1900–1906)

Sir Henri-Gustave Joly de Lotbinière was the only French Canadian, and indeed the only outsider with no previous ties to the province, to be appointed Lieutenant Governor of British Columbia. The owner of a former seigneury, a politician with high ethical standards and a pioneer in forest conservation in Canada, he was the "product of two quite different worlds—patrician Catholic Quebec on his mother's side and bourgeois Protestant France . . . on that of his father."[92] Biographer Jack Little has called Joly de Lotbinière "undoubtedly the most influential Lieutenant Governor British Columbia has ever had."[93] This was due to his role in ushering in government along party lines, which would "stabilize the state in order to restore the investor confidence that would ensure the continued growth of British Columbia as a satellite economy of central Canada."[94]

The first of his mother's ancestors, Louis-Théandre Chartier de Lotbinière, had arrived in New France in 1651. Louis-Théandre's great-great-grandson, Michel-Eustache-Gaspard-Alain Chartier de Lotbinière, served the colony as a soldier during the American War of Independence in 1776 and as a battalion commander in the War of 1812; he was also appointed to Lower Canada's Legislative Council. His second wife was Mary Charlotte Munro; the youngest of their three daughters, Julie-Christine Chartier de Lotbinière, born in 1809, became Henri-Gustave's mother.

Henri-Gustave's father, Pierre-Gustave Joly, was born in Geneva in 1798 to a Protestant French family based in Épernay. As a young man, he travelled widely to promote his family's wine export business. Around 1827 he came to Montreal where he met Julie-Christine de Lotbinière. Julie-Christine's father had died in 1822, and he had arranged for his daughters to receive their inheritance once they came of age. Shortly after Pierre-Gustave and Julie-Christine were married in 1828, her father's three seigneuries were divided among his daughters. Julie-Christine claimed the seigneury of Lotbinière, which had less arable land than the other two and a relatively small number of *habitants* or *censitaires* but contained valuable timber resources. When Julie-Christine gained legal ownership of the seigneury, she transferred its management to her husband.

In December 1829 Henri-Gustave Joly was born in Épernay, France, where his parents—Julie-Christine and Pierre-Gustave Joly— were holidaying. Although the Quebec seigneury had never been the traditional residence of the Lotbinière family, after the birth of their son they returned to Canada where Pierre-Gustave Joly became deeply involved in managing and modernizing the property, building two gristmills and a steamboat dock, and promoting the timber trade by constructing two sawmills beside the Rivière du Chêne. In 1846 he purchased a property next to the seigneury and fronting on the St. Lawrence River to build a summer house, which they called the Maple House; it is now recognized as one of Canada's National Historic Sites and a *Site et monument classés du Québec.* On this property he also built a laboratory in which his son Henri-Gustave later experimented with the propagation of native and exotic trees.

Although the French-born Henri-Gustave Joly de Lotbinière spent his early childhood in Canada, from the age of eight he studied in Paris, first at the Keller Institute, a Protestant school, followed by the Collège royal Saint-Louis and then the Université de France, from which he earned a bachelor of letters degree in 1849. He returned to Lower Canada in 1850, articled in law and was called to the bar five years later. In 1856 he married Margaretta Josepha "Lucy" Gowen, the daughter of an Anglican merchant in Quebec City, and soon after his marriage he converted to the Church of England. Around this time, his parents' marriage was disintegrating, and in 1860 Julie-Christine transferred title to the seigneury of Lotbinière to Henri-Gustave. (Pierre-Gustave moved to France and died in Paris in 1865.) After his mother's death in 1887, Joly added "de Lotbinière" to his family name.

In managing the seigneury that he received from his mother, Henri-Gustave Joly was inspired by his father's sustained-yield approach to forestry and soon became noted for his practice and promotion of forest conservation. He was, according to his biographer, J.I. Little, "the only Quebec lumberman of the nineteenth century to manage a sizeable forest on a sustained-yield basis, and he was the country's most prominent proponent of forest conservation when that movement was still in its infancy." Joly satisfied both his paternalist bent and his conservation philosophy by creating timber reserves and hiring local farmers and contractors to cut and transport the wood for his sawmills. As a result, "the Lotbinière forest resource provided income and long-term security for families who would not have been able to survive for long on the farms had the forest reserve been sold to an outside lumber firm."[95]

In 1851, just a year after he returned from Paris, Henri-Gustave Joly ran unsuccessfully for a seat in the Legislative Assembly; a decade later, however, he was elected when he ran as an independent against an Irish-Canadian opponent. In the Legislature he formed alliances with reformers who opposed Conservative leaders John A. Macdonald and George-Étienne Cartier; initially he also opposed Confederation, and in response to the Quebec Resolutions of 1865, he spoke in the Legislature for an entire day, arguing that such unions promoted tribalism rather than integration, that Confederation was not necessary for economic development, and that it would be difficult for French Canada to survive culturally within Confederation. Once the four colonies agreed to a larger union, however, he accepted it. In 1867 he was elected to the Quebec Assembly, though by now he also sat in the House of Commons. When Quebec abolished the double mandate in the early 1870s, Joly decided, unlike many of his colleagues, to give up his federal seat, despite pressure from the federal Liberals. Instead he became the leader of the Opposition in the provincial Legislature as he was now one of the older and more experienced of the remaining Liberal MLAs.

Throughout his political career Joly supported provincial rights and opposed corruption and waste. He advocated the modernization of agriculture, diversification of crops and improvements in agricultural training. He supported more effective management of Crown lands to conserve timber resources, and he did whatever he could to ensure that logging companies followed regulations and paid reasonable fees for access to provincial timber. At the same time he supported the construction of railways to promote settlement and trade.

In March 1878 Quebec Lieutenant Governor Luc Letellier dismissed Premier Charles-Eugène Boucher de Boucherville for attempting to force municipalities to help pay for railways, and he asked Joly to form a government. Since he did not have enough support within the Legislature, Joly had to call an election, but the vote resulted in his Liberal numbers being so evenly matched with the Conservative Opposition that his government was destined to last just eighteen months. During that time his administration focused on promoting railway construction and cutting the provincial budget.

Meanwhile, in the federal election of September 1878,

Macdonald's Conservatives were returned to power in Ottawa, and Macdonald asked Governor General Lord Lorne to dismiss Letellier. Joly travelled to England to express his support for Letellier to the colonial secretary and, in doing so, became involved in the process of defining the role of Lieutenant Governors in Canada. As the

Sir Henri-Gustave Joly de Lotbinière inherited a former seigneury from his mother, Julie-Christine de Lotbinière. A committed forest conservationist, he served as the premier of Quebec from 1878 to 1879.

Image courtesy of Royal BC Museum and Archives, G-O9834.

result of this crisis, the "imperial government concluded that the lieutenant-governor did have the constitutional right to dismiss his ministers, though he must take care to act impartially in his dealings with rival parties, but that the governor general must follow the advice of his ministers with regard to removing a Lieutenant Governor from office."[96] This ruling meant that Letellier had behaved within his rights, but since the federal government opposed his decision, he could still be dismissed for his actions—which he was. The experience that Joly gained in dealing with this issue would be remarkably pertinent two decades later when he was appointed to replace Canada's second dismissed Lieutenant Governor and used his own prerogative to dismiss a premier.

In 1878 Quebec's new Lieutenant Governor, Théodore Robitaille, was more sympathetic to the Conservatives, while popular backlash against Joly's proposals to reduce government spending lost him the support of a crucial number of Liberal members. He resigned as premier in the fall of 1879 and left provincial politics altogether in 1885 when he found himself at odds with the pro-Riel sentiments held by fellow Liberal MLAs and by his constituents.

With Confederation in 1867, the provinces had become responsible for managing Crown lands, and the Quebec government had followed Joly's recommendation to establish a forest committee to regulate wood cutting. A decade later he wrote a report on the state of forests in Canada in which he recommended a number of reforms to avoid overexploitation, forest fires, illegal cutting, overproduction and the wasteful practice of cutting hemlock just for its bark. In 1882 he became president of the Forestry Association of the Province of Quebec and the following year the vice-president of the American Forestry Conference. In his talks he promoted the planting of a variety of trees in settled areas. Like other conservationists of the time, he believed that caretaking natural resources had moral benefits, and that "tree planting would ensure that youths became responsible citizens."[97] To this end, in 1886 he introduced to Quebec the equivalent of American Arbor Day, a holiday on which schoolchildren planted trees.

After Joly had taken a few years off from provincial politics, the federal Liberal leader, Wilfrid Laurier, enlisted his help in dealing with the Manitoba school question. Joly gave talks in towns and cities in Ontario promoting inter-ethnic understanding between

Prime Minister Wilifrid Laurier (left) had a great deal of confidence in Joly's (right) abilities, encouraging him to enter federal politics in the 1890s.
Image courtesy of Royal BC Museum and Archives, G–00386.

French and English speakers and spoke in support of the right of Catholics to have their own schools. Knighted in 1895, Joly ran in the next year's federal election, winning the seat for Portneuf. Laurier then made him responsible for the portfolio of inland revenue, under the jurisdiction of the ministry of trade and commerce. Joly's general refusal to dismiss employees so they could be replaced with patronage appointees loyal to the Liberal government made him unpopular with his colleagues. Fortunately, the dismissal of Thomas Robert McInnes as BC's Lieutenant Governor in 1900 gave Laurier the perfect opening for Joly because of his honesty, fairness, integrity and constitutional experience.

At this time governments in BC were not formed along party lines as they were in eastern Canada, but were instead composed of loose affiliations of MLAs with similar interests, and since loyalties frequently shifted, governments were short-lived. Joly, an outsider, was expected to sort out this political chaos, not least so that companies could safely invest in British Columbia. At first he focused on simply maintaining political stability, so when James Dunsmuir attempted to resign as premier in the fall of 1901, he refused to accept his resignation, knowing as Laurier did that forcing him to stay in office would "prevent another crisis and possibly another general election."[98] However, Joly did allow Dunsmuir to resign the next year after other MLAs accused him of corruption over an attempted sale of his Esquimalt and Nanaimo Railway. In such circumstances, a resigning premier is allowed to recommend a successor, and in November 1902 Joly followed Dunsmuir's advice by naming Edward Gawlor Prior as the next premier.

Meanwhile, the idea of party-based government was slowly gaining traction in BC, and in March 1902 Joly wrote to his son, Edmond, "With our English parliamentary system, party discipline is absolutely necessary. It's utopian to dream of a stable parliamentary government in a place where those who support it refuse to take responsibility for its acts."[99] That September Robert Borden and several members of his federal Opposition Party met in Revelstoke, BC, with provincial MLAs for a Liberal-Conservative convention (as the federal Conservatives referred to themselves at that time). As early as 1899 the Liberal-Conservative Convention had endorsed party lines in provincial politics, but this time even more delegates were in favour, and the *Revelstoke Herald* reported on September 18 that the convention had passed a resolution stating "That, in the opinion of this Convention, the stability of government and beneficial legislation can best be secured by the introduction of party politics in local elections, and that such a policy be adopted."[100]

In June 1903, after Premier Prior's hardware company won the successful bid to provide material for a bridge on the Cariboo Road, and Prior admitted to having seen the competing bids, the scrupulous Joly dismissed him, citing lack of confidence in Prior's judgment. The time had now come for Joly to select a premier who would introduce party lines, and he called on thirty-three-year-old Richard McBride, the leader of the provincial Opposition, to form a new government. In some ways McBride was an odd choice because of his youthfulness and the fact that he had not won his party's leadership at the previous year's convention, but it was out of the question for Joly to appoint Joseph Martin, who was the leader of the Liberals. McBride, on the other hand, had been publicly supporting the introduction of party lines since at least 1899, so Joly may have thought he would be good at collaborating with individuals of varying opinions, and he may also have thought that his age would make him more amenable to guidance. Once McBride was installed in office, Joly advised him in a way that was more interventionist than usual for a Lieutenant Governor or, as Joly put it, he was acting as "an advisor to my advisors!!!!"[101] And he wrote to his son Edmond that, "Our Prime Minister [premier] is the youngest member in the House, and I think he is well disposed to do what is right. I treat him as if he were my son, so far as advice and encouragement can do it, and he trusts me."[102]

McBride did respect Joly's advice and felt his influence even after Joly left BC, writing to him that he still considered that "an important part of my work is to account to you for what is going on."[103] Yet they did not always see eye to eye. For example, McBride sought to increase provincial revenue by selling timber licences, while Joly promoted the conservation of the forest resource. As Lieutenant Governor, his agency in this regard was limited, but he worked with the Canadian Forestry Association (of which he was president) to provide conservation information to BC MLAs in order to influence forestry reforms. On the issue of federal-provincial relations, as the former premier of Quebec, he tended to support BC's campaign for better terms.

The second half of Joly's term in office was marked by sadness after his wife, Lucy, passed away in August 1904. She had always been active in organizing literary societies, and in BC she had also been honorary president of the National Council of Women. Susan Crease, a friend of the Jolys in Victoria, noted in her diary the despair that Joly felt as his wife's health failed: "Poor Henri's face a study—such grief when out of sight [of her] such courage when in."[104] After Lucy's death one of Joly's daughters came to live with him as chatelaine. Although he agreed to Laurier's request to extend his term as Lieutenant Governor by eleven months, on May 11, 1906, he left office without any fanfare to return to his estate at Lotbinière. He died in Quebec City on November 15, 1908.

Joly had represented the Crown with dignity and integrity, and even though he was a newcomer to the province, he became highly regarded by British Columbians. Part of this admiration may have been due to Joly's presence at community events in Victoria and further afield, for example, when he opened agricultural fairs in Kamloops, Ashcroft and New Westminster in the fall of 1902. Travelling beyond Victoria and the Lower Mainland for social and ceremonial purposes seems to have been unusual for Lieutenant Governors at the time. As Richard McBride stated, "Coming to British Columbia a stranger, he grew quickly to love this part of Canada, and in a short space of time had so identified himself with our life and ways that he soon gained in wonderful degree the respect and admiration of the people."[105]

James Dunsmuir (1906–9)

James Dunsmuir, who had served as British Columbia's premier from 1900 to 1902, was one of the last of the province's politically experienced Lieutenant Governors and the first of the extraordinarily wealthy ones. He was appointed as the vice-regal position was shifting away from constitutional expertise toward a more social and ceremonial role, but his term was plagued by controversy, and he was one of the few Lieutenant Governors who chose to leave the position before the end of the usual five-year term.

James Dunsmuir was born on July 8, 1851, in Fort Vancouver, a stopping point for his parents, Robert and Joan Dunsmuir, as they travelled from Scotland to Vancouver Island where Robert planned to work in the new Hudson's Bay Company coal mines. The family's association with coal went back to the mines of Kilmarnock, Scotland, where Robert's grandfather had started acquiring coal leases in 1816. But in the summer of 1832 seven-year-old Robert was orphaned when his mother, father, grandmother and two sisters died in quick succession, probably from typhoid or cholera. Fortunately for the boy, before his grandfather also died just three years later, he assigned part of his estate to the care of Robert and his surviving sister, Jean, allowing Robert to attend the Mercantile and Mechanical School in Paisley. At sixteen he left school and began working as a coal miner under the supervision of his uncle, Boyd Gilmour, and at twenty-two he married Joan White, whose father was a local spade maker.

In December 1850 Robert and Joan Dunsmuir and their two young daughters, along with Boyd and Jean Gilmour, left Scotland for Vancouver Island. Gilmour had secured a three-year contract with the Hudson's Bay Company (HBC) for work at their Fort Rupert coal mine, near the northern tip of Vancouver Island. Less than a week before they left Scotland, however, he learned that the Scottish miners who had preceded them to Fort Rupert had deserted the mines there the previous July due to the poor working conditions. Although some of their prospective co-workers opted out, Gilmour and Dunsmuir were determined to go. The family would stay in Fort Rupert only a short time, however, as the HBC transferred its mining operations to Nanaimo in 1853 in search of better quality coal.

Robert Dunsmuir was not a supporter of strikes, and when his co-workers in Nanaimo struck in 1855, he did not join them. To reward his loyalty, the HBC gave him a free-miner's licence to work an abandoned shaft. In 1862 the Vancouver Coal Mining and Land Company (VCMLC) acquired the HBC mines and hired Dunsmuir to work as a supervisor. Two years later he left the VCMLC to become a manager for the Harewood Coal Mining Company, formed by naval officers at Esquimalt, but when that company folded in 1869, he returned to the VCMLC. During his time with Harewood he had also been prospecting for other coal seams, and in 1869 he discovered the Wellington coal seam northwest of the Nanaimo harbour. With another group of naval officers, in 1873 he formed Dunsmuir, Diggle, Limited, a company that was under his control and included his sons James and Alexander (born in 1853) in the partnership.

By this time James Dunsmuir was in the midst of the education that would prepare him to manage his father's mining ventures. He had attended public schools in Nanaimo, and when he was sixteen his father sent him to the Willamette Iron Works in Oregon to apprentice as a machinist. Two years later, as his father's finances improved, he was sent to the Wesleyan Boy's Institute in Dundas, Ontario, and in 1874 enrolled at the Virginia Agricultural and Mechanical College in Blacksburg, Virginia, to study mining engineering.

In Virginia James Dunsmuir met his future wife, Laura Miller Surles, the sister of one of his classmates. They married on July 6, 1876, and returned to Nanaimo where James assumed the management of his father's Wellington Mine. During crises, however, such as a strike in 1877 and a fire and explosion in 1879, Robert took over the helm. In 1881 James transferred to a mine at Departure Bay.

The two major mining companies operating in Nanaimo in the late 1880s had very different practices when it came to working and living conditions for their employees. The VCMLC tended to hire British miners, recognized a union, accepted an eight-hour workday and offered such benefits as five-acre lots for lease or purchase; in contrast, Robert and James Dunsmuir were strict employers who refused to negotiate with unions, fired union organizers and evicted strikers from company housing. If these tactics did not bring strikes to an end, they enlisted government help in the form of special constables and the militia.

As a strategy to reduce wage costs and divide the workforce, the Dunsmuirs became major employers of Chinese workers, who were willing to work for less in part because they were supporting families in China where the cost of living was significantly lower. In contrast to the VCMLC mine, the Dunsmuirs also employed Chinese labour underground. Skilled white miners refused to form labour alliances with Asian workers, complaining that their labour was too cheap, and that as unskilled workers who could not communicate well in English, they created dangerous working conditions underground. This argument seems to have been unsound, however, as the all-Chinese crew in the South Wellington mine had an excellent accident record in the 1890s.[106]

Robert Dunsmuir increased his wealth substantially when he negotiated with the federal government to build a rail link between Esquimalt and Nanaimo. In exchange the federal government gave him $750,000 and two million acres (800,000 ha) of land, the equivalent of one-fifth of Vancouver Island. This grant included not only surface rights but also the rights to all subsurface coal and other minerals. Railway construction began in February 1884 and the line was completed by August 1886.

James Dunsmuir was the driving force behind the opening of the

Comox coalfield in Cumberland in 1887, where he employed new technology such as diamond drills and mechanical coal cutters. His brother-in-law, John Bryden, was also involved in this project, and the two men organized camp construction and a rail link to Union Bay. By 1890, its third year of operation, the mine had produced 114,792 tons of coal.

When Robert Dunsmuir suddenly died in April 1889, he left everything to his wife, Joan, and it took seventeen years for James to seize control from her and his sisters; the battle included a lawsuit begun by his mother in 1903 that promoted the family to headline news. When it was over, however, James was confirmed as the sole owner of the railway and collieries, which made him the richest man in British Columbia. James had moved his family to Victoria

James Dunsmuir and his brother-in-law, John Bryden, expanded the family enterprise in 1887 when they established a coal mine in Cumberland. The company constructed simple cabins, seen here, to accommodate miners and their families.
Image courtesy of Royal BC Museum and Archives, A–O4531.

in the early 1890s, and although he was intolerant of any kind of labour organization, in 1898 he convinced miners and others living around his mines to elect him to the provincial Legislature as the representative for Comox. Two years later he was premier, his rise to power hastened by the downfall of Lieutenant Governor Thomas Robert McInnes; on March 1, 1900, when McInnes had entered the Legislature to prorogue the session and introduce Joseph Martin as the new premier, Dunsmuir had been the first to stand up and leave. He later denied that he had orchestrated the protest, but the fact that he had walked out first gave him a reputation for political leadership, whether he wanted it or not.

In the election Martin called for June 9, Dunsmuir ran in South Nanaimo where he promised the voters who worked in his Extension Mine that he would remove Chinese labourers from underground work and replace them with white workers as soon as they were available. That election gave Martin just five supporters in the Legislature, while thirty-two seats were held by politicians with little in common except their opposition to him. Observing that Dunsmuir had a reputation for being non-partisan and believing he would strive for provincial order and stability to protect his business interests, McInnes invited him to become premier. Four days after he accepted the role, Dunsmuir and the other government members passed a motion condemning McInnes's decision to invite Martin to be premier in the first place. Prime Minister Wilfrid Laurier immediately dismissed McInnes and replaced him with Henri-Gustave Joly de Lotbinière.

Dunsmuir has been characterized as a caretaker premier as he maintained stability but did not provide innovative leadership. He was also criticized for conflict of interest in his railway and mining policies, though he was unable to see a problem with this. "I consider when I am watching the people's interests," he explained, "I am watching my own. I have very large interests here and, if I don't look after the interests of the country, my own interests will not be looked after."[107] During his premiership, a number of railway companies negotiated with the government to build lines connecting the Coast and the Interior, but he ended the policy of paying with land grants in advance—a policy that had greatly profited his own family—and replaced it with paying cash subsidies once the railways were completed. Like previous premiers, he also argued that

BC should have better terms within Confederation since the province had not yet caught up in the construction of public works.

Even before he entered politics, Dunsmuir had been looking forward to retirement, but he had to wait until 1902 before Joly would accept his resignation thanks to accusations of corruption over an attempted sale of the E&N Railway to the Canadian Northern. (Three years later the Canadian Pacific Railway bought the E&N for $2.3 million.) Dunsmuir sold his coal mines in 1910 to Canadian Northern Railways for $11 million.

As soon as Joly retired in the spring of 1906, James Dunsmuir was rumoured to be the likely replacement. The *Toronto Globe* explained his suitability by stating, "First, that the British Columbia people want a lieutenant-governor of their own province; and second, that few prominent British Columbians can make the financial sacrifice required of the lieutenant-governor."[108] Wealth, in fact, would be a deciding factor in the appointment of Lieutenant Governors from then on.

Dunsmuir's term started out on a positive note on May 11, 1906. He opened the new YWCA in Vancouver and shot a bull's eye at a meeting of the Rifle Association in Richmond. He was a generous patron of sports organizations and community development, donating a trophy to the Northwest International Yacht Racing Association and a $1,000 prize to the Pacific Northwest Golf Association in addition to investing in local improvement bonds in Victoria.

Dunsmuir's popularity, however, did not last long. In 1907 he fell out of favour for his position on Asian immigration. Since Canada had raised the head tax on Chinese immigrants to $500 in 1904, major employers such as railway companies and mines had been turning to Japan for new workers. They, like the Chinese, had no option but to accept the lower wages they were offered in BC, causing resentment among white workers. In April 1907 the provincial government passed An Act to Regulate Immigration into British Columbia, which was intended to put an end to Japanese immigration into BC as well, even though similar acts passed by the BC Legislature almost annually since 1900 had always been disallowed by the federal government because immigration was within federal, not provincial, jurisdiction. In addition, the federal government had recently signed a trade agreement with Japan and could not afford to offend. Dunsmuir, though a well-known employer of

Asian workers, withheld royal assent for this latest version of the immigration act since he assumed that it would simply be disallowed by Ottawa as previous bills had been.

In the summer of 1907, in response to the arrival in BC since the previous January of at least 5,500 Japanese immigrants, the Vancouver Trades and Labour Council formed an Asiatic Exclusion League, and on September 7 the League organized a parade to protest Japanese immigration. They laid the blame for the recent influx on Dunsmuir, burning him in effigy in front of city hall, "accompanied by the howling of the crowd and the waving of white flags labelled for a 'White Canada.'" One speaker at the protest proposed a resolution "asking the Dominion government to instruct the lieutenant-governor to consent to the act."[109] Both the effigy burning and the resolution suggest that citizens saw the Lieutenant Governor as exercising considerable power and influence, rather than being simply bound by the Canadian Constitution.

In the aftermath the federal government sent William Lyon Mackenzie King to investigate the riots, and in reviewing the records of the Canadian Nippon Supply Company, King discovered that Dunsmuir had asked this company to supply him with 500 Japanese coal miners. MLAs James Hawthornthwaite, a Socialist, and John Oliver, a Liberal, reacted by calling for Dunsmuir's impeachment. When he opened the next sitting of the Legislature in January 1908, Dunsmuir was prepared: he announced that a new immigration bill would be presented, as the federal government had instructed him to assent to the bill, which would then transfer responsibility to Ottawa to disallow it. The BC government, however, decided to enforce the new law immediately, though given the precedence of the Anglo-Japanese treaty, court cases quickly established that the act was illegal.

His reputation with many white British Columbians now thoroughly tarnished, Dunsmuir made plans to retire early, and he asked Victoria architect Samuel Maclure to redesign "Burleith," the family home on the Gorge. He subsequently changed his mind when Hatley Park, Roland Stuart's 250-acre (100-ha) estate on the Esquimalt Lagoon, became available. He purchased it in 1907 for $50,000, and by 1910 had expanded the estate to 800 acres (320 ha). Maclure created a stone castle for the site, designing it to look as though it had stood on the property since the Middle Ages. Dunsmuir installed a Chinese labour force at a discreet remove from the main house to take care of the animals and crops that supplied the family, their visitors and the local market with basic farm produce as well as tropical fruits, vegetables and flowers from the greenhouse. The woods were stocked with game so Dunsmuir and his friends could enjoy hunting on the weekends.

Dunsmuir took a vacation from March to August 1908, travelling with his family to Scotland where they took delivery of his new yacht, the *Dolaura*, and went for a cruise in the North Sea. Near the Kaiser-Wilhelm Kanal (now the Kiel Canal), they encountered

James Dunsmuir and his youngest daughter, Dola, stand in front of Hatley Castle, which was constructed during his term as Lieutenant Governor.
Image courtesy of Royal BC Museum and Archives, H–O2831.

the *Hohenzollern*, a yacht owned by the German Emperor, Kaiser Wilhelm II, who invited the Dunsmuirs aboard his vessel, and they in turn gave him a tour of the *Dolaura*. Back in Victoria, Dunsmuir served one more year as Lieutenant Governor, then resigned from his post on December 3, 1909, two years before his term was due to end, in order to enjoy a peaceful retirement at Hatley Park.

James and Laura Dunsmuir had ten children who survived infancy: two sons and eight daughters. As their elder son, Robin, enjoyed travelling, gambling, drinking and womanizing, James intended to train his more serious, younger son, James Jr.—nick-named "Boy"—to manage the family fortune. Boy, a keen eques-trian, joined the mounted militia as soon as war broke out in August 1914. After training in Winnipeg, he became a lieutenant in the 2nd Regiment, Canadian Mounted Rifles. His friend Robert Brackman Ker often visited him at Hatley Park and later recalled a clash that had occurred between father and son one evening in the library of Hatley Castle. James Jr. had finished his training in Winnipeg and, worried that the war would be over before he could go overseas, told his father he planned to quit the CMR and join a British regi-ment. "'Oh no, you won't. You're not twenty-one,' retorted his father. 'I'll be twenty-one in another month or two, then you can't stop me,' replied the defiant young man."[110] James Jr. did resign from the CMR, travelled to New York and booked passage on the Cunard liner, RMS *Lusitania*, despite public warnings that the German navy was targeting vessels flying the British flag. On May 7, 1915, within sight of Ireland, a German submarine sank the *Lusitania*. James Dunsmuir Jr. died along with another 1,197 passengers. When the news reached Victoria, where the young man had been a popular member of the CMRs, anti-German riots broke out. In his grief James Dunsmuir donated large sums to the war effort, supporting a hospital in Paris and the Red Cross, and purchased $500,000 in Victory Bonds. He spent increasing time at his cabin on the Cowichan River and died there on June 6, 1920.

Thomas Wilson Paterson (1909–14)

Thomas Wilson Paterson, British Columbia's ninth Lieutenant Gov-ernor, had both origin and elite economic status in common with his predecessor. Both the Paterson and Dunsmuir families came from Scotland to North America with young children; neither family was wealthy at the time; and both became involved in the construction of the Esquimalt and Nanaimo (E&N) Railway.

Paterson was born on December 6, 1850, in Darvel, Ayreshire, Scotland, and his parents, William and Margaret, emigrated to Canada West with their family when Thomas was three years old. They settled in Ontario but relocated several times in an effort to find work. Thomas did not go to school for long since his wages were needed to help support his family. One of his first jobs was shovelling dirt for railway construction along the Welland Canal, but he was a hard worker and understood mechanics, and before long he became a partner in the construction company Larkin, Connolly and Paterson. In the early 1880s Paterson moved the company west to work on various sections of the Canadian Pacific Railway, and at thirty-two he was awarded a contract to build a section of the Dunsmuir family's Esquimalt and Nanaimo Railway.

The surveying and construction of the Esquimalt and Nanaimo Railway Company had been divided into two sections, the first from Esquimalt north for 38.4 kilometres (24 mi) to a point along Shawnigan Lake, and the second from Shawnigan Lake north to Nanaimo, a distance of 80 kilometres (50 mi). Paterson and his new company, Bell, Larkin and Paterson, got their chance after the company awarded the contract to clear and grade the northern section went broke, and by the summer of 1885 they were employing about 900 men, including both Chinese and white labourers. On August 13, 1886, the last spike of the E&N Railway was driven by Prime Minister John A. Macdonald on the east side of Shawnigan Lake near the point where the two sections of the line met.

That same year Paterson married Emma Elizabeth Riley, the daughter of a Victoria merchant, George Riley. Shortly after the Esquimalt and Nanaimo Railway was completed, Thomas and Emma Paterson and George Riley set off for the Interior to build the Shuswap and Okanagan Railway, a branch line connecting the Canadian Pacific Railway with the Okanagan Valley. The railway was completed in May 1892 with much of the labour being done by Chinese workers, and the CPR took over its operation the following year. The Patersons and Rileys enjoyed a leisurely lifestyle while the railway was under construction, the two families living in the large "railroad house" where they had "two Chinamen servants, & everything very comfortable—later dinners—and no early rising."[111]

Thomas Wilson Paterson and his business partner (and father–in–law),
George Riley, built the Shuswap and Okanagan Railway, seen here under
construction. The railway connected the Okanagan to the Canadian Pacific Railway
at Sicamous by 1892.
Image courtesy of Royal BC Museum and Archives, A–O6871.

After completing the Shuswap and Okanagan Railway, Paterson moved back to Victoria where he built 8 kilometres (5 mi) of the downtown section of the new street railway along Fort, Government and Douglas Streets. In March 1893 he won the contract to construct a railway connecting Victoria with the town of Sidney to the north. Not only did Paterson earn $15,833.33 per mile of the Victoria & Sidney (V&S) Railway, but he also took advantage of an option to purchase stock in the holding company, the Saanich Land Company, and soon became secretary of the company. He completed the railway and its associated buildings and stations for the V&S Railway in April 1895, then remained with the company as general manager for a monthly wage of $250. He also had a contract to provide the cordwood that was used to fuel the locomotives.

The new railway promoted settlement on the peninsula, provided a way for farmers to deliver their produce to market in Victoria and gave them a source of income in the winter months cutting cordwood for the line. However, the V&S was not a commercial success, and to increase ridership and freight transportation, in 1900 Paterson purchased the 22-metre (72-ft) shelter-deck steamer *Iroquois,* to carry passengers, freight and mail from Sidney to Nanaimo and the Gulf Islands. The *Iroquois,* "an ungainly, top-heavy little vessel of 195 tons,"[112] operated six days a week, and on two of those days made the trip north to Nanaimo. As business increased, Paterson broadened the upper deck by 1 metre (3 ft) to make space for more cargo, although this increased the instability of the vessel. The provincial government supported Paterson's endeavour by building wharves at various Gulf Island harbours and even dredged a canal between North and South Pender Islands to make the route of the *Iroquois* shorter. (It was not until 1955 that a bridge was built to reconnect the islands.)

While the *Iroquois* provided an essential service, delivering the mail daily, carrying supplies to the islanders and bringing their produce to Sidney, the *Victoria Daily Times* also recommended it as "an unique opportunity to the man of affairs who finds it impossible to take a protracted vacation, to snatch a day from the desk and counter and to undertake a cheap, yet ideal outing with his family."[113]

In 1908 the *Iroquois* capsized off Jack Point near Nanaimo, and after it was salvaged and put back into service, Paterson sold it. Then on April 10, 1911, it left the Sidney dock in windy weather and fifteen minutes later, when some of the cargo shifted, the vessel tipped to one side, capsized and sank. Although there are different accounts of the number of survivors, about eleven of the thirty-one passengers and crew were saved, three of them rescued by Cowichan men in a dugout canoe. Ultimately, owner and Captain Arthur A. Sears, who survived the incident, was found guilty of negligence for failing to secure the cargo safely.[114]

Thomas Paterson was defeated in his first run at provincial politics when he attempted to win the seat for Victoria North in 1898, but four years later he gave up the management of the V&S and tried again in the same riding. This time he was elected, though his success was somewhat suspect since the *Iroquois* had made a special run to Vancouver to gather up men to vote on Galiano Island under assumed identities. In the ensuing court case, however, the blame was laid not on Paterson but on Philip Robinson, who was found guilty of recruiting and paying the fake voters. Paterson served in the BC Legislature for the next five years, during which time he was also involved in civic politics in Victoria and elected president of the Board of Trade in September 1905. He was defeated as a Victoria mayoral candidate in January 1907 and two weeks later lost his provincial seat to A.E. McPhillips.

By this time, thanks to his railway contracts, his management position with the Victoria and Sidney Railway and his contract to supply that rail line with cordwood, Paterson had become a wealthy man who could afford to invest in land and expensive leisure activities. A farm he owned near Ladner that was managed by his nephew, A.D. Paterson, employed the latest tractor technology and won prizes for its shorthorn cattle. In 1906 he had also bought Moresby Island near Sidney and established a dairy farm there that was managed by a Quaker farmer, Stanley Harris, while much of the heavy work was done by Japanese labourers.

When James Dunsmuir left the position of Lieutenant Governor prematurely in December 1909, Laurier was in a rush to find a replacement, and within ten days of Dunsmuir's resignation, Paterson received a telegram inviting him to take up the post. Like Dunsmuir, he had the wealth necessary to take on a position that involved entertainment expenses that far exceeded the salary provided by the government.

Paterson's term began on December 3, 1909, in a period of economic prosperity and optimism, and Victoria was experiencing a building boom. Intent on beautifying Government House as some of his predecessors had done, Paterson hired Vancouver land-scape architect G.K. Maclean to design the first overall plan for the gardens. As the house had been built on a hill overlooking Fairfield, it had plenty of rocks but not much water, and Maclean, therefore, proposed building rock gardens hydrated by water flowing through concealed pipes that would allow the creation of pools and small waterfalls. His plan also included the enlargement of the small pond in front of the house with a tennis court built next to it and driveways meandering through the property to accommodate auto-mobiles. A gasoline-powered lawn mower was acquired, a state-of-the-art sprinkler system installed, a heating plant was built to keep the greenhouses warm year round, and a wrought iron gate added at the entrance. Although not all of the roads in the Maclean plan were paved while Paterson was living at Government House, in 1913 he was able to drive his newly purchased automobile, a Winston Six, which cost $6,000, around the grounds.[115]

Paterson took up golf and on April Fool's Day 1910 he captained a team of civil servants playing against the military. Professional hockey had just arrived in the city, where the mild climate required artificial ice, and on January 12, 1912, he dropped the puck for a game featuring the Victoria Aristocrats and the New Westminster Royals, the first professional hockey game played west of Toronto.

In late September 1912 Paterson hosted the Governor General, the Duke of Connaught, his wife and daughter, and the Duke was invited to lay cornerstones on new buildings such as the provincial library and the seamen's institute. After their sojourn in Victoria, which also included a visit to Paterson's farm on Moresby Island, the vice-regal party explored coastal British Columbia on the CPR steamer *Princess Alice,* going as far north as the Alaskan boundary,

As Governor General, the Duke of Connaught visited British Columbia in September 1912. Seated, from left to right, are Princess Patricia of Connaught, Emma Paterson, the Duke and Duchess of Connaught and Thomas Wilson Paterson.
Image courtesy of Royal BC Museum and Archives, G–07099.

then stopping in Port Simpson where they met Tsimshian Chief Dudoward and his wife, who presented the Duchess with a painted paddle. On the way back they stopped in Alert Bay, where the Kwakwaka'wakw residents paused in their potlatch to perform a dance, which the vice-regal party viewed from the rail of the steamer. Potlatches, central ceremonial events held by West Coast First Nations, marked a wide range of important occasions and established claims to property and resources. They were banned by the federal government in 1884 but continued with minimal enforcement until after the First World War. The *Victoria Daily Colonist* reported that at the end of the dance, "one of the dancers came forward and presented his headgear to His Royal Highness. Mr. Halliday, Indian Agent, took the headgear from the dancer, and handed it up to His Royal Highness who was standing at the rail."[116]

Paterson's term came to an end on December 5, 1914, four months after Canada had entered the First World War. In preparation for his retirement, Paterson had commissioned architect Henry Sandham Griffith to design a new house for his family to be built on waterfront property at 3150 Rutland Road in the new and elite Uplands subdivision. A photo of Paterson's house, which reflected "an adapted mission-revival style with stucco arches forming a large porte cochere and supporting a wrap-around veranda" was chosen to grace the cover of a brochure advertising the Uplands.[117] Thomas Paterson enjoyed his retirement home until his death in Victoria in 1921 at the age of seventy; his wife Emma lived until 1944.

Unlike many of his immediate predecessors, in Thomas Paterson's five years in the vice-regal post he did not have to face any political crises that required him to exercise his reserve powers. Instead, as the second of British Columbia's extraordinarily wealthy Lieutenant Governors, he concentrated on building the reputation of Government House as an elegant vice-regal estate.

IV

BC's Lieutenant Governors and the First World War

PATRIOTISM, DEEPENING ETHNIC divisions and a desire for reform all shaped British Columbia's experience of the Great War. Because of the "British character" of BC and the high proportion of males in the population—67.8 per cent British and 70 per cent male, according to the 1911 census[118]— the province had relatively high enlistment rates. Almost 10 per cent of British Columbia's population volunteered, and of the 55,570 who served in the forces, 6,225 died and 13,000 were wounded.[119] Reformers, however, gained concrete achievements during these war years, such as the vote for women in 1917 and the adoption of Prohibition from 1917 to 1920.

Meanwhile, the war was creating divisions in BC between citizens of British origin and people from Germany and the Austro-Hungarian Empire who had immigrated to Canada in the years before the war. Now considered enemy aliens, some were interned while others were required to report regularly to local authorities. One's loyalty could be questioned during the war, even that of the Lieutenant Governor. Grief and anger over the sinking of the *Lusitania* were especially strong in Victoria, where rioters threatened to march on Government House because the chatelaine was of German descent.

On the other hand, there was also a new generosity of spirit on the home front. When Canada entered the First World War alongside Great Britain on August 4, 1914, the Governor General, the Duke of Connaught, created the Canadian Patriotic Fund to raise money for soldiers' families who found themselves in need. BC Lieutenant Governor Thomas Paterson, who was nearing the end of his term, volunteered to become a member of the national executive and assist in initiating the Victoria branch of the fund. Members of the Victoria board included BC's Premier Sir Richard McBride and Frank Stillman Barnard, who would succeed Paterson as BC's Lieutenant Governor. Both Paterson and Barnard gave generously as did Colonel Edward G. Prior, who would follow Barnard as Lieutenant Governor in 1919.

Participation in the First World War played an integral part in the construction of a Canadian identity and in increasing Canada's sovereignty. In 1919 Canada signed the Treaty of Versailles separately from Britain. Canada also had a seat at the League of Nations. In time, service in the war seemed to become a prerequisite to appointment as Lieutenant Governor in this province. In fact, every BC Lieutenant Governor from 1941 to 1968 had fought in the First World War. As representatives of the Crown, Lieutenant Governors and their chatelaines before, during and immediately after the war served as role models in their support of the armed forces and war-related fundraising efforts. After the war, they helped usher in a new peace, representing the Crown in commemorative events in an attempt to come to terms with the incomprehensible losses.

Francis Stillman Barnard (1914–19)

Francis "Frank" Stillman Barnard, who replaced Thomas Paterson as Lieutenant Governor on December 9, 1914, and remained in that role for the remainder of the war, was a businessman who, like his father, Francis Jones Barnard, had been an innovator in the province's transportation industry. Francis Jones Barnard was descended from a Loyalist family in Quebec. When his own father died, it fell to then-twelve-year-old Francis Jones to support his family. He married Ellen Stillman, an Irish immigrant, in 1853, and their son, Francis Stillman Barnard, was born on May 16, 1856. But lured by British Columbia's gold rush, Barnard soon left his wife and young son behind to head west. Settling in Yale, he started out doing odd jobs, such as cutting cordwood, working as a constable, building trails and serving as purser on the steamer *Fort Yale*. By 1860 he was offering a mail delivery service to the new gold diggings in the Cariboo; the job entailed walking from Yale to the Cariboo, a return trip of over 1,200 kilometres (750 mi), with a sack full of letters, which he delivered for a dollar each. In that same year the family was reunited when Ellen and their son moved west; the Barnards had two more children, George Henry and Alice. Frank attended school in Yale until the age of ten, then spent four years at the Collegiate School in Victoria; while he was studying there, his family relocated to the capital city.

In 1863 Francis Jones Barnard began purchasing horse-drawn wagons to carry the mail between Lillooet and Alexandria, then partnered with George Dietz and Hugh Nelson (Lieutenant Governor 1887–92) to transport government mail from Victoria to Yale. The Cariboo Wagon Road, which reached Soda Creek in 1863 and Barkerville in 1865, allowed Barnard to expand his business and carry travellers in relative comfort in fourteen-passenger coaches, each drawn by six horses. The horses for this venture, raised on the BX Ranch, which Barnard had established just outside Vernon in 1860, pulled the freight wagons and stagecoaches of Barnard's Express until 1892 when the Shuswap and Okanagan Railway connected Vernon to the Canadian Pacific Railway. By the mid-1860s Barnard's company had thirty-eight employees and four hundred horses. According to historian Margaret Ormsby, in 1864 "Barnard's stagecoaches travelled some 110,000 miles [176,000 km], carried all the mail to the Interior, transported 1,500 passengers to and from Soda Creek at the one-way fare of $130, and conveyed $4,619,000 worth of gold from the Cariboo to Yale."[120]

In 1866 Barnard bought out Dietz and Nelson in order to gain control of the entire express route from Victoria to Barkerville. The following year he was elected to the Legislative Council of BC. He favoured union with Canada and the construction of a transcontinental wagon road to BC, which would have furthered his transportation empire; instead, the federal and provincial governments agreed on a railway. In the 1870s two unlucky business decisions resulted in financial losses for Barnard: the six steamrollers he ordered from Scotland to use on the Cariboo Road proved unsuitable for local conditions, and in 1879 his contract to build part of a telegraph line via the Yellowhead Pass was cancelled after the government decided against that route for the transcontinental railway. Possibly as a result of these financial stresses, Barnard suffered a stroke in 1880. His ill health brought his son, Frank Stillman Barnard, back to BC from London, Ontario, where he was studying at Hellmuth College, to take over the business.

Although only twenty-four, the younger Barnard showed that he was a dynamic manager and investor by developing influential energy, resource and transportation companies that would shape the emerging economy and society of the province. These included the purchase of the Columbia and Kootenay Steamship Navigation Company and the Okanagan Land and Development Company, which promoted the emerging city of Vernon. He invested in a number of mining companies and, with a group of investors, purchased the Hastings Mill. He turned Barnard's Express into the Victoria Transfer Company, offering freight and passenger transportation, and in April 1894 became manager of the newly formed Consolidated Railway and Light Company. Over the next two years, with support from London financier Robert Horne-Payne, Consolidated Railway and Light purchased the Vancouver street railway and lighting system, the New Westminster and Vancouver Tramway Company, and the Victoria Electric Railway and Lighting Company, the three major electrical streetcar and lighting companies in the province.

However, disaster struck the city of Victoria and its streetcar system on May 26, 1896, the third day of local celebrations marking Queen Victoria's birthday. Victorians heading to Esquimalt to watch a Royal Navy sail-past crowded onto Streetcar No. 16, and it started across the Point Ellice Bridge with 142 passengers, far too many for its size. When it was halfway across, the bridge collapsed and the car plunged into the Gorge, killing fifty-five people.

Frank Stillman Barnard was manager of the Consolidated Railway and Light Company, which included the Victoria electric railway system, when an overcrowded streetcar caused the collapse of the Point Ellice Bridge on May 26, 1896. Fifty–five people died.
Image courtesy of Royal BC Museum and Archives, A–04605.

In the aftermath, the Consolidated Railway Company went into receivership and was sold at auction in Vancouver that November. The company changed hands a couple more times before April 1897 when Horne-Payne repurchased what was by then called the BC Electric Company. With Barnard reinstated as managing director, the new company rebounded from its loss, and in 1898 the company built BC's first hydroelectric plant on the Goldstream River, northwest of Victoria. Barnard managed the company for just a year before resigning, though he remained a director.

Frank Barnard had served as a Victoria city councilor in 1886–87 and, following in his father's footsteps, as the Conservative MP for Lillooet–Cariboo from 1888 to 1896. He also ran for provincial election in 1902 but was unsuccessful. However, he was a supporter of party government and that same year participated in the Conservative Party committee, which led to the election of Richard McBride as premier in 1903. He decided not to run again for office but set off with his wife to explore Europe, Australia and Asia.

In November 1883 Frank Stillman Barnard had married Martha Amelia Loewen, the eldest daughter of Joseph Loewen, a wealthy Victoria brewer. The Prussia-born Loewen had been drawn to the North American west—in his case California—by the lure of gold before he made his way north to Victoria, where in 1870 he had partnered with Louis Erb to purchase the Victoria Brewery. Loewen and Erb's business prospered, and in 1892 they demolished their brewery in order to construct the imposing six-storey Victoria Brewing and Ice Company, which after a merger the following year became the Victoria-Phoenix Brewing Company. In Victoria Joseph Loewen had married Eva Laumeister, whose father, Frank, had achieved some notoriety by introducing camels as pack animals on the route to the Cariboo goldfields. In 1892 the Loewens had a Queen Anne-style mansion built, which they called "Rockwood," overlooking the Gorge just west of the rapids at what is now Tillicum Road. Joseph and Eva Loewen raised a musical family—six daughters who all sang and played the piano—and they enjoyed entertaining.

Frank Stillman Barnard began his term as Lieutenant Governor of British Columbia on December 5, 1914, and many of his and his wife's subsequent activities were oriented toward promoting the success of Britain and its allies in the war in Europe. Together the Barnards hosted Allied guests, while Martha held garden parties to raise funds for the Red Cross and organized parties to sew clothing for soldiers. Despite her efforts to support the war effort, however, Victorians were critical of her German heritage, and the public mood turned uglier after the sinking of the RMS *Lusitania* on May 7, 1915. In particular, Victorians grieved the loss of James "Boy" Dunsmuir, the popular son of the former premier and Lieutenant Governor. Communities across the province had already been expressing anger and suspicion toward German-Canadians, calling for their wholesale internment, and now rioters in Victoria damaged businesses that appeared to be German-owned, including breweries and the Kaiserhof Hotel (later re-christened the Blanshard) until the mayor was forced to call in the militia. On May 10 a mob threatened to march on Government House after malicious rumours circulated that the Barnards had pro-German sympathies and had celebrated the kaiser's birthday; fortunately, the *Daily Colonist* was able to report the next day that the authorities had the situation in hand after twenty-five soldiers were stationed on the

Anti–German riots broke out in Victoria in response to the sinking of the *Lusitania* in May 1915. After targeting establishments such as the Kaiserhof Hotel, seen here, rioters threatened to march on Government House because of Chatelaine Martha Barnard's German heritage and due to malicious rumours that the Barnards had celebrated the kaiser's birthday.

Image courtesy of Royal BC Museum and Archives, A–02709.

grounds for the protection of the vice-regal couple.[121] It is not clear how close the rioters came to Government House. The Lieutenant Governor's private secretary, Henry Joseph Salisbury Muskett, placed public notices in the newspaper assuring the public that no celebration of the kaiser's birthday had taken place and that the Lieutenant Governor was thoroughly loyal to Britain and its allies.

In fact, the King's representative and his Victoria-born wife likely felt the loss of James Dunsmuir, Jr., more keenly than many Victorians, given their close friendship with the Dunsmuirs. The two families moved in the same social circles, and a photo that Frank Barnard took in 1893 shows four of the young Dunsmuir girls in fur-trimmed coats in front of Rockwood.[122] In 1897 Martha Barnard had invited one of the Dunsmuir sisters to vacation with her at the BX Ranch in Vernon. Alice Barrett Parke, wife of ranch manager Harold Parke, observed primly in her diary that Mrs. Barnard, her two sisters and Miss Dunsmuir "are all nice happy, giddy girls, but a little too 'awfully' intense & emphatic for really good style. Mrs. Barnard is the prettiest & has the best manners I think."[123]

Despite the negative attention the Barnards received during the

Lusitania riots, just a few weeks later they hosted a concert to raise funds for the Red Cross. Martha Barnard regularly coordinated events with organizations such as the Imperial Order of Daughters of the Empire (IODE) and held "working parties" at Government House for the Red Cross every few weeks. The Barnards also allowed organizations such as the King's Daughters and the Women's Canadian Club to use Government House as a site for fundraising events, and they acted as patrons of, or supported, organizations such as the Blue Cross Fund, which raised funds for horses in wartime, the Victoria Branch of the Navy League, which sent parcels to sailors, and the Sister Susie Club, which fundraised for widows and orphans. In July 1918 the band of a visiting Japanese cruiser gave a concert at Government House with admission fees going to the Red Cross.[124]

The Barnards hosted a number of distinguished visitors during the war years. The Governor General of Canada, the Duke of Connaught, and the Duchess of Connaught visited Victoria in the summer of 1916. The next Governor General, the Duke of Devonshire, visited western Canada in 1917, and the Prince of Wales, the future King Edward VIII, toured Victoria in September 1919. The Duke and Duchess of Devonshire returned that October, and Admiral and Lady Jellicoe came in November. John Jellicoe had been commander of the Royal Navy from the outbreak of war to 1917 and would become Governor General of New Zealand in 1920.

Meanwhile, the high turnover in provincial leadership following Premier Richard McBride's twelve years in office required an active constitutional engagement from Frank Barnard. When McBride retired on December 15, 1915, Barnard swore in his successor, William John Bowser, but Bowser was defeated at the polls less than a year later on November 23, 1916. Harlan Carey Brewster formed the next government, but he died in office on March 1, 1918, and Barnard then called on John Oliver to be the next premier, a position Oliver held until his death in 1927.

Following a referendum during the 1916 election, British Columbia introduced Prohibition on October 1, 1917. It was a limited success, since those who wanted a drink could import it from outside of British Columbia, buy it at a bootlegger's or pay for a doctor's prescription for medicinal liquor available from a drugstore or government store. According to historian John T. Saywell, Barnard's family ties to the brewing industry may have led him to exceed his constitutional

During his term as Lieutenant Governor, Frank S. Barnard swore in a succession of three premiers following the retirement of Richard McBride, and gave royal assent to Prohibition in 1917.

Image courtesy of Royal BC Museum and Archives, B-01964.

role when it came to the prohibition of alcohol. Barnard reportedly "refused to assent to prohibition in British Columbia unless the government promised to appoint a commission to determine damages to be paid to the liquor interests and [he] continued to put pressure on successive premiers for three years."[125]

Even during Prohibition, however, champagne was available for special events, and on March 27, 1919, Martha Barnard christened the steamer *Strasbourg*, which had been constructed by Foundation Shipyards in Victoria. The *Daily Colonist* reported that "Lady Barnard stood on the launching platform with beribboned champagne bottle poised; the shipyard band ceased playing; the big crowd stood tensely waiting," but the vessel, stuck on hardened grease, failed to slide down the ways and into the water. She broke the champagne bottle anyway, and after a spray of champagne landed on workers attempting to dislodge the steamer, bystanders "pictured them with their tongues out trying to lap up some of the precious liquid which was dripping from their caps."[126] Following a plebiscite in October 1920, British Columbia became the first province in English Canada to repeal Prohibition, and after June 1921 British Columbians could purchase alcohol, though only from government stores.

Despite a challenging start to their residency at Government House, Frank and Martha Barnard proved well-suited to the tasks required of a vice-regal couple, and along with several other Canadian Lieutenant Governors of the day, Barnard was knighted for his services in 1919. When the couple left Government House on December 9, 1919, they resumed their travels in Europe and spent time in California. Francis Stillman Barnard died in Victoria at age eighty on April 11, 1936; Martha Barnard was seventy-six when she died in 1942.

Edward Gawlor Prior (1919–20)

Edward Gawlor Prior was well qualified to follow Frank Barnard as British Columbia's Lieutenant Governor in the immediate post-war period. A mining engineer and inspector of mines, he had left the provincial civil service in the 1880s to start a hardware company. He had experience in both provincial and federal politics, and although he had been too old to go to war, he was firmly entrenched in military traditions through his leadership in the BC militia. Serving briefly as an aide-de-camp for two Governors General had given him an insider's perspective into the vice-regal role.

Edward Gawlor Prior, the second son of an Anglican minister, was born May 1, 1853, in Dallowgill, Yorkshire. He was educated at Leeds Grammar School and studied mining engineering at Wakefield. When he was twenty years old, he sailed from England and travelled overland across the United States to take a job as an engineer and surveyor with the Vancouver Coal Mining and Land Company in Nanaimo. While working there, he helped found the Nanaimo Rifles, a division of the volunteer force whose first West Coast units had been formed in Victoria and New Westminster in the 1860s in response to threats related to the American Civil War and Fenian raids. As a result of the mobility of British Columbia's workforce at that time, these early militia units were generally short-lived, but in 1871 BC's units became part of the Canadian militia, giving them more legitimacy.

Appointed provincial inspector of mines in 1877, Prior relocated to Victoria. There on January 31, 1878, he married Suzette Work, the youngest daughter of retired fur trader John Work (ca. 1792–1861), who was born in Ireland, and Josette Legacé, who had French-Canadian and Spokane ancestry. Work's family had moved with him throughout the Columbia and Northwest Coast regions as he held positions at various fur trading posts. When his children were young, he had been concerned about the discrimination they might face in white society, and in 1834 he wrote to a colleague, "I have now here four fine little girls, had I them a little brushed up with education and a little knowledge of the world, they would scarcely be known to be Indians."[127]

In 1852 Work became one of the Hudson's Bay Company fur traders who retired with their Indigenous or Métis partners and families to Victoria where, as early settlers, they could become part of the landed elite. He bought 823 acres (330 ha) of farmland on the city's northern edge and built a mansion he called "Hillside"; by the time of his death in 1861 he had enlarged his estate to 1,800 acres (720 ha) and become one of the colony's largest landowners. Colonists arriving after the gold rush, however, often looked down on mixed families such as Work's, though the daughters of these founding families tended to be economically and socially more successful than the sons, marrying elite newcomers who could see the advantages to be had from political connections and access to land.

Edward and Suzette Prior returned to Nanaimo where he continued to work as inspector of mines. When they moved to Victoria a few years later, Prior partnered with Alfred Fellows to open a hardware store on Yates Street. When Fellows left for England three years later, Prior bought him out and expanded the business, now called E.G. Prior & Company, opening branches in Kamloops and Vancouver.

Thanks to his thriving hardware business, in 1884 Prior commissioned the construction of a twelve-room Italianate mansion on a four-acre plot on Rockland Avenue; the family christened it "The Priory." His eldest daughter, Nellie, who was six years old when the house was built, recalled that "we moved up to—they called it Nob Hill—near Government House, and in later days they called it Snob Hill because so many big houses went up there."[128] A community-oriented couple, Edward and Suzette enjoyed singing and acting. Suzette sang in a group that included Chief Justice Sir Matthew Baillie Begbie, and Edward Prior played the pirate king in *Pirates of Penzance* at the Victoria Theatre.

Throughout his life, Prior remained a dedicated member of the British Columbia militia. From 1888 to 1896 he was head of Victoria's Fifth Regiment, Canadian Artillery. Although the militia volunteers were unpaid and had to supply their own uniforms, they enjoyed the prestige associated with membership. In addition, militia activities included social events, sports and travel. Nellie Prior recalled that one of the popular events staged by the militia units were "sham fights" on Beacon Hill in Victoria in which "they'd disappear behind the hill and then they'd run up . . . and pop their little guns off." From the top of the hill, spectators could see the army "sneaking round and pretending to surprise the navy." Great crowds, including children, came out to watch these battles, which were accompanied by much fanfare: "Flags were flying everywhere, and the bands playing."[129]

For officers such as Prior, service in the militia actually involved significant expenditures of money as well as time. The BC Rifle Association, established in 1874 with both civilian and militia members, regularly sent marksmen to the shooting competitions in Bisley, England, and in 1890 Prior led the Canadian team. While there, he displayed photographs of western Canada, which, according to family lore, caught the eye of Queen Victoria's eldest son, Albert Edward, who "came down twice to see them because he'd heard it was such a wild and woolly place, you know, just out in the wilds somewhere, and he couldn't believe it when he saw the photographs. It was a bit civilized . . . But the views were lovely, and it advertised Victoria a lot."[130] In his role as commander of Victoria's 5th Regiment, Prior welcomed dignitaries to the city, and when Prince Roland Bonaparte, ethnographer and grandson of Napoleon's brother, visited Victoria in May 1893, Prior held a dinner for him at which Lieutenant Governor and Mrs. Dewdney were also present.[131] In 1898 Prior covered the travel expenses for his regiment to visit Seattle for the Fourth of July celebrations.[132]

Patriotic !—At the Sham Fight, Beacon Hill, May 24.

Papa's Boy—" Gee !   Don't I wish I was a cannon firing solger."
Mama's Boy—" I'd rather be a solger hidin' in the broom."
Sally—" And I'm glad I'm a wummon !"

As the head of Victoria's 5th Regiment, Canadian Artillery, Edward Prior helped
organize "sham fights" between the army and the navy at Beacon Hill Park in
Victoria. Artist Emily Carr sketched children watching one such fight.
Image courtesy of Royal BC Museum and Archives, B–08161.

In addition to running his hardware company and volunteering in
the militia, Prior had an active political career. After a two-year stint
as MLA for Victoria, he was elected to Parliament as the Conservative Member for Victoria in 1888 and appointed to the cabinet of
Prime Minister Mackenzie Bowell as controller of Internal Revenue
in 1895. While serving as an MP, Prior divided his time between
Ottawa and Victoria, and was therefore available to serve as aide-
de-camp for Governors General Lord Stanley (1888–93) and Lord
Aberdeen (1893–98) when they visited Victoria. When Lord and
Lady Aberdeen came in November 1894, Prior also organized an
evening party at the Drill Hall. Impressed with the food, decorations
and decorum of the event, Lord Aberdeen wrote in his wife's diary
that "the arrangements were most admirably carried out" by Prior.[133]
When the Aberdeens returned to Victoria the next summer, Prior
accompanied them on their tour of the navy in Esquimalt as they had
none of their "regular ADCs with staff uniforms in attendance."[134]

In 1897 Prior journeyed to London to attend the Diamond Jubilee of Queen Victoria, "the only Conservative that Liberal Sir Wilfrid Laurier took over for the coronation."[135] Unfortunately, that was also the year that Prior's wife, Suzette, died from cancer. In 1899 Prior married a second time; the bride was Genevieve Boucher Kennedy Wright, a widow visiting Victoria from San Francisco.

Edward Prior held his federal seat until the election of 1900 when it was discovered that some of his supporters had run afoul of the Elections Act. However, BC Premier James Dunsmuir, who regarded Prior as a potential cabinet member, encouraged him to run for provincial office again, and when Prior was elected in 1902, Dunsmuir appointed him Minister of Mines.

When Dunsmuir resigned as premier of British Columbia in November 1902, he advised Lieutenant Governor Henri-Gustave Joly de Lotbinière to ask Prior to form a government. It would prove to be the last in a series of short administrations, surviving only to the

Elected as the Conservative MP for Victoria in 1888, Edward Prior is seen here (standing at right) with other British Columbian members of Parliament. This group also includes Frank S. Barnard, standing second from left, and his brother-in-law John Mara, seated in the centre.

Image courtesy of Royal BC Museum and Archives, G–00024.

end of May 1903. Prior faced several problems during that time. In exchange for building a railway from Trail to Midway, the Columbia and Western Railway (a subsidiary of the CPR) had received large land grants in the Crow's Nest Pass where the company expected to find petroleum and coal. Dunsmuir's cabinet had agreed to the grants, but in April 1903 MLA John Oliver proposed that a select committee of the Legislature should investigate them. As a result of that investigation, Prior asked two cabinet ministers who had supported the grants to resign, but the loss of these ministers weakened his government, and after MLAs passed a non-confidence motion, Prior asked Lieutenant Governor Joly to dissolve the Legislature. At about this time some MLAs had been investigating a government contract won by Prior's company to provide wire rope for a bridge at Chimney Creek on the Cariboo Road. It appears that Prior had seen the bids, although he denied informing his company of their content and argued that there was nothing wrong with the outcome since the province was going to save money. When Joly was informed, he refused to dissolve the government and instead dismissed Prior, explaining he was no longer confident of Prior's judgment and could not act on his advice.

In his study of Canada's Lieutenant Governors, historian John T. Saywell argues that if Joly's "principles had been universally applied, there would have been scores of dismissals in the Canadian provinces. However, [Joly's] dismissal [of Prior] was extremely gentle and it passed without criticism and with very little comment. Dismissal was old news to British Columbians."[136] Joly then called on Conservative Richard McBride to form a government, helping to usher in more than a decade of stability and, in the longer term, the introduction of party politics to British Columbia.

After his dismissal, Prior returned his attention to federal politics, but he was defeated in his bid to represent Victoria at the federal level in 1904, and he left politics to focus on his hardware business, volunteering and travelling. He served as president of the Board of Trade of Victoria and chairman of the Returned Soldiers' Employment Committee, and he and his second wife travelled to England several times. In 1908 they were presented to King Edward VII, who had admired Prior's photographs in 1890, and Queen Alexandra.

On December 9, 1919, Edward Gawlor Prior was installed as the first Lieutenant Governor of the post–World War I period. One of his first tasks, in January 1920, was to inspect a Chinese workforce at William Head, west of Victoria. At the beginning of the war about 84,000 workers had been recruited in China to labour on the battlefields of France to repair roads and railways, load cargo and clean up after the battles. They had been shipped across Canada in sealed railway cars before being loaded onto ships and sent to France, and now with the war over, about 50,000 of them were being returned home the same way.[137]

Prior's duties focused on commemorating the generation who had served in the war and those who had fallen, and on supporting the regeneration of society. On July 9, 1920, he unveiled a memorial in Oak Bay to men who died in the war. In August he inspected a summer camp for the naval brigade on the Gorge, after which eight boys attending the camp rowed him, the camp leader and the provincial president of the Navy League back to town. He became a patron and promoter of the Boy Scouts, gave a speech at a banquet for Canadian veterans and attended a dance to raise money for nurses.

The Priors hosted both international visitors and local residents. Among the guests at Government House in September 1920 was the Governor General, the Duke of Devonshire, and he was followed by Viscount Cave, who had served as British home secretary during the war and would later be appointed lord chancellor. Genevieve Prior was a dedicated hostess, holding "at homes" on a monthly basis, and in August the Priors held a large garden party, "a strictly formal affair," on the lawn in front of the summer house with music provided by the Great War Veterans' Association's band. And when a group of pilots flew across Canada in October 1920, they delivered messages to Prior from other Lieutenant Governors.[138]

Edward Gawlor Prior's term as Lieutenant Governor ended on December 12, 1920, when he died after a five-week illness. He had served for a scant year, but he had brought to the position of Lieutenant Governor a wealth of political experience, knowledge of the role of vice-regal representatives and a background of hosting distinguished visitors. Prior was the last of a series of politically experienced "Ottawa's men" to serve in this role. After Prior, the role of the Lieutenant Governors in British Columbia would undergo a dramatic shift.

V

Reaching Out to British Columbians in the 1920s

AS EARLY AS Confederation, the Governors General of Canada had made an effort to travel the country from coast to coast. As Scottish novelist and historian John Buchan (later Canada's Governor General, 1935–40) recommended, vice-regal representatives should show "an interest in every form of public activity" and visit "every corner of [their] dominion."[139]

In British Columbia, however, it was not until the 1920s that Lieutenant Governors were expected to travel throughout the province
and attend community events large and small, a shift in their role
that was partly brought about by the expanding rail and road systems that made it physically possible to reach more communities.
They may also have been influenced by the British monarchy's search
for popular relevance after the war. George V was making an extra
effort to reach out to the general population, increasing his public
appearances, radio broadcasts and support of charities. He involved
his sons and daughter in this project, too, hanging a map on the wall
of Buckingham Palace to "mark the extent of the family's expeditions
and at the end of the year calculated who had travelled furthest."[140]

It is also significant that the Lieutenant Governors appointed in
BC before the 1920s all had political experience, which had been
especially useful when it came to making constitutional decisions.
From 1920 to 1960, political and legal experience were not essential
for the job, while a willingness to travel, promote British Columbia
and host large events became increasingly important.

Walter Cameron Nichol (1920–26)

When Edward Prior died in office in December 1920, Prime Minister Arthur Meighen had to choose a replacement quickly, and he
selected a newspaper editor and owner, Walter Cameron Nichol. This
new Lieutenant Governor and his manner of carrying out his role
would change the game for all future incumbents in this office. Walter
Nichol was not only the first journalist appointed to the position, but
more significantly, he was the first Lieutenant Governor since Trutch
who did not have experience as a politician or senator.

Walter Nichol was born in Goderich, Upper Canada, on
October 15, 1866, the year before Canadian Confederation, the
sixth and youngest son of Robert Ker Addison Nichol and Cynthia
Jane Ballard. His paternal grandfather, Lieutenant-Colonel Robert
Nichol, had served with distinction in the War of 1812 and become
a prominent politician, but Walter Nichol's father was an unsuccessful barrister, and growing up in Hamilton, Ontario, the boy was
mostly educated by his mother. By age twelve he was working as a
messenger in a law office and in 1881, while still in his mid-teens, he
went to work for the *Hamilton Spectator*. He also served as editor
and writer for the short-lived monthly journal *Bicycle*, the official

organ of the Canadian Wheelmen's Association, which was at the leading edge of the new bicycling trend in Canada. Over the next decade he wrote for the *Evening News* in Toronto, helped found the Toronto weekly paper *Saturday Night,* then established another weekly paper, *Life,* also in Toronto, before returning to Hamilton and the *Hamilton Herald* in 1889 as a reporter. Seven years later he had risen to editor-in-chief when he left to found the *News* in London, Ontario.

In 1897 Nichol married Quita Josephine March Moore and together they went west, drawn by a mining boom in the Kootenay district of British Columbia. In July of that year he took the job of editor of the Kaslo *Kootenaian,* but by October he was in Victoria as editor of the weekly *Province,* owned by businessman and politician Hewitt Bostock. By now Nichol had established an aggressive editorial style, and he had no sooner settled into the editor's chair than he attacked the *Daily Colonist* for its support of Premier John Herbert Turner, stating that the *Colonist's* sole purpose was to protect the Dunsmuir family "in the enjoyment of the money-making monopolies which they have secured from hypnotized and venal legislatures."[141] In December, Turner and Attorney General Charles E. Pooley sued Nichol for libel, a case that was not resolved until October 1901 when Nichol was found not guilty. In March 1898 Bostock started a daily version of the *Province* in Vancouver, and Nichol moved there to edit it; he bought the controlling interest in the paper in 1901. By 1910 the *Province* was the most influential newspaper in British Columbia.

Walter Nichol was just fifty-four years old in December 1920 when he was appointed Lieutenant Governor to replace the late Edward Gawlor Prior, whose death had created a constitutional emergency: until a new Lieutenant Governor was appointed, no orders-in-council could become law. While it was unusual for a journalist to be appointed to this post, the *BC Veterans' Weekly* commented that "as a journalist in daily touch with world-wide affairs,"[142] Nichol might possess the qualities of good judgment and broad experience necessary for the position. He was installed in his office in the Legislative Buildings early in January and "immediately set to work signing orders and crown grants, piled up on his desk by Mr. H.J. Muskett, the secretary," before he met with Premier Oliver and his ministers.[143]

At the time of Nichol's appointment, his family was away. Quita Nichol had spent Christmas in Switzerland and in January 1921 had moved on to London, England, where she was studying music and their daughter, Maraquita, was attending school. Walter and Quita's son, Jack, had served in the Air Force during the war, and by 1921 was studying at McGill University. After Quita returned to Victoria in March 1921, she was guest of honour at a reception sponsored by the Women's Canadian Club at the Empress Hotel. Later that month the Nichols hosted about three hundred guests at a ball for naval officers at Government House, which had been transformed into "a veritable fairyland with masses of hothouse blooms and springtime flowers, which adorned the dining room, reception hall and drawing room, while palms and foliage were the decorations noticed in the ballroom."[144] In late April 1921 Quita Nichol received almost a thousand guests at Government House at an event for which debutantes had been enlisted to serve the tea; the *Colonist* commended it as a "brilliant function."[145]

Quita Nichol also participated in community events such as the opening in July of an exhibition of crafts, baking, garden produce and sports organized by the Esquimalt Women's Institute. One of the highlights of the exhibition was a baby show in which twenty-nine babies were judged by two physicians, two nurses and Mrs. F. Campbell, "convenor of the child hygienic committee of the institute." Mrs. Nichol handed out the prizes for the babies and decorated perambulators.[146]

As Nichol's appointment to office had come just two years after the end of the war, many of the ceremonial activities he presided over commemorated the sacrifices British Columbians had made in the conflict. At a ceremony attended by about five thousand people in early October 1921, he planted the first tree in a "Road of Remembrance" along a straight stretch of Shelbourne Street in Saanich that leads to Mount Douglas Park. It was inspired by the tree-lined country roads that Canada's soldiers had marched along in France and represented new life conquering death. The trees chosen were London plane and American mountain ash, which were planted every 9 metres (30 ft); the ash trees grew quickly and were removed once the plane trees had matured. In his speech at the opening ceremony, Nichol dedicated the road "to the memories of those who fought and fell in the service of their Empire in South Africa and in France and Flanders that peace and civilization might endure." Trees, he said, were a living entity that would continue beyond the lifetime of those who planted them, but "he who plants a tree plants a hope."[147] In July 1925 Nichol unveiled a statue honouring Canada's war dead on the grounds of the Legislature.

Although Sir Henri-Gustave Joly de Lotbinière did visit BC communities beyond Victoria and Vancouver in an official capacity, it does not appear that this became a customary responsibility of the Lieutenant Governor until the 1920s. In this way, Nichol initiated a significant change to the vice-regal role. In July 1921 he and his private secretary, H.J. Muskett, opened an irrigation convention in Vernon, then proceeded south through Kelowna to Penticton, returning to Vancouver on the Kettle Valley Railway. In August he made an unofficial visit to Cumberland where he spoke to the Board of Trade and officials from Canadian Collieries and stayed at the home of James Savage, the manager of the collieries.[148] He supported city beautification, donating $300 in 1923 to promote gardening in Nelson; this prompted the city council to offer a trophy for the most beautiful gardens, which were judged by the Nelson Horticultural Society. In response to the increasing popularity of the automobile, he also promoted tourism and the expansion of the province's highway system. In May 1923 he opened a new auto camp at Curtis Point in Victoria. Two months later he and Alberta Lieutenant Governor Dr. Robert G. Brett opened the federal government's new Banff–Windermere Highway, one of the first road links between BC and Alberta; to protect wildlife along the new road, the federal government had also created Kootenay National Park. Two processions of automobiles, one from the east and one from the west, arrived for the ceremony, which took place "over the headwaters of the Kootenay, as the latter provided larger parking space."[149] At the opening ceremonies Ktunaxa people from Fort Steele, Tobacco Plains, Creston and other regional reserves performed ceremonial dances and displayed Indigenous arts; Nichol purchased a beaded buckskin dress made by Chief Louis la Bell's daughter.

In addition to travelling more widely in British Columbia, Nichol was the first Lieutenant Governor to shine a spotlight on the province's history by unveiling cairns for the federal Historic Sites and Monuments Board (HSMBC), which had been created in 1919 "to identify people, places and events of national historic

When Walter Cameron Nichol went to Yuquot (Friendly Cove) to unveil a memorial to Captain James Cook, Nuu–chah–nulth chief Captain Jack used the opportunity to deliver a speech arguing for the repeal of the potlatch ban. Here, Nichol is shaking hands with Chief Napoleon Maquinna, a descendant of Chief Maquinna, who welcomed Captain Cook in 1778.

Image courtesy of Royal BC Museum and BC Archives, A–06089.

significance."[150] The board had chosen Yuquot, on the west coast of Vancouver Island, as the site for British Columbia's first monument, and in August 1924 Nichol, along with several historians and members of early settler families, went to Nootka Sound to unveil a cairn commemorating Captain James Cook's arrival there in 1778.

Participants at the commemoration event expressed two fundamentally different perspectives: a settler appreciation of imperial achievements, versus Nuu-chah-nulth protest over restrictive laws. At the beginning of the Lieutenant Governor's speech, he thanked the Nuu-chah-nulth people for granting land for the cairn, then surveyed the history of European exploration of the Northwest Coast. Judge Frederick William Howay, who served as the western representative on the board from 1923 to 1943, described the cairn as "a memorial to Cook and the triumph of two British imperial ideals: that sovereignty over waste lands went to the first civilized nation that took real possession and that the oceans of the world are free to all nations."[151] Victor Harrison, chief factor of the Native Sons of British Columbia (representing the descendants of Euro-Canadian settlers), argued that colonialism in the form of law, Christianity and Western education had benefited Indigenous people, whom he mistakenly asserted shared the same rights as other Canadians. In contrast, Nuu-chah-nulth chief Captain Jack took the opportunity of an audience with the Crown's representative to argue that the anti-potlatch law of 1884 should be withdrawn. (Instead, three years later an amendment to the federal Indian Act was passed that prohibited Indigenous people from "raising money or hiring lawyers to pursue land claims.") Despite the conflicting points of view expressed at the meeting at Yuquot, a respectful exchange took place in the weeks that followed when Dominic Jim of the Ehattesaht village sent Nichol the gift of a 42-foot (13-m) war canoe, the *Weetatset,* which was installed on the grounds of Government House. In return Jim requested a power saw, which Nichol sent to him.[152] The following year HSMBC monuments were erected at Fort Langley, Gonzales Hill, Prince George, Stanley Park and on the Yale-Cariboo Road, although Nichol only participated in the event at Gonzales Hill in Victoria, which recognized early Spanish exploration of the coast.

Walter and Quita Nichol travelled abroad for four months in the fall of 1922, visiting England, France, Germany and Italy, and Nichol returned to London two years later. On his travels, Nichol promoted immigration to British Columbia. In his absence, James Alexander Macdonald, chief justice of the British Columbia Court of Appeal, acted on Nichol's behalf. In September 1925 the Lieutenant Governor of Quebec, Narcisse Pérodeau, invited all the other Lieutenant Governors and their wives to meet at Spencerwood in Quebec City for a conference, the first time such a meeting had occurred in Canada. "The object of the assembly," the *Daily Colonist* reported, "was largely that of letting the various lieutenant-governors become acquainted and of permitting them to discuss the many problems which they have in common."[153] Nichol later reflected that such a meeting could help develop Canadian unity and provide guidelines for future Lieutenant Governors.

Narcisse Pérodeau, the Lieutenant Governor of Quebec, organized the first meeting of Lieutenant Governors from across Canada in Quebec City in September 1925. At rear, left to right: Henry William Newlands (Saskatchewan), Walter Cameron Nichol (British Columbia), Frank Richard Heartz (Prince Edward Island), James Albert Manning Aikens (Manitoba); in front, left to right: James Robson Douglas (Nova Scotia), Narcisse Pérodeau (Quebec), Henry Cockshutt (Ontario), William Frederick Todd (New Brunswick). Missing: Robert Brett (Alberta).
Image courtesy of Bibliothèque et Archives nationales du Quebec, P600, S6, D2, P46.

During Walter Nichol's term in office, he and Quita hosted two Governors General. The Duke and Duchess of Devonshire came to Victoria in April 1921 to unveil the statue of Queen Victoria in front of the Legislative Buildings. Lord and Lady Byng arrived in Victoria on the *Princess Alice* in August 1922. Julian Byng, first Viscount Byng of Vimy, was the British cavalry officer who commanded the Canadian Corps during the First World War and planned the Canadian attack on Vimy Ridge in April 1917. On arrival in Victoria, he immediately inspected the guard of honour, speaking with the veterans and paying special attention to a soldier in a wheelchair and a blinded veteran in the crowd on the lawn of the Legislature. In his speech in the Legislature he spoke with optimism about the future of the province, praising the "good-fellowship," "collective responsibility" and character of the soldiers from British Columbia he had witnessed in the war.[154] The next day he unveiled a Cross of Sacrifice at the Ross Bay Cemetery. He also spoke to a joint meeting of the Canadian Club, Kiwanis Club and the Women's Canadian Club at the Empress Hotel, urging them to reach out to young men and women to teach them "the highest principles of citizenship."[155]

The Prince of Wales, the future Edward VIII, came to Victoria in October 1924 for an informal two-day visit. He stayed at the Empress Hotel and played golf in Oak Bay and Colwood with Major Selden Humphreys, Nichol's aide-de-camp. (Major Humphreys was married to Kathleen Dunsmuir, a daughter of James Dunsmuir, and although Nichol had once been critical of the *Colonist*'s support for the Dunsmuirs, relations seem to have improved.) A dinner dance was held in honour of the prince at Government House that evening, and he left for Vancouver the next day. Sir Robert and Lady Baden-Powell, originators of the scouting and guiding movement, visited in April 1923, and Field Marshal Sir Douglas Haig, who had served as commander of the British Expeditionary Force on the Western Front in France and Belgium, came to Victoria in 1925.

Nichol attended or officiated at the openings of cultural landmarks built during the prosperity and optimism of the mid-1920s such as Crystal Gardens in Victoria, which contained the largest saltwater pool in the Empire, and the first permanent buildings on the Point Grey campus of the University of British Columbia in Vancouver. He had always been a supporter of the arts, and as Lieutenant Governor he became president of the BC Art League and the Arts and Crafts Society of Victoria. The Arts and Crafts Movement, which was a reaction against the mass production that had resulted from industrialization, supported craftsmanship in everyday life and allowed individual craftsmen the time to create beautiful objects from start to finish. At that time some of the finest arts-and-crafts homes in Canada were to be found on the West Coast, especially in Victoria, where architect Samuel Maclure led the movement. Therefore, in 1925 as Walter Nichol anticipated the end of his term in office, he commissioned Maclure to build a summer house for his family in Sidney that reflected elements of arts-and-crafts style. The exterior of the house they named "Miraloma" featured slabs of Douglas fir still covered in bark, so that the building would blend into nature. Animal forms were carved into the staircase, and the dining table was painted with images inspired by Indigenous designs. The landscapers cut as few trees on the property as possible so the garden would be an extension of the living space. According to a contemporary newspaper article, "Shrubs and trees stand as nature planted them years ago, informally jostling against the walls or standing back with native courtesy to leave room for the grassy slopes which curve their way upwards from the east entrance towards the miniature mountain."[156]

Walter Cameron Nichol remained in office until the end of February 1926. Soon after being appointed Lieutenant Governor, Nichol had sold his interest in the *Province* to William Southam, so after his term was over, he retired, dividing his time between a house that he and Quita had purchased in the Rockland area and Miraloma in Sidney. He died in December 1928 at the age of sixty-two, leaving an estate of over $2.7 million. Quita Nichol, who remained actively involved in musical societies, charities for people with disabilities and the Girl Guides, outlived her husband by four decades. She passed away in November 1968 at the age of ninety-three.

As Lieutenant Governor, Nichol honoured the sacrifices of British Columbia's soldiers, promoted tourism and acted as a patron of the arts and crafts. His reinterpretation of the vice-regal role to include official visits to BC communities and commemoration of historic events set a new standard for those who would follow.

Robert Randolph Bruce (1926–31)

Robert Randolph Bruce, who became Lieutenant Governor in 1926, was born in St. Andrew-Lhanbryde, Scotland, on July 16, 1861. He was home-schooled by his father, a Presbyterian minister, before attending a grammar school in Aberdeen. Graduating with a BSc in Civil Engineering from the University of Glasgow qualified him for a job with a civil engineering firm in Dumbarton, where he worked until 1887. Then he set off for Canada via New York with a letter of introduction to Lord Mount Stephen in his pocket; it was enough to secure him a job as a surveyor with the Canadian Pacific Railway, building a branch line to Boston. In 1895 he helped survey the route through the Crow's Nest Pass in southeastern British Columbia, then, in order to take advantage of BC's mining boom, he took a degree in mineralogy at McGill, though his first job after completing his courses was supervising the construction of a street railway in Cornwall, Ontario.

Bruce had returned to Britain, possibly planning to head for the gold and diamond mining fields of South Africa, when he received an offer to install a stampmill on Perry Creek near Fort Steele, and he set off for British Columbia again. Perry Creek yielded little of value, but in 1900 Bruce invested with two partners in the three claims that formed the Paradise Mine near the north end of Lake Windermere. The mine workings eventually extended to a depth of 120 metres (400 ft) with a 10.5-metre (35-ft)-wide productive vein, and the small townsite of Wilmer grew up nearby for the workers who extracted the mine's silver, zinc and lead.

Meanwhile, Bruce had become interested in farming in the Windermere Valley, and in 1912, as one of the founders and the vice-president of the Columbia Valley Irrigated Fruit Lands Ltd., he wrote an attractive and persuasive brochure that was distributed through the CPR's travel agents in Britain. This brochure, which drew numerous settlers to the valley, was "a clever example of the widespread, often fraudulent, orchard land promotions in British Columbia before the First World War."[157] It promised land where settlers could grow luscious strawberries, large red apples and rich hay, and ship their agricultural produce to market in Calgary. At the time the brochure was published, however, there were no direct road or rail connections to Calgary.

The settlers who came to the Windermere Valley with visions of running successful farms were soon frustrated by the lack of amenities and the length of time it took for Columbia Valley Irrigated Fruit Lands Ltd. to fulfill its promises to dig the necessary irrigation ditches and build houses, stores, churches and schools. One such disillusioned couple were Jack and Daisy Phillips. Newly married in 1912, the Boer War veteran and newspaper publisher's daughter had read Bruce's pamphlet and immigrated to Canada, even though "Jack knew nothing about farming [and] Daisy, nothing about housekeeping."[158] They camped on their land while "the Company" built their house. At first they were patient, accepting that the company was dealing with a larger number of settlers than expected, but by late August they could see snow on the tops of nearby mountains, and their fireplace would not yet draw. They complained directly to Bruce, who had established his own agricultural estate nearby. The meeting had the desired effect as the next morning a workman came to rebuild the fireplace.

Over time Bruce purchased 1,100 acres (445 ha) and planted an orchard, winter wheat and hay. He also commissioned his own fine house in Invermere, complete with electric lights, indoor plumbing and steam heat. Later in 1912 he went to Scotland where, at the age of fifty-one, he married Lady Elizabeth Northcote, the thirty-seven-year-old daughter of the Earl of Iddesleigh. Bruce had amassed a considerable fortune by this time, part of which he spent on gifts for his bride, including jewellery and a motor boat. The couple spent their honeymoon in Algiers, but when they finally arrived in Invermere in May 1914, the Settler's Association was fighting Bruce's company for compensation for leaking cisterns and overpriced land. Bruce's new house was still not finished, so he and his bride lived aboard a houseboat on the lake. About a year after she arrived in the Windermere Valley, Elizabeth Bruce developed appendicitis. As Invermere's only doctor had volunteered to serve overseas, a doctor was summoned from Cranbrook, but he was too late. Lady Elizabeth died on September 27, 1915.

After his wife's death, Bruce remained in the Windermere Valley, and in 1917 he bought out his mining partners to become the sole owner of the Paradise Mine. Unfortunately, because of his exposure to the lead in the mine and to the chemicals involved in assaying ore, he was now losing his eyesight, though this affliction did not prevent him from continuing to promote settlement and tourism. In 1922 he initiated the construction of the David Thompson Memorial Fort, "western Canada's first purpose-built historically themed tourist attraction,"[159] and he played a major role in finally achieving a road connection between Windermere and Banff as well as a national park straddling the new highway. Construction of this road had begun on BC's side of the provincial border in 1911, but the province had run out of funds at the start of the war. Work started again at the war's end when the CPR helped the BC government pay for the section of the road from Windermere to Vermillion Pass; the federal government then paid for the connection to Banff. Bruce helped negotiate the transfer of land on either side of the road to the federal government for Kootenay National Park, which was established in 1920. He wanted to name the park "Columbia" to appeal to American tourists. Always keen to encourage tourism, Bruce commented, "One might say that the calling of this park 'Columbia' might be pandering to our cousins across the line. Well, we want to pander to them all we can. We want their cars and their money and their business, and that is a good deal why this road was started originally. I know it because it was me who started it."[160] The Banff–Windermere Highway was opened in July 1923 by Lieutenant Governors Walter Cameron Nichol of British Columbia and Dr. Robert G. Brett of Alberta.

Bruce had made his fortune in the Columbia Valley thanks to the miners at work in his Paradise Mine and the settlers who had purchased land from Columbia Valley Irrigated Fruit Lands Ltd. He gave some of this back by donating a building for a Legion club house, providing awards for local sports competitions and grub-staking prospectors in search of gold. He renovated "Pynelogs," the home where he had hoped to live with his wife, and donated it to the community as a hospital. The Lady Bruce Memorial Hospital was opened in May 1937.

Robert Randolph Bruce was in London when his appointment as the new Lieutenant Governor of BC was announced on January 21, 1926. At the time it was customary for Lieutenant Governors, who were all male, to be assisted by a female hostess, usually his wife. Since Bruce was a widower, he asked his twenty-one-year-old niece, Helen Mackenzie, to return to Canada with him to act as his hostess, and they arrived in Victoria in March 1926. Mackenzie later recalled that, although her official role was to assist her uncle as his hostess, the new Lieutenant Governor was now legally blind, and she also acted as his eyes. He preferred not to reveal this disability to the general public, so she read official papers and speeches to him, allowing him to memorize them, and at gatherings she would cue him in advance, enabling him to "recognize" guests.

Helen Mackenzie also met with the Chinese cook on a daily basis to discuss upcoming menus, but she did not have to manage the house or garden as a butler was responsible for housekeeping, and "there was one footman, two maids, three kitchen staff and eight gardening staff under a head gardener." Bruce also had a chauffeur who drove him in his Packard or on special occasions in a Lincoln.[161]

Like his predecessor, Walter Nichol, Bruce travelled widely and celebrated British Columbia's pioneer history. What he had already

In September 1928, Robert Randolph Bruce and his niece Helen Mackenzie attended a centennial re-enactment of Hudson's Bay Company governor Sir George Simpson's arrival at Fort St. James. While Bruce celebrated the "courage, endurance and fortitude" of fur traders, Indigenous people used the occasion to gather for a secret potlatch. Pictured here are Nak'azdli Chief Charles Martin and Hudson's Bay Company chief factor C.H. French, who played the part of Sir George Simpson.
Image courtesy of Royal BC Museum and Archives, A-04219.

done for the East Kootenay area, highlighting its economic poten-tial, natural beauty and heritage, he now applied to the province as a whole. Indeed, tourism and settlement worked hand in hand as early promoters understood that tourism would draw settlers and agricultural and industrial development to the province. Organi-zations big and small were eager to attract publicity and prestige by inviting the Lieutenant Governor to their events, and Bruce was happy to oblige, willing to "travel long distances to say a few kind words of encouragement in some little village where no previous lieutenant-governor ever troubled to show himself."[162]

In spite of his visual impairment, Bruce undertook several extensive tours of the province. In the fall of 1926 he toured the newly rebuilt Cariboo Road. In August 1927 he travelled on the HMS *Patrician* with historian and Judge Frederick W. Howay to unveil a cairn to Alexander Mackenzie on Dean Channel west of Bella Coola. In September 1928 he spoke at the celebrations in Fort St. James commemorating the centenary of HBC governor Sir George Simpson's arrival in New Caledonia. In his speech he commended the Hudson's Bay Company for its role in nation-building and called Simpson "not only a pioneer, but a great statesman and empire builder," without whom this territory may not have remained British. He celebrated the "courage, endurance and fortitude of those old pioneers—sentinels of outposts of empire . . . who at great sacrifice tenaciously held this great domain." Like Nichol at Yuquot, he emphasized the friendly and fair relationship between the newcomers and the Indigenous people and told his audience that the HBC had gained the "confidence of the Indians— at first antagonistic, but by fair treatment and kindness converted into close and loyal friends." [163] Historian Frieda Klippenstein points out, however, that by celebrating the HBC and the British Empire, the pageant re-enacting Simpson's entry to the fort did not "reflect the reality of the Native peoples at the gathering" since the "Carrier [people] were asked to commemorate a person who had humiliated them and to celebrate the anniversary of an event which was not a happy one for them."[164] Indigenous people came from great distances to participate in the event, but according to an oral account, they attended mainly to take part in a potlatch, which had to be done secretly since potlatches had been outlawed since 1885.

In June 1929 Bruce and his niece visited the north coast and the northwest of the province, stopping at Prince Rupert, the Queen Charlotte Islands (now called Haida Gwaii) and Atlin. A month later he officiated at the opening of a new trail along Dove Creek west of the Comox Valley, the work of local booster Clinton Wood, who had named this area the "Forbidden Plateau" and was promoting it for skiing and mountaineering. He had persuaded the provincial government to finance this access route. The opening, attended by about seventy-five people, was marked with great ceremony, speeches, presentations and ribbon-cutting, and Helen Mackenzie, who

Having lost his seat in the British election of 1929, Winston Churchill went on a tour of Canada with Robert Randolph Bruce that September. From left: Churchill's son Randolph, Lieutenant Governor Robert Randolph Bruce, Winston Churchill, Helen Mackenzie, Churchill's nephew Johnnie and Churchill's brother Jack.
Image courtesy of Royal BC Museum and Archives, F-05006.

accompanied her uncle to the opening, was honoured by having a lake named after her.

Bruce hosted a number of distinguished guests during his years at Government House, among them Field Marshall Lord Allenby and Queen Marie of Romania in 1926, Scottish comedian and singer Harry Lauder, the Prince of Wales, the Duke of Kent and Prince Henry of Gloucester in 1929. Bruce and his niece also accompanied the Governor General and his wife, Lord and Lady Willingdon, on a cruise on the Canadian Pacific steamship *Princess Norah* to points on Vancouver Island, including Yuquot, Port Alberni and Qualicum.

In September 1929 Bruce and Mackenzie received a visit from Winston Churchill. As Chancellor of the Exchequer in Britain from 1924 to 1929, Churchill had overseen the return to the gold standard, a decision he later regretted since it depressed industries such as coal mining and cotton manufacturing. When the Conservatives lost the election of May 1929 to the Labour Party, Churchill had found himself out of a job at age fifty-five, and that August he embarked on a speaking tour of Canada and the United States with his brother Jack and their sons, Randolph and Johnnie. Although Churchill was a popular speaker, he did little to refresh the content of his talks, and Helen Mackenzie would later note that he had given the same speech everywhere he stopped across the country. Churchill enjoyed his visit to Victoria, which he described as "English with a splendid climate thrown in." He reported that he was treated royally by Bruce, a "splendid old Scotsman . . . who landed forty years ago with £1 in his pocket and is now very wealthy."[165]

When Helen Mackenzie married Julian Piggott in the spring of 1930, her sister Margaret came from Scotland to replace her as their uncle's hostess. Thus it was Margaret Mackenzie who accompanied Bruce in late June 1930 when he joined the "Golden Twilight" caravan tour of BC. This tour by Canadian and American motorists, which included BC Premier Simon Fraser Tolmie, had been organized to promote the construction of a highway connecting Washington and Alaska through British Columbia, which would draw tourists to its scenic wonders and create a corridor providing access to natural resources and the industries based on them. The two groups of motorists, driving about fifty automobiles in all, met at the Peace Arch on the international border in Surrey, BC, and proceeded north through the Fraser Valley and Canyon, detoured to the ghost town of Barkerville, then drove north to Prince George and west through Vanderhoof to the end of the road at Hazelton. Bruce and Mackenzie did not drive north with the group but instead sailed to Prince Rupert and travelled by train to meet the caravan in Hazelton. They accompanied the group on the return trip south, along with Alaska's governor.

In May 1930, less than a year after she arrived in BC from Scotland, Margaret Mackenzie married Captain William Hobart Molson, a member of the Montreal brewing family and a widower with two young sons, who had been an aide-de-camp to Bruce for several years. Although women had joined the workforce in great numbers in the interwar period, it was still customary for them to leave their jobs when they married, and Margaret resigned her job as hostess for her uncle in 1930. As the wife of an aide-de-camp, however, Margaret continued to be invited to events at Government House, where nine years later she was a guest at an exclusive dinner for the King and Queen of England.

The loss of a second trustworthy chatelaine, who had acted not only as hostess but also as Bruce's "eyes," made it challenging for him to carry on as Lieutenant Governor, and he requested a leave of absence starting in March 1931. While he was away, the provincial chief justice, the Honorable J.A. Avondale, acted in his place. Bruce did not return from his leave, and that August John William Fordham Johnson agreed to replace him as Lieutenant Governor.

Robert Randolph Bruce married again in October 1931 to Hobart Molson's sister, Edith Molson. In October 1935 he ran for federal office in East Kootenay but Henry Herbert Stevens, who had left the Conservative Party to form the Reconstruction Party, won the seat. A year later Prime Minister Mackenzie King appointed Bruce Canada's "Minister Plenipotentiary" to Japan, a position he held until October 1938 when he retired to live in Montreal. He died in February 1942. Under the terms of his will, the residue of his estate was to be donated to a number of hospitals in BC after his wife's death, which came in 1962.

Bruce had been an enthusiastic Lieutenant Governor who believed that the province had great potential, and he visited more of British Columbia than any preceding Lieutenant Governor. He began his term during a time of economic optimism in BC, and even after the stock market crashed in 1929, he continued to promote road building, settlement and tourism.

VI

Retrenchment and Extravagance in the Great Depression

DURING THE GREAT Depression the office of the Lieutenant Governor came under fire in every province across Canada for the financial burden it placed on taxpayers. Widespread unemployment and the need for federal, provincial and municipal governments to funnel more and more money into relief programs led citizens and provincial governments to question the validity and expense of the office.

In Ontario, Premier Mitchell Hepburn threatened to abolish the position of Lieutenant Governor altogether, and even Governor General Lord Bessborough, saw "little use in having nine lieutenant-governors as well as a Governor General."[166] Prime Minister Mackenzie King met with both Hepburn and Ontario's Lieutenant Governor, Herbert Alexander Bruce, to discuss the issue.

Their conversations, recorded by Mackenzie King in his diary, reveal his arguments for keeping the position. Bruce's hosting of international dignitaries had relieved Hepburn to accomplish other tasks and had the potential to channel wealth into the province. One of his guests was the wealthy Lord Queensbury, whom Bruce hosted "with a view to having him brought in touch with people so he could invest money in the development of the Northern part of Ontario." But King would not publicly challenge Hepburn in case it became "an issue of my standing for Royalty against the rights of the common people to save taxes, get rid of social trappings, etc., etc."[167] In the end, both Ontario and Alberta reduced expenses by closing the Lieutenant Governor's official residence.

In the early 1930s the economy of British Columbia, which was almost wholly dependent on the export of its natural resources, faltered as the demand fell for lumber, salmon, coal and fruit, and the grain that was stored in Vancouver's elevators. The province was also impacted by the migration of unemployed men west where the winter was milder for those who had no other option but to live outdoors. The provincial government, led by Conservative premier Simon Fraser Tolmie, was slow to provide aid for them, waiting instead for the federal government to come up with subsidies and relief works. However, by 1931 when Canada's unemployment rate reached 28 per cent, the provincial government set up relief camps for single unemployed men; it was another year before the federal government took over the camps and placed them under the control of the Department of National Defence.

During these desperate years, the elite status of the Lieutenant Governors made them even more incongruent with the general population. The first was John William Fordham Johnson, a wealthy businessman, who had retired after the stock market crash and was travelling the world when he received the invitation to take up residence at Government House. While he and his family were largely cushioned from the impact of the Depression, he dealt with public opposition to his role by cutting back on extravagant events at Government House. However, hosting more modest functions did not increase his popularity. At the same time the provincial government was also unwilling to maintain Government House in a manner that would show respect to visiting dignitaries. Eric Werge Hamber, who followed Johnson in the post, was a former banker and timber baron who was living off his investments. Despite his extravagant lifestyle, he was a popular Lieutenant Governor, partly due to his outgoing nature but also because of his generosity, not only in hosting large events but also in his philanthropy. Despite debates over the role and usefulness of the Lieutenant Governor, the office survived the Depression without significant changes in either constitutional or ceremonial responsibilities.

John William Fordham Johnson (1931–36)

John William Fordham Johnson, who succeeded Robert Randolph Bruce as Lieutenant Governor in 1931, was born in Spalding, Lincolnshire, England, on November 28, 1866. He trained as a book-keeper and at age twenty-two moved to Portland, Oregon, to work for the Portland branch of the Bank of British Columbia. In Portland he married Helen Dudley Tuthill. A decade later the bank transferred Johnson to Vancouver as manager.

In January 1901 the Bank of BC merged with the Canadian Bank of Commerce, and shortly after, Johnson left the bank to work for one of its clients, the British Columbia Sugar Refining Company, generally known as BC Sugar. Established in Vancouver in 1890 by Benjamin Tingley Rogers, BC Sugar was the city's first major industry that did not process wood or fish. After Rogers purchased a sugar plantation in Fiji in 1905, he appointed Johnson president of his new Vancouver-Fiji Sugar Company, and Johnson left for Fiji that summer. He was soon joined by his wife and two young daughters, Beatrice and Helen, but the family found the living conditions unsafe. Five-year-old Beatrice suffered from "poisoning from mosquito bites," and Johnson himself contracted amoebic dysentery, which developed into an abscess of the liver. He was hospitalized in Fiji, then had to seek medical treatment in Sydney, Australia. With conditions in Fiji so unpleasant, the family returned to Vancouver in 1907, and after that, Johnson travelled to Fiji on his own to inspect the plantation.

John William Fordham Johnson spent most of his career with the British Columbia Sugar Refining Company (BC Sugar). The company's refinery in Vancouver is pictured here, ca. 1910.
Image courtesy of City of Vancouver Archives, AM1592–1–S5–FO16–: 2011–092.2124.

In May 1915 Johnson's wife, Helen, died, and a year later Johnson married Adelaide Alice (Mcdonell) Ridley, a widow. She had studied at the University of Toronto and married a lawyer, Henry E. Ridley, who had practised in Dawson City in the Yukon before moving to Vancouver.

After Johnson was appointed president of BC Sugar in 1920, the company prospered, shareholders earned large dividends, and the company invested in prominent transportation and utilities companies such as the Canadian Pacific Railway and Bell Canada. However, by this time Johnson had earned a reputation for cutting costs; even though the company was doing well financially, he hesitated to invest in modern equipment or new structures, and in an attempt to maintain a monopoly over the supply of sugar, he lobbied the federal government to prevent sugar from competitors entering BC below cost or without paying duty.

Possibly due to the worsening economic situation, Johnson retired from BC Sugar in May 1930. He was now one of the wealthiest men in the province and owned a grand home in the Shaughnessy Heights neighbourhood of Vancouver as well as a summer home at Qualicum Beach on Vancouver Island where he enjoyed a variety of outdoor activities, including fly-fishing. In January 1931 John and

John William Fordham Johnson, pictured here with his second wife, Adelaide Alice (Mcdonell) Ridley, was sworn in as Lieutenant Governor in August 1931.
Image courtesy of City of Vancouver Archives, Port N527.1.

Alice Johnson embarked on a round-the-world vacation with stops in New York, Italy, the Middle East, India, Indonesia, Korea, Japan and Hawaii. They were still travelling when his appointment as Lieutenant Governor was announced on July 18, 1931. At his swearing-in ceremony in Victoria in early August, he stated, "My long residence in BC has made me a fanatic on the subject of its beauties and its wonderful opportunities. For many years I have regarded it as a land of promise."[168] He moved into Government House with his wife and younger daughter, Helen.

Two months into Johnson's term, the King and Queen of Siam visited Victoria; they were on their way home from New York where King Prajadhipok had undergone an eye operation. An unlikely heir to the throne, Prajadhipok was the youngest of the nine children born to King Chulalongkorn and Queen Saovabha Bongsri, but due to the deaths of his older brothers, he had become king in 1926 at the age of thirty-two. Although he came from a line of absolute monarchs, he favoured the decentralization of power and the introduction of a parliament to Siam. The royal party had passed through Vancouver in April on their way to New York, and on their return journey had toured Canada and the Rockies, visiting Qualicum before driving down the island to stay at the Empress Hotel. Johnson hosted them at a state dinner at Government House and accompanied them to Butchart Gardens.

Lieutenant Governor Johnson travelled the province, probably since Nichol and Bruce had set the precedent, but he made only two significant trips, suggesting there was a diminished interest in such ceremonial tours in those years both on his part and among the population. With his aide-de-camp, Major A.S. Humphreys, and private secretary, A.M.D. Fairbairn, he spent a month in the fall of 1931 touring coastal communities on board the HMCS *Skeena*. The tour began in Victoria and included stops at New Westminster, Powell River, Alert Bay, Carter Bay, Lowe Inlet, Prince Rupert, Port Simpson, Skidegate, Safety Cove and Port Alberni, returning to Vancouver in time for Remembrance Day.

The second trip occurred in the summer of 1935 when Johnson toured the Okanagan to celebrate the Silver Jubilee of the reign of King George V and Queen Mary. Despite this effort by the Lieutenant Governor, there was minimal celebration of this anniversary; as historian Margaret Ormsby notes: "A mood of intense anxiety prevailed in all corners of British Columbia, and the citizens, who had always hitherto been noted for their resilience, were close to losing their fortitude."[169]

In April 1932 a group representing BC businesses and service clubs and led by lumber company owner H.R. MacMillan approached the provincial government to advocate for a reduction in government spending. The Conservative government of Simon Fraser Tolmie agreed to allow a committee led by George Kidd, the former president of the BC Electric Railway Co., to investigate the provincial budget and suggest improvements. One expense targeted by the committee was that of the Lieutenant Governor's office, which they saw as "an expensive and unnecessary luxury."[170] The report proposed that the Lieutenant Governor should earn his keep (a salary of $9,000 plus $33,000 to maintain Government House[171]) by requiring him to warn the government against excessive spending. This attempt to advise the Lieutenant Governor or modify his role was a controversial move and some observers pointed out that the recent appointees did not have the political experience to act as government advisors. The Vancouver *Province* defended the Kidd Report, arguing that Lieutenant Governors had become figureheads without political power but did not explain how, as unelected officials, they could exercise more power and not overstep the boundaries of responsible government. Facing overwhelming negative reaction, the government did not implement the recommendations of the Kidd Report.

As the Depression deepened, the Johnsons entertained on a smaller scale, which may have been appropriate for the times but had a negative effect on their reputation. The problem stemmed not only from his decision to cut back on formal events but also from reduced government spending on the upkeep of Government House; the carpet in the front hall, for example, was badly worn. Despite this belt-tightening, the Johnsons did host national and international visitors. The Governor General, the Earl of Bessborough, and his wife visited on two occasions, and in October 1935 the vice-president of the United States, John Nance Garner, visited Victoria on his way to the Philippines.

Toward the end of his term in May 1936 John William Fordham Johnson was suffering from poor health, and after he retired from office, he and Alice returned to Vancouver, where he died two years

later on his seventy-second birthday. He had served during a difficult economic time when the very position of Lieutenant Governor
was questioned, and it had not helped his public image that he had
appeared to be a frugal host.

Eric Werge Hamber (1936–41)

British Columbia's Lieutenant Governor from 1936 to 1941, Eric
Werge Hamber was the eldest child of Frederick and Ada Hamber,
who arrived in Canada from England in 1877. Both had been raised
in middle-class families, but economic misfortune had led them
to start a new life on a farm near the southern shore of Lake Winnipeg. Eric was born in 1879, followed a year later by a daughter,
Kathleen. In 1881 Frederick was hired to teach music at St. John's
College, and the family was able to move to a small house in the
Anglican parish just north of Winnipeg; two more sons were born
in 1882 and 1885, Harold and Hereward. Then, in addition to caring
for their young children, Ada became assistant painting mistress at
St. John's College Ladies' School.

Eric Hamber was enrolled at St. John's College School in 1886
and attended classes with the sons of Winnipeg's elite, although the
school imposed a spartan lifestyle on all its students with simple
meals and chores such as splitting wood and hauling water. Later
he attended St. John's College where he studied classics and soaked
up the values associated with British imperialism, including an
"unshakeable trust in God, King, and Country."[172]

At nineteen, Hamber was hired by the Dominion Bank as a clerk
and within a short time had risen to branch manager. As his biographer Richard Mackie observes, Hamber's athletic accomplishments
were an asset here, since his employers thought that confident,
athletic clerks and managers were likely to attract new clients. He
played hockey for the bank's team in the Winnipeg Bank Hockey
League and belonged to the Winnipeg Rowing Club, competing
in regattas in a team of four. In 1900 his team won their race in
the Nelson Water Carnival in BC, and in July 1901 he competed in
an eight-oared shell in Philadelphia. After he was transferred to a
branch of the bank in Toronto, he showed his leadership skills by
acting as captain of rowing, hockey and rugby teams. He also joined
the Argonaut Rowing Club and in 1902 went with them to England
to compete in the Royal Henley Regatta.

In May 1906, when he was twenty-seven, Hamber was transferred to Calgary to open and manage a new branch of the Dominion
Bank. A year later he was tasked with opening a branch in Vancouver
where he found an entry into society through the Springer brothers,
whom he had raced against in Nelson. But in Vancouver his taste in
sports changed, and he gradually shifted from rowing, hockey and
rugby to yachting, golf and equestrian sports. He also helped found
the 72nd Canadian Infantry Battalion of the Seaforth Highlanders
of Canada.

In June 1911, Hamber went with a group of Canadian military
men to London for the coronation of George V and remained
there to open the Dominion Bank's first overseas branch, which
was intended to facilitate international investment in Canadian
enterprises and resource extraction. Among the other Canadians
attending the coronation were Vancouverites Adeline Hendry and
her daughter Aldyen, who at age twenty-six was being presented
at court. Aldyen's father, John Hendry, owned the largest sawmill
in the British empire, the BC Mills, Timber and Trading Co., and
had investments in power, coal mining and railway companies. The
only child of this elite Vancouver family, Aldyen had studied art and
languages in Germany. Hamber may have met Aldyen Hendry previously in Vancouver; they grew close in London and were married
there on May 14, 1952. After their wedding, Hamber resigned from
the bank to work for his father-in-law as vice-president and general
manager of BC Mills, Timber and Trading Co.

Eric and Aldyen Hamber returned to Vancouver in 1913, and
that August, as a member of the Seaforth Highlanders, he was
called to Nanaimo, where striking miners had attacked some of the
Chinese and Japanese strike breakers and started a riot in Lady-
smith. However, when war broke out in August of the following year,
Hamber, now thirty-five, did not volunteer for overseas service but
stayed in Vancouver to manage Hendry's mill and seek new markets
for its lumber since the Depression and now the war had reduced
demand. Together with BC's chief forester and minister of Lands, he
began courting British buyers, encouraging them to purchase wood
from the Empire's mills, even convincing the British Admiralty
that its vessels should stop in Vancouver on their way back from
the Pacific to pick up lumber, a move that allowed the company
to re-open some of its logging camps and increase sales of milled

lumber. In 1915 Hamber and Hendry also established a company to tow logs to their mills, improving their delivery efficiency, and it was about this time that Hamber also stepped up his campaign for the construction of a Canadian fleet of lumber carriers. The result was the formation of the British Columbia Merchant Marine Company in January 1916, an initiative that stimulated both the shipbuilding industry, which had been focused on coastal vessels, and the lumber industry. BC's lumber exports tripled between 1916 and 1917, and by January of the following year sixty wooden or steel vessels were under construction at shipyards in Victoria and Vancouver, with lumber being cut specifically for the new ships.

After John Hendry's death in 1916, Hamber became president and managing director of BC Mills, and in January 1917 the Forest Products Bureau, which he now chaired, met with the buyer for the Imperial Munitions Board, Major Austin Cottrell Taylor. Their goal was to convince Taylor to buy Sitka spruce, the strong but light wood that was needed for aeroplane construction, from BC mills instead of Washington State mills. The result of that meeting was that in 1918, 11 million metres (36 million ft) of airplane spruce went from BC to the aircraft industry. At the same time, Hamber was beginning to recognize the value of the province's standing forests, especially the old growth, and had begun arguing for conservation, the reduction of waste and the processing rather than export of raw logs.

After the war Hamber lobbied on behalf of employers in the forest industry. As president of the Timber Industries Council (TIC) from 1921 to about 1925, he challenged government efforts to introduce workmen's compensation, an eight-hour day and a minimum wage. He also raised concerns about damage from pine beetles, continued to campaign against the export of raw logs and in the mid-1920s managed to convince the government to keep timber royalties low. Toward the end of his presidency of the TIC, however, Hamber began his exit from the lumber industry. He sold the Hastings Mill site in 1925 and dismantled BC Mills in 1928. By 1932 he had divested himself of most of his companies, though he remained a director of nine local firms, and he continued to manage his investments, which allowed him to live well during the Depression years. He told a reporter that he had earned a fortune because "he needed the money for his sports."[173] He played golf, tennis and polo, owned race horses, won sailing races with his yacht and took guests to his coastal resort on his 146-foot (45-m) schooner. After the Vancouver Polo Club closed in the early 1930s, he transferred his polo-playing to his 1,000-acre (400-ha) country estate, Minnekhada, near Coquitlam. Here he kept his race horses, bred polo ponies and held polo matches; he also created a marsh for waterfowl and built a hunting lodge where he could entertain his friends in style.

The Hambers also entertained lavishly at their Vancouver home, Greencroft, and even before they moved to Government House, they were hosting Canada's Governors General. For example, Aldyen Hamber invited Lady Willingdon to sail on their schooner, and in 1932 the Earl and Countess of Bessborough travelled with the Hambers on a cruise up Howe Sound to visit Britannia Mines.

Both before and during the Depression years Eric Hamber made major charitable contributions to education, sporting and military establishments. In 1922 he gave the Vancouver Rowing Club the four-oared shell with which they won their silver medal at the 1924 Olympics. To commemorate his father's teaching years at St. John's College School in Winnipeg, he donated $30,000 for the construction of Hamber Hall. He and Aldyen gave the Seaforth Highlanders $5,000 toward a new armoury in Vancouver and contributed to the Red Cross and the Vancouver General Hospital. Through an inheritance and the sale of Hastings Mill, Aldyen was independently wealthy, and she made her own donations to charities and other organizations. When three hundred unemployed men built a shack town at the old Hastings Sawmill site in 1931, she sent packages of boots and socks to the residents and gave Christmas and Easter gifts to workers and their families at Minnekhada.

The wealthy, generous and outgoing Eric Werge Hamber replaced the frugal John William Fordham Johnson as Lieutenant Governor on April 29, 1936. Like his predecessors since 1920 Hamber had never held an elected office and, as a result, had always been free to voice his opinion on political matters. In commenting on his new constitutional role a month after accepting the post, he observed that, despite their important responsibilities in government, Lieutenant Governors were more restricted than private citizens in their freedom to speak their minds about current issues. But in his new role, he said, "I have to be impartial. I have to adhere to the rules and regulations of a high office."[174]

As Johnson had, Hamber received an annual salary of just $9,000,

Eric Hamber brought to the role of Lieutenant Governor not only great wealth and generosity, but a deep loyalty to the Crown. He had travelled to London for the coronation of King George V in 1911, and he and his wife, Aldyen, attended the coronation of King George VI in 1937. In the spring of 1939 the Hambers hosted King George VI and Queen Elizabeth on the Victoria stop of their Canadian tour, and in 1947 they were invited to attend the wedding of Princess Elizabeth and the Duke of Edinburgh.

Image courtesy of Royal BC Museum and Archives, H–03596.

and the province contributed another $31,000 for the maintenance of Government House, but according to Aldyen Hamber's secretary, Hamber and his wife spent about $50,000 a year of their own money on entertainment and other expenses while he held the post.

They held garden parties for six hundred guests and entertained an estimated hundred thousand visitors at Government House during the five years they lived there.

Hamber's senior aide-de-camp during those years was Brigadier James Sutherland Brown, who had been a senior staff officer in the Canadian Expeditionary Force during the First World War and director of Military Operations and Intelligence in Ottawa after the war. Then, as District Officer Commanding in BC and the Yukon from 1928 to 1933, he had set up work camps for unemployed men. Sutherland Brown and his wife had the dignity and elegance required to stand in for the Lieutenant Governor and his chatelaine when necessary, yet his son recalled:

> Having no car and little money for taxis they frequently travelled to Government House by bus or streetcar dressed in their finery. After alighting, they would then have to walk the half mile from Fort Street to the great house on Rockland Avenue.[175]

The Hambers had a deep loyalty to the monarchy and the empire, and in the spring of 1937 Eric and Aldyen, their secretaries—A.M.D. Fairbairn and Mae Rice—and Aldyen's mother travelled to England to attend the coronation of King George VI at Westminster Abbey. In September 1937 President Franklin Roosevelt and Eleanor Roosevelt arrived on a battleship from Seattle, and as the president and Hamber drove through Victoria in an open convertible, crowds lined up to greet them. Governor General Lord Tweedsmuir (the author John Buchan) and Lady Tweedsmuir also visited British Columbia that year and travelled by floatplane and on horseback through the area that would be named Tweedsmuir Provincial Park in his honour the following year. Two years later the Tweedsmuirs returned and stayed at Government House and at the Hambers' Minnekhada estate.

However, the visitors who most caught the public imagination were King George VI and Queen Elizabeth. On May 30, 1939, just months before Britain declared war on Germany, the royal couple arrived at Government House at the end of their tour across Canada. An important purpose of this first visit to Canada of a reigning monarch was to strengthen ties with Canada and increase support for Britain in the face of imminent hostilities. The Hambers had redecorated Government House for their visit with new colour schemes, carpets, furniture and ornaments, and Prime Minister Mackenzie King, who had accompanied the royal party, reported in his diary that "Victoria was at its best, trees in full foliage. Flowers everywhere. Children wearing garlands in their hair . . ."[176]

After the royal party drove through the city, there was an intimate dinner at Government House. Former chatelaine Margaret Molson (née Mackenzie) attended this dinner with her husband, Hobart Molson, who was serving Hamber as aide-de-camp, and she described the evening in a letter to her uncle, former Lieutenant Governor Robert Randolph Bruce and his wife Edith (Hobart's sister):

> Fairy tale of fairy tales! Hobart and I dined with the King and Queen, not a state banquet, but informally and en famille. They had asked that they might enjoy a quiet dinner by themselves at G.H. in dinner jackets, so Hobart as senior ADC was the only outsider besides the Premier and his wife, but the Hambers in the kindness of their hearts arranged that I should be included.

Seated next to Margaret Molson was Mackenzie King, "who is always a charming dinner partner, and who talked much of you, saying that very day he had received a Japanese book from you." Even though this was an "informal" dinner, the Queen wore a gown decorated with crystal embroidery in addition to "magnificent jewels."[177]

The women and men retired to separate rooms for after-dinner conversation. Margaret was thrilled that "the Queen beckoned *me* to draw up a chair beside her! There we sat until nearly an hour later when we were joined by the others! She is charming to talk to and chatted away happily on all sorts of topics." [178] Mackenzie King had a conversation with Hamber and George VI, and noted in his diary that Hamber had told some "interesting stories" about Prohibition and rum-running, then the conversation turned serious with King George expressing his concerns about the Munich Agreement and who would succeed Chamberlain as prime minister.[179]

With Canada's declaration of war on September 10, 1939, the Hambers turned their attention to supporting the Allied war effort. Aldyen and staff members at Government House knitted clothing for soldiers and sent it overseas. When actress and singer Gracie Fields visited Victoria in 1940, she was guest of honour at a garden party the Hambers hosted to raise funds for the Red Cross. After the fall of France the Hambers gave the Canadian government

It was common for appointees to accept a pay cut when serving as Lieutenant Governor, and some even made their own financial contributions to cover the cost of travel and entertainment. Eric Hamber, formerly the president of BC Mills, and his wife, Aldyen (née Hendry), reportedly spent about $50,000 per year to host events, travel and update Government House, when the salary of the Lieutenant Governor was $9,000.
Image courtesy of Royal BC Museum and Archives, G–04600.

$100,000 toward the war effort, and they also handed over their yacht, *Vencedor,* to the navy.

With his five-year term as Lieutenant Governor drawing to a close in the spring of 1941, Hamber was encouraged to take on a second term, but early in May he submitted his resignation.

Mackenzie King then offered him the post of Canada's minister in Japan, but according to King's diary, Hamber was unwilling to take on this responsibility without a knighthood, an honour that the prime minister refused to support.

Following his term as Lieutenant Governor, Hamber remained president of the British Columbia Red Cross Society. A new provincial park in the Rocky Mountains was named after him in September 1941. Hamber Provincial Park initially spanned the immense area connecting Mount Robson Provincial Park with Yoho National Park, but in 1961 it was reduced to a small park with no road access. Hamber served as Chancellor of the University of British Columbia from 1944 to 1951, during which time he donated $50,000 to the university. Although he never received a knighthood, after the war he was made a Companion of the Order of St. Michael and St. George. Having put much effort and expense into making the king and queen feel welcome and comfortable during their brief stay at Government House in 1939, the Hambers were rewarded by an invitation to the November 1947 wedding of Princess Elizabeth to the Duke of Edinburgh where they were hosted privately by the king and queen. Eric Werge Hamber died on January 10, 1960, at eighty years of age, and in his memory Aldyen Hamber gave $500,000 to UBC to create a chair of medicine in his name.

While Hamber's lifestyle had been in obvious contrast to that of the majority of British Columbians during the Depression years, this did not seem to adversely affect his popularity as Lieutenant Governor. He had taken on the role with enthusiasm, spending his own money on entertaining and redecorating Government House in preparation for the royal visit of 1939 and giving generously to the war effort. However, his reluctance to extend his term or accept the post of Canada's minister in Japan suggests that he was also seeking prestige as the reward for his services, and that, denied a knighthood, he did not feel duly compensated for his labours by the Canadian government.

VII

Lieutenant Governors and the Second World War

WITH THE SURRENDER of France in June 1940 and the evacuation of British forces from the Continent, Canada suddenly had to consider mobilizing on a greater scale for the war effort, and the federal government passed the National Resources Mobilization Act (NRMA), allowing the state to conscript soldiers for home defence, though not for fighting overseas.

Of equal importance, the NRMA also gave the government powers over economic resources. At the head of this economic mobilization was Clarence Decatur Howe. Born in the United States and educated as an engineer at the Massachusetts Institute of Technology, Howe had moved to Halifax in 1908 to teach engineering at Dalhousie University. In 1913, having decided that his future lay in Canada, he became a British subject and went to work for the federal Board of Grain Commissioners. Three years later he left the board and started his own engineering company that specialized in building grain elevators. He was elected as the Liberal MP for Thunder Bay in 1935 and in April 1940 became minister of the Department of Munitions and Supply (DMS). When it became apparent that the government would need to move into the manufacturing realm, he created Crown corporations to produce commodities such as bombers and the synthetic rubber needed by the armed forces of Canada and its allies. The DMS also regulated all materials that could be used for war production.

Howe and the DMS are significant for this study because five of the six Lieutenant Governors appointed between 1941 and 1973 worked for the DMS directly or indirectly during the war years. These men all had business and management experience, all had a record of active service in the Canadian forces during the First World War, and all had earned the complete trust of the decision-makers in Ottawa.

William Culham Woodward (1941–46)

William Culham "Billy" Woodward was born on April 24, 1885, one of the nine children of Charles A. Woodward, the founder of Woodward's Department Store. Charles Woodward had opened his first store in 1875 on Manitoulin Island in Lake Huron, but after the completion of the transcontinental railway, he left his young family in Ontario to start fresh on the West Coast. In 1891 he bought two lots on Main Street in Vancouver and built a store where he sold boots and shoes, menswear, groceries and dry goods. The next year he returned to Ontario to bring eight of his nine children west, leaving his wife, Elizabeth, to follow a few months later with their infant daughter. Elizabeth, however, was suffering from tuberculosis, and both she and their infant daughter died soon after arriving in Vancouver. Their sixteen-year-old daughter died of tuberculosis the same year.

Meanwhile, Charles Woodward was intent on building up the store with help from his older children, and in 1895 his eldest son, Jack, having studied at the Ontario College of Pharmacy, opened a drug department. The Klondike gold rush also provided a great boost to the company, with miners purchasing their supplies at Woodward's before heading north. But Jack died, also from tuberculosis, in May 1900, and sixteen-year-old William, frustrated by his father's devotion to his business to the detriment of his family's health and well-being, left school to take a job with the Royal Bank of Canada. Undaunted by his son's defection, in 1903 Charles opened a much larger store on West Hastings Street with help from his other children.

William's work for the Royal Bank took him to Nelson, Grand Forks and the Lardeau Valley in the Kootenays, then to the town of Republic in Washington State. Next the bank transferred him to its branch in Havana, Cuba, where in 1906 he witnessed the revolution that toppled the government of Cuba's first president, Tomas Estrada Palma. Leaving the bank, William went into stockbroking, but when that business failed a year later and he lost his savings, he had little choice but to return to Vancouver and work as a bookkeeper for his father. His seventeen-year-old brother, Reginald Percival "Reggie" Woodward, joined the company as a salesman at about the same time. Both helped to manage the company, although their personalities were quite different: "William was extroverted, open-handed and liked to be liked. Percival kept his own counsel, was suspicious of other men and their motives, demanded efficient performance, spurned popularity."[180]

In 1916 William enlisted with the 1st Canadian Artillery and served with the Canadian Expeditionary Force (CEF) in France and Belgium, then remained with the CEF in Germany after the war, returning to Vancouver and the family department store in the spring of 1919. A year later a wartime friendship gave Woodward the opportunity to meet his future wife; in the summer of 1920 fellow officer Clare Underhill invited William to join him on a visit to the Wynn-Johnson family at their ranch at Alkali Lake, 64 kilometres (40 mi) south of Williams Lake. Their eldest daughter, Ruth, had also just returned from Europe. After studying at a finishing school in Paris, she had spent the war years living with relatives in Wales and Ireland and volunteering at the Soldier's Central Club and a hospital in Dublin and cooking at the Waverley Abbey Hospital in Surrey. William Woodward and Ruth Wynn-Johnson were married at Alkali Lake in the fall of 1921; she was twenty-four and he was thirty-six.

The family company expanded with the opening of a store in Edmonton in 1926 and extension of the mail-order business, and Charles Woodward gradually turned the operational supervision over to his sons. The business weathered the worst of the Depression years fairly well, and when Charles died in 1937, he left a solidly rooted business with William and Percival in charge as president and vice-president. They expanded Woodward's main store in downtown Vancouver to eight stories with a larger main floor, a basement for its famous Food Floor, and a new auditorium where the staff could meet for meals and recreation. However, in 1938 the Vancouver store was one of the establishments that suffered broken windows after police broke up sit-in protests by unemployed demonstrators at the post office, Georgia Hotel and art gallery.

At the outbreak of the Second World War, William C. Woodward was one of the successful businessmen recruited by Clarence Decatur Howe, minister of the Department of Munitions and Supply (DMS), to work for his War Supply Board. In Ottawa William worked as Howe's executive assistant, and in December 1940, he set off with Howe, financier E.P. Taylor and Montreal businessman Gordon W. Scott for England via New York to assess England's needs in aircraft and munitions. At 5:30 on the morning of December 14 in a 112-kilometre (70-mi)-an-hour gale, a German torpedo struck their ship, the *Western Prince*. The passengers were evacuated into lifeboats before the ship went down, and after eight hours on the open ocean, they sighted a small freighter, the *Baron Kinnaird*, which was on its way to Florida, and signalled to it with flares. The freighter had accommodation for only forty but took all 160 survivors on board despite instructions from the Admiralty that Navy vessels, not merchant ships, should rescue the survivors of torpedoed ships. Howe, Woodward and Taylor survived, but Scott died when the lifeboat he was in capsized against the side of the *Baron Kinnaird*. The rescue ship turned around for Glasgow, where it arrived four days later. The three men stayed in England for a month conducting business before returning to Canada.

In Ottawa Woodward and his wife operated within an elite circle, forming connections that subsequently opened a pathway to his appointment as Lieutenant Governor of BC. Indeed, Woodward's appointment signalled a return to Ottawa's practice of assigning men with experience working for the federal government—individuals known to and trusted by the prime minister—as vice-regal representatives in BC. Thus, Woodward was the first in the second wave of "Ottawa's men." In February 1941, shortly after his near-fatal experience on the North Atlantic, William and Ruth hosted a dinner in Ottawa for Prime Minister Mackenzie King and BC Lieutenant Governor Eric Hamber and Aldyen Hamber. Mackenzie King was favourably impressed by Ruth Woodward, whom he presumed was responsible for the "sumptuous repast" and "exquisite" flower arrangements. He characterized William Woodward, however, as "a rough diamond. Generous, good natured, etc. but not a diplomat."

In this photograph from December 4, 1941, William Culham Woodward opens his first legislative session three days before Japanese forces attacked Pearl Harbor. On December 9, Woodward swore in Premier John Hart as the head of a coalition government.
Image courtesy of Royal BC Museum and Archives, D–O5922.

Mackenzie King's diary note was in reference to Woodward's disparaging remarks at the dinner table about the Americans, who were still officially neutral. "It is a marvel that Britain has any friends left in the States," Mackenzie King reflected, "the way in which some of our people say unpleasant things about the U.S."[181]

Despite his reservations, six months later Mackenzie King invited W.C. Woodward to become BC's next Lieutenant Governor, and Woodward began his term on August 29, 1941. It is possible that the appointment may also have coincided with a desire to remove him in an honourable way from the Ministry of Munitions and Supply. Howe's biographers suggest that Woodward was somewhat superfluous there, since he "cheerily roamed the corridors of power, looking for something to do, until Howe sent him packing back to British Columbia to become that province's lieutenant-governor."[182] Officially, appointing Lieutenant Governors was Mackenzie King's job, not Howe's, but given the number of men who worked with Howe who were appointed Lieutenant Governors in the following decades, it is likely that Howe may have had an influence over these decisions.

In addition to his routine constitutional responsibilities, just three months into his term Woodward was called upon to make a decision regarding a coalition government. In the provincial election of October 21, 1941, the incumbent Liberal Party under Thomas Dufferin Pattullo had retained just twenty-one seats, the CCF remained the official Opposition with fourteen seats and the Conservatives increased their representation to twelve members. A few days after the election the Conservative leader, R.L. (Pat) Maitland, called for a union government and invited the CCF to join, but CCF leader Harold Winch was not interested. However, on December 3 when a Liberal convention voted in favour of a coalition government, Pattullo left the room in disgust. He then offered his resignation to Woodward, who accepted his recommendation that John Hart become head of a coalition government. In the meantime, Pattullo and Hart had gone to Ottawa, on separate trains, to negotiate a tax-rental agreement with the federal government.

At that time BC's Lieutenant Governor did not have to pay income tax because the allotted salary of $9,000 fell short of the annual travel and entertainment expenses he was expected to pay out of pocket, an amount estimated at $30,000 (although this was less than Hamber's annual expenditure). Concerned that the tax transfer agreement Pattullo was attempting to negotiate would reduce his net income to $4,000, "which would not even pay one-half of the expense of [his] personal staff," Woodward asked Pattullo to consider the matter while in Ottawa. Despite being president of Woodward's Stores and a director of several companies, Woodward claimed it was a burden for him to pay for two households, and he suggested that raising the Lieutenant Governor's salary to $11,000 would increase the pool of candidates "who would do great honour to the position."[183] Appropriations were subsequently increased for Government House, but the cost of maintaining it continued to come under scrutiny during the war, with the CCF suggesting that the building could be better used as "home for the aged" or "a tuberculosis hospital."[184] Neither recommendation was implemented.

John Hart was sworn in as premier on December 9, 1941, just two days after Japan bombed Pearl Harbor. As Japan and China had been at war since 1937, the Chinese Canadian community in BC had for years called for a boycott on Japanese goods sold in Canada. The Woodward family, as retailers, had opposed a boycott because of its impact on sales and the effect it would have on BC's natural resource exports to Japan, but on February 11, 1942, Woodward wrote to Mackenzie King to ask for further "precautions" against "the Japanese menace on our coast."[185] On February 26 the Minister of Justice ordered all persons of Japanese origin to leave a 100-mile (160-km)-wide protected zone along the coast; it was apparent that, although Lieutenant Governors were supposed to be politically neutral, the definition of non-political would change over time.

During the war Government House welcomed Canadian and international dignitaries and royalty. The Governor General, the Earl of Athlone and his wife, Princess Alice, came in 1942. They were followed by British Admiral James Somerville, who was the commander-in-chief of the Eastern Fleet, Field Marshal Montgomery, Princess Juliana of the Netherlands, who was in exile in Ottawa during the war, and Prince Olav of Norway. The next Governor General, Earl Alexander of Tunis, who had served as senior army commander in the Mediterranean after 1942, came to stay in 1946.

Because of the war, fundraising activities and military events replaced state balls and garden parties at Government House. Four American youths, the Quiz Kids, stars of a popular radio program,

During the war, William Culham Woodward hosted fundraising activities and military events at Government House. An April 1944 event included actress Mary Livingstone (third from right) and comedian Jack Benny (far right); William Woodward is third from the left and Ruth Woodward is second from the right.
Image courtesy of Royal BC Museum and Archives, B–01466.

came to Victoria to raise funds for British children by answering trivia questions. Herbert Marshall and other American actors held a fundraiser for the Red Cross. In April 1944, the Woodwards hosted a luncheon for American radio comedian Jack Benny and his "comedy troupe," who had come to BC to take part in a Victory Loan campaign.

On a tour of the Kootenay district Woodward urged his audiences to support Victory Loan Campaigns, stating, "We've got to do more than we are doing now if we are going to win this war. This war can be easily lost. The time to sugar the pill is gone. We want the Government to tell us, not ask us. I'm not going to ask you to buy bonds, I'm going to tell you. It's your job and mine."[186] Toward the end of the conflict, he presented medals to local veterans, and he and his wife also supported a number of charitable causes and heritage groups. Then in April 1945 he joined Saskatchewan premier Tommy Douglas on a tour of the battlefields of Holland and Germany.

Woodward remained in office for a year after the war ended and, together with Ruth, revived some of the traditional social events at Government House. When his term ended on October 1, 1946, he returned to his business concerns, opening new branches of Woodward's, including one in Victoria. He was also free to spend more time at the farm he and Ruth had purchased in North Saanich in 1944; they called it Woodwynn and raised prize cattle there. He retired from his involvement in the department store in 1956, but he had little time to enjoy retirement as he died suddenly on a trip to Hawaii in February 1957.

Woodward, who had known the realities of combat in the First World War and had nearly lost his life in the sinking of the *Western Prince* in the Second World War, had adapted the position of Lieutenant Governor to the exigencies of a country at war, eliminating the more celebratory functions yet maintaining a social presence appropriate to supporting the war effort. He also adopted the popular opinions of the day, becoming outspoken on matters of Japanese internment and Victory Loans, while later Lieutenant Governors would be expected to maintain a more neutral position.

VIII

Lieutenant Governors in Postwar British Columbia (1946–60)

BETWEEN 1945 AND 1960 Canada and other Western capitalist nations enjoyed a period of economic growth that was mostly fuelled by military spending, consumerism, construction of suburbs and megaprojects and the use of new materials and fuels. In this affluent period, Lieutenant Governors were expected to entertain lavishly, and the three Lieutenant Governors who served in British Columbia— Charles Arthur Banks, Clarence Wallace and Frank Mackenzie Ross—were all wealthy owners of large companies.

Little is known about those who rejected the position, but Victoria businessman Robert Henry Brackman Ker, who had served as an aide-de-camp to Lieutenant Governor Walter C. Nichol, was one individual who was not interested due to the expense. In 1946 Ker wrote to a colleague that "It is important that they get the right man for the position and also one who can afford the expense. Personally I am not interested and never will be."[187] As well as all being wealthy men, Banks, Wallace and Ross had all served in the First World War, and during the Second World War they assisted or worked for C.D. Howe's Department of Munitions and Supply, so they had a special relationship to Ottawa.

These post-war Lieutenant Governors also oversaw the broadening of civil rights in British Columbia as disenfranchised groups received the right to vote. As late as 1944, Chinese, South Asian and Indigenous British Columbians as well as members of some religious groups did not have the right to vote, but after 1945 service in either world war allowed members of these prohibited groups to vote. In 1947 Chinese and South Asians gained the right to vote; two years later Indigenous and Japanese residents of British Columbia could also vote in provincial elections; and in 1951, when a revision of the Indian Act removed the prohibition on pursuing land claims, groups such as the Nisga'a started to organize in order to gain official recognition of Aboriginal title in BC.

Charles Arthur Banks (1946–50)

Charles Arthur Banks was born in Thames, New Zealand, on May 18, 1885. Family history held that he was a collateral descendant of Sir Joseph Banks, the British naturalist who sailed with Captain Cook to the South Seas. After graduating with an engineering degree from the Thames School of Mining, Charles Banks' subsequent employment with mining companies took him to many sites around the world. In France he married Jean (or Jane) de Montalb (or Montalk),[188] the daughter of French and Scottish parents, and the couple returned to North America where, as a team, they "went prospecting together from the Kootenays to Alaska."[189] With the outbreak of the First World War, they sailed for England where Charles joined the Royal Engineers and Jean worked for the Women's Volunteer Services. After the war they settled in Vancouver where Banks became manager of British Columbia Silver Mines, Ltd.

In 1925 Banks and Australian lawyer William Addison Freeman co-founded a minerals exploration company, Placer Development Limited, to "inspect and acquire rights to likely placer (alluvial) deposits"[190] worldwide. One of their most profitable holdings was the Bulolo Gold Dredging Co. in New Guinea, which they started working at the beginning of the Depression. Until then, gold mining in New Guinea had been carried out by individual prospectors and small companies, but the New Guinea Administration could not afford to build a road from the goldfields at Edie Creek and along the Bulolo River to the coast, so the gold there had been difficult to process and remove. Banks's Placer Development company stepped in with the capital and the resources to do large-scale dredging of silt and gravel, and Banks made the somewhat risky decision to build a camp there and bring in dredges and the hydroelectric generators to power them. But because of the cost of building and maintaining a road, he calculated that it would be cheaper to fly in the equipment. The idea of carrying in all this equipment, especially the 1-million-kilogram (1,100-Imperial-ton) dredges, to a mining camp by air was relatively unproven, and planes that could manage such heavy equipment were not readily available in that part of the world. But in 1931 Banks helped Guinea Airways acquire three Junker G-31 cargo planes from Germany that could each handle loads of up to 3,182 kilograms (7,000 lbs), and the dredges were dismantled into sections that would fit into the Junkers and be re-assembled on site. Guinea Airways made up to five flights per day from the airport at Lae to the airstrip at Bulolo flats, and in the first year of operation, the company flew in 4 million kilograms (3,947 Imperial tons) of freight. This was more freight than the total carried that year by the air services of Britain, France and the United States combined.[191]

The first dredge, described as a "monster" that "groaned and wallowed like a mammoth lumbering from the midday mud,"[192] went into operation at Bulolo on March 21, 1932. By 1940 eight dredges were in operation, powered by three hydroelectric plants generating 10,000 horsepower, and 85 million yards of gravel had been dredged to recover one million ounces (28 million g) of gold.

During the war the mining camp at Bulolo was destroyed, though not by the Japanese. On January 21, 1942, Japanese fighter planes destroyed the three Junker G-31s, but nothing else was damaged, and four days later all the camp personnel were evacuated.

Placer Development Limited, co-founded by Charles Arthur Banks and William Addison Freeman, flew in the parts for 1,100–ton dredges like the one above and assembled them on site to establish a gold mining operation on the Bulolo River in New Guinea in the early 1930s.
Image courtesy of Michael Waterhouse.

Ultimately, it was Australian forces that destroyed the camp and its equipment so nothing of value would come into Japanese control. As a result, after the war Bulolo Gold Dredging had to rebuild from scratch, the only consolation being that an army-built road to the mining area helped with the reconstruction.

Meanwhile, Placer Development was investing in mining operations elsewhere in the world—Emerald Tungsten in British Columbia, Pato Gold Dredging in Colombia, Rutherglen Gold Dumps in Australia, and the Coronet Oil Company in Texas. In Colombia, the company found fish hooks and ornaments made of gold when dredging through gold deposits that had been mined by Spanish and Indigenous people in the centuries preceding them.

At the beginning of the Second World War, Charles Banks was focused on operating his businesses, which he saw as vital to the war effort. He told a commencement class at the Colorado School of Mines in the spring of 1940 that "the products of mining, which have been such a large factor in building our civilization, can be used for the comfort and benefit of mankind, or for his destruction and enslavement." He urged the mining students to put their efforts toward projects that promoted "peace and freedom" and the "continued development and progress of the civilized world."[193]

A.M. Healy, in his book, *Bulolo: A History of the Development of the Bulolo Region, New Guinea,* describes Charles Banks as "the perfect mixture of technical engineer and adventurous businessman." In his mining operations, he "demanded the closest examination of every factor in every proposition, he was able to take a long term view, to sort out transient difficulties from disqualifying obstacles, and, when necessary, to act swiftly on his own judgement." These qualities, in addition to his "capacity for compromise, and for reconciling factions"[194] were no doubt what made C.D. Howe reach out to recruit him in the spring of 1940 for his Department of Munitions and Supply. They also made Banks the most suitable candidate to head the London office of the department, which Howe had opened in order to circumvent British bureaucracy; his responsibilities there included gathering information on British war production, sending military supplies to Britain and acquiring equipment for Canada.

While stationed in London, Banks gave £10,000 to the Beaver Club where Canadian soldiers could meet, enjoy Canadian foods and catch up on the news from home. Jean Banks worked at the Beaver Club and also helped found the United Nations Club in London. When BC Lieutenant Governor Woodward visited in May 1945, he and Banks "mingled together with the London crowds on V-E Day."[195] In recognition of his wartime services, Charles Banks was named a Commander of the Order of St. Michael and St. George.

After the war ended, Banks was busy dealing with mining operations that had been destroyed during the war or needed to be modernized, but in the fall of 1946 he accepted an appointment to replace Woodward as BC's Lieutenant Governor. His term began on October 1, 1946, but from the start it was not a very good fit. Although Charles and Jean Banks were adventurous, they were not very outgoing, and they found meeting large numbers of people and hosting elaborate events daunting. In fact, when asked about his upcoming ceremonial role, Banks responded, "I hope there won't be too much of it. It can all be very strenuous."[196] In Victoria the

Bankses were not as popular as other Lieutenant Governors had been since they did not host lavish parties, though they did hold parties for children with disabilities and attended naval and military events. Fortunately, few high-profile visitors came to BC in the immediate postwar years so their hosting duties were limited, but they visited the Kootenay district, a tour that must have reminded

Appointed Lieutenant Governor in 1946, Charles Arthur Banks enjoyed travelling throughout British Columbia with his wife, Jean, but neither was very enthusiastic about hosting large events.
Image courtesy of Royal BC Museum and Archives, C–O8131.

them of their prospecting trips when they were young, and Banks reported with enthusiasm, "We are both in love with the Kootenays; we hope to come again at the very next opportunity."[197] They were often absent from Government House—they had homes in Vancouver, San Francisco and London—and in early 1950 they spent three months in England.

During Banks's term as Lieutenant Governor, the government of British Columbia extended the right to vote in provincial elections to Canadians of Chinese and South Asian origin in 1947 and to those of Japanese origin and Indigenous residents in 1949 (Indigenous people would have to wait until 1960 for the federal vote). In recognition of this momentous occasion, Chief William Scow, president of the Native Brotherhood of BC, and Chief Frank Assu, president of the North American Brotherhood, spoke at the opening of the Legislature on February 14, 1950, wearing full ceremonial regalia. Both pointed out that the franchise was just the first step in achieving equitable relations. As Chief Scow stated, the franchise "is the beginning of giving [our people] many privileges which they have not had in the past."[198] This opening ceremony, the first one to be filmed, was also remarkable as it included the first Indigenous MLA in Canada, Frank Calder, the Nisga'a member for Atlin, and the first female Speaker of the House in the British Commonwealth, Nancy Hodges.

According to Clarence Wallace, who followed Charles Banks as Lieutenant Governor, the Bankses had not been overly happy at Government House. Privacy, in particular, was an issue for Jean Banks. She had prospected throughout British Columbia, explored New Guinea with her husband—a feat for which she had been named a Fellow of the Royal Geographical Society—and volunteered in Britain in both world wars. However, she was not comfortable with the level of public access to Government House while it was her home, especially as the gardens had become very popular with both locals and tourists after the war. Clarence Wallace would later recall, "The dear old people just walked through the gardens. The gardens were lovely, and the flowers were beautiful, and it was such a wonderful place for these old gals to sit and do their knitting. The old fellows used to go in and read books." But according to Wallace, Jean Banks was annoyed that people were "peeking in her windows" so the vice-regal couple "ordered guards to be put on the gates and the gates kept shut so taxis couldn't come in."[199] This resulted in a public backlash since the grounds—though not a park—were public property, and foot traffic had always been allowed during certain hours of the day. Subsequent Lieutenant Governors would make greater efforts to open Government House and grounds to the public.

Although the Hambers had renovated the building for the royal visit of 1939, some parts of the interior needed updating, but strained relations between the Bankses and the provincial government delayed improvements. When Banks invited Wallace and his wife to see their future residence in 1950, Wallace was "shocked at the way that Government House was looking." He tripped over holes in the rugs of the drawing room and dining room. Banks told him ominously, "You know, I don't think you're going to like it here, and I don't think you're going to last more than two years . . . I don't think that Government House will last any longer." But when Wallace told Premier Byron "Boss" Johnson that he was reluctant to live in Government House in its present state, Johnson assured him that "when you come, we'll fix all that." When he asked why the government had not already done so, Johnson explained that "we couldn't get on with His Honour." [200] Despite this gloomy outlook, during Banks's term, Government House did acquire a new laundry, an improved kitchen and a new garage.

Charles Banks resigned in June 1950, a year before the end of his term, a move that he explained was due to his responsibility to his companies and their shareholders. In any case, the Bankses must have enjoyed the city of Victoria, as it remained their base for the next few years. Banks continued as chairman of Placer Development until his retirement in 1959 when he and Jean moved back to Vancouver.

When he died in 1961, Charles Arthur Banks left an estate worth $2.2 million. Since he and his wife had no children, the money from their estate, apart from what Jean would use in her lifetime, was divided among the University of British Columbia, which received $1.1 million for scholarships and student loans, the Salvation Army, the Vancouver Foundation and Central City Mission.

It was likely the qualities that had induced C.D. Howe to recruit Charles Arthur Banks for his Department of Munitions and Supply also contributed to his appointment as Lieutenant Governor in 1946. Yet ultimately, due to the Bankses' preference for privacy and their lack of interest in ceremony, they proved to be a less than ideal choice for the social roles of Lieutenant Governor and chatelaine.

Clarence Wallace (1950–55)

Clarence Wallace, the first Lieutenant Governor of BC who was born in this province, came from a family of shipbuilders. His father, Alfred, was a shipwright's son from Devon, England, who immigrated to Canada with his wife, Eliza, in 1887. They first settled in Toronto where Alfred worked on Great Lakes vessels. The Wallaces moved to Vancouver in 1891, and by 1894 Alfred co-owned a shipyard on False Creek, though he soon bought out his partner. Wallace's shipyard was highly efficient, with a crew of just five or six men completing an average of three Columbia River fishboats per day. These wooden vessels, 15 to 20 feet (4.5 to 6 m) long with a mast and sail, were used by the northern canneries. His company also built two of the ferries that provided a link between Vancouver and North Vancouver. In 1906 the Wallace Shipyard moved from False Creek to North Vancouver.

Alfred and Eliza Wallace had three sons, William, Clarence and Hubert, but William died in a bicycling accident when he was just six years old. Clarence, born in 1894, attended elementary school in Vancouver and completed his secondary education at St. Andrew's College in Toronto. On his return to Vancouver in 1912, he began working at the shipyard, and by 1914 he was responsible for the purchasing department.

Three days after Britain declared war on Germany in August 1914, taking Canada into the conflict as well, twenty-year-old Clarence Wallace and a friend joined the 31st Regiment (BC Horse), even though neither of them had ridden before. As Wallace recalled, "We thought we'd better learn to ride a horse so we went and hired a horse ... and we rode for three or four days around town, you know, and out in the country, and God, we got so god-damned stiff neither one of us could hardly move."[201] The BC Horse went first to Kamloops to train, then to Valcartier, Quebec, for five weeks before travelling via convoy to Britain. Wallace served part of his time at the front as a dispatch runner, and he narrowly escaped death when he and seven other volunteers were sent to scout the German position; a conversation with French-speaking Algerian troops gave them the false impression it was clear to proceed, but German soldiers discovered them, and only three of them returned. Wallace was gassed during the second battle of Ypres in the spring of 1915 and spent seven months recovering in a British hospital. Once he was well enough, he was returned to Canada where he went back to work at the shipyards.

In 1921 Wallace married Charlotte Chapman, whose father, Edward, had operated a Vancouver clothing store and outfitting business since 1891. Clarence had met Charlotte before the war when he accompanied his mother to a florist shop one Saturday morning. His mother started talking to Mrs. Edward Chapman, and Clarence asked to be introduced to her daughter. While he was overseas, Charlotte had written to him every day. Clarence and Charlotte had four sons: Blake, Richard, Philip and David.

After the war there was a slump in business for most Vancouver shipbuilders, but in 1921 the Wallace Shipyard landed the contract to build the coastal steamship *Princess Louise* for the CPR. Meanwhile, Alfred's request for a federal subsidy to build a dry dock was rejected. Not easily discouraged, his son Clarence purchased the property adjacent to the shipyard for $25,000. Then he went to Ottawa where he brought in an expert from New York to update the plans and budget for the dock. In a 1977 interview he recalled, "I stayed [in Ottawa] for three months, and then came home for the birth of our twins, then went back."[202] Clarence kept submitting estimates to the government, which were regularly rejected. Finally he asked if the man in charge of approvals would take the plan and estimates home and look them over in the evening on his own time; he agreed and the plan was approved. The dry dock was opened on August 11, 1925. Three years later, Wallace Shipyards built the *St. Roch*, the RCMP's Arctic patrol ship, which became the first vessel to sail through the Northwest Passage. When Alfred's health began to decline in 1929, Clarence became head of the company, and with the dry dock in place, the shipyard was able to carry out substantial repair work during the Depression years.

During the Second World War, the new Burrard Dry Dock completed contracts for both the British and Canadian governments, building minesweepers as well as corvettes for anti-submarine work and carrying out aircraft carrier conversions. However, the shipyard became best known for its 10,000-ton supply ships, an essential support for the war effort as they carried food, steel, lumber, nails, motorcycles, bombs and the aluminum to build bomber aircraft in

Clarence Wallace's Burrard Dry Dock built over a hundred 10,000-ton supply ships for the Canadian government during the Second World War. Here, Wallace poses with a model cargo supply ship in 1943. A portrait of his father, Alfred Wallace, hangs on the wall.
Image courtesy of North Vancouver Museum and Archives, 27–523.

Britain. Construction of these ships began in the fall of 1940 after the British Admiralty had toured shipyards in Canada and the United States to assess their suitability for building naval and maintenance vessels. As a result of this tour, Burrard Dry Dock received an order for eight 10,000-ton ships based on the "North Sands" design. As there were few experienced shipbuilders in Canada, Wallace hired British shipbuilders to show them how to do it, then contracted out the fabrication of engines, boilers and even frames to other companies, with Burrard's workers assembling the final product.

Then, at the request of C.D. Howe, head of the Department

of Munitions and Supply in Ottawa, forest company owner H.R. MacMillan investigated the possibility of building more freighters in Canada. Wallace committed Burrard to building another thirty North Sands ships, vessels that were "not only completed . . . on time, but also for less than the amount contracted."[203] In the end over three hundred of these supply vessels were launched by Canadian shipyards during the war, and Burrard built 109 of them.

Burrard had begun the war with about two hundred employees, but this rose to about thirteen thousand men and a thousand women at the peak of wartime employment. The company was, in fact, one of the first shipyards in Canada to hire women in large numbers. General manager Bill Wardle was reluctant to hire them, but Wallace saw female employees as a necessity if the company was to fulfill its orders. The women were offered jobs that were considered to be "light," such as welding, electrical installing and helping carpenters and pipefitters, leaving the "heavy" work for the men. But concerned about socializing between male and female workers, the company built a separate lunchroom for female employees. They took their breaks in separate quarters and entered and left the shipyard by different gates. After the war Burrard, like many other war industries, expected women to vacate their jobs to make way for returning soldiers, despite the abilities that they had demonstrated. Burrard did not hire another woman welder until 1981.

After the war, although the company bought out other shipyards such as Yarrows of Victoria and took on a French contract to build coal transporters as part of a program to rebuild European infrastructure, Wallace downsized the workforce at Burrard Dry Dock and focused the company primarily on repairing ships and building ferries. Re-armament during the Cold War led to contracts for anti-submarine vessels and destroyer escorts, and the federal Department of Transport, interested in unlocking Canada's northern resources, ordered a number of Arctic icebreakers to help with the task. With the increasing mechanization of logging, Burrard also built barges to carry logs rather than rafting them, while the shipyard's active industrial division built equipment for hydroelectric generators, plywood processing and the petrochemical industry, which was essential to postwar projects and resource extraction in Western Canada.

With his contributions to the war effort, his outgoing nature and his wealth, Clarence Wallace was a natural for the job of Lieutenant Governor of BC, but he was surprised to receive the phone call from Prime Minister Louis St. Laurent asking if he would take the position. It probably had not hurt that, although not a member of any particular political party, Wallace had been good friends with Premier Byron Ingemar ("Boss") Johnson, one of the individuals who forwarded names of potential Lieutenant Governors to Ottawa. Wallace recalled, "I knew [Johnson], you see. I was always very close to the family. I had a place up on the Pitt River where the family had the big quarry, and I was director of their Ocean Cement . . . But he was a very likable chap and a very sincere person, and I liked Boss very well."[204] After taking a day or two to persuade Charlotte, who was "not too receptive of the idea"[205] of leaving their social circle in Vancouver, Wallace phoned the prime minister to accept the position. It was a decision he did not regret, and he later recalled his term in the post as "the happiest five years we've ever had."[206]

Wallace enjoyed travelling the province and meeting British Columbians. In July 1951 he went on a tour on HMCS *Ontario* to meet First Nations leaders and visit coastal communities, and early that fall he and his wife visited the Kootenays. His biggest challenge was giving so many speeches: "It's a hell of a job—and I'm no speechmaker—to have to go to all these little places and make speeches, about two a day and several a week. You'd go out to lunch and dinners and they'd have the same thing everywhere you went— cold roast beef and ham and apple pie and cheese, every damned meal! However, it was most enjoyable."[207]

Clarence Wallace met Queen Elizabeth on several occasions. The first time was in the fall of 1951 when she was still Princess Elizabeth, and she and Prince Philip toured Canada, staying with the Wallaces at Government House. Two years later Wallace attended her coronation at Westminster Abbey. (He was not the first member of his family to attend a coronation as his parents had gone to London for the coronation of King George V and Queen Mary on June 22, 1911.) When Wallace next toured coastal Indigenous communities, he travelled on his own yacht, the *Fifer,* and invited residents to come on board and watch films of the 1953 coronation. He met Prince Philip again in 1954 when the prince came to Vancouver for the British Empire and Commonwealth Games.

The Wallaces were generous hosts at Government House,

Clarence Wallace hosted Princess Elizabeth and Prince Philip when they toured Canada in the fall of 1951. At this state luncheon on October 22, Wallace was seated next to the princess, with Premier Byron Johnson and the Duke of Edinburgh to the right.
Image courtesy of Royal BC Museum and Archives, NA-40829.

entertaining about thirty thousand guests during their term. International dignitaries who visited included Prince Axel of Denmark and Prince Akihito of Japan. Two Governors General, Earl Alexander and Vincent Massey, visited Victoria several times during Wallace's term, while other guests included Prime Minister Louis St. Laurent, the Archbishop of Canterbury, and singer and author Margaret Truman, the daughter of President Harry S. Truman.

During his tenure as Lieutenant Governor, Clarence Wallace was required to exercise his reserve powers twice, first in 1952 to select a premier following a close election, and then in 1953 when he agreed to the premier's request for a dissolution. From 1941 to 1952 British Columbia had been governed by Liberal-Conservative coalitions, but the second coalition fell apart in January 1952 after a conflict arose between Liberal Premier Johnson and Herbert Anscomb, finance minister and head of the Conservative Party. Anscomb had offended Johnson by releasing information to the press about a new fiscal agreement with Ottawa before informing the cabinet, and at the next cabinet meeting, Johnson asked for Anscomb's resignation. Anscomb walked out, as did the other Conservative members. The Liberals were left with only a slim majority.

An election was set for June. With the Liberals and Conservatives now separated, space had opened up on the political spectrum for a third party to gain a majority, either the CCF or the relatively unknown Social Credit Party. The results of this election were slow to emerge as it was organized as a transferable ballot vote: voters ranked candidates in order of preference. Candidates gaining clear majorities won their seats outright, but if no candidate on the ballot had a majority, then second choices came into play; thus it took over a month for the results to be calculated. Overall the CCF party had gained 31 per cent of the popular vote and Social Credit 27 per cent, but Social Credit had elected nineteen members to the CCF's eighteen. BC historian Jean Barman points out that with the transferrable ballot, "Social Credit and the CCF came out ahead [of the Liberals and Conservatives] because they were so often mutual second choices. Protest against the status quo won the day."[208]

Even though the Social Credit Party had elected one more member than the CCF, it was not clear who should govern, and it was now Wallace's responsibility to decide. Among the elected Social Credit members only W.A.C. Bennett—he was only chosen as party leader after the election—and one other member, Tilly Rolston, had previous experience as MLAs. The CCF, led by Harold Winch, had more members with previous experience in the Legislature and also claimed the support of one independent MLA.

Wallace was concerned that even though "Winch would have the same number in the House as Bennett, he would be turned down the first time there was a vote by the Liberals and Conservatives." He spoke to the heads of both these parties to find out if they would support Winch as premier. "They said definitely not, and they weren't too sure about Bennett." Wallace thought that if he appointed Bennett, the government might be more stable: "Bennett had the chance of lasting out a hell of a lot longer than Winch." Wallace even went to Ottawa to ask "Mr. St. Laurent if he could give me any advice. He said no, I was on my own, which didn't make me feel too happy."[209] He also consulted Chief Justice Gordon Sloan, who told him he could not call on Bennett to form a new government, adding, "If you let those Socreds in there, you'll never get them out."[210]

Finally Wallace decided in favour of Social Credit after Bennett was able to produce a letter from the one independent promising his support, but when he informed Sloan of his decision, Sloan told him he would not come to the swearing-in ceremony at which he was to preside. The ceremony was set for nine o'clock that evening, and Wallace had some difficulty eating his dinner. Finally Sloan phoned to say he would come, and Wallace was able to have "a couple of good slugs and ate a real dinner."[211] That evening, Bennett and his cabinet members were sworn in at Government House as the new premier and executive council.

Wallace's next constitutional dilemma occurred in March 1953. The Social Credit Party had a minority government and seemed to be offering the other parties opportunities to defeat them in the house. The other parties resisted until the Socreds introduced the Rolston Formula, a convoluted Act to Amend the Public Schools Act, which would increase funding for rural schools while decreasing funds for urban schools. According to the leader of the CCF Opposition, Harold Winch:

> Bennett was not content to stay on as a minority government, but he knew that we weren't going to give him an opportunity; he knew that he'd have to force it by bringing in something that neither we nor the five Liberals nor three Conservatives in the House could possibly support . . . And that's when they brought in the Rolston Formula for education finances. It was just brought in for the very purpose of bringing about the dissolution of the house.[212]

Bennett's biographer, David Mitchell, noted that "The government was defeated on the Rolston Formula by a vote of twenty-eight to seventeen—the first administration defeated on the floor of the BC Legislature in over half a century."[213] The premier had achieved his goal: he wanted to dissolve the Legislature and have a new election. Meanwhile, Winch came to ask Wallace if he could form a government, but when Wallace asked if he could command a majority of support in the House, Winch could not guarantee it. Wallace then agreed to Bennett's request for a dissolution. In the general election of June 19, 1953, Social Credit gained a majority with twenty-eight members elected. As Chief Justice Sloan had predicted, the Social Credit party would continue to win elections, with Bennett as premier, until 1972.

After Clarence Wallace's term as Lieutenant Governor ended in 1955, he returned to work at the shipyard, which built several vessels for the BC Ferry Authority, and his family bought a farm in Coquitlam where he hosted international guests and took them on hunting expeditions. In 1966 the province awarded him with the prestigious Order of the Dogwood, which was created that year to recognize exceptional public service. It was awarded to only thirteen people, among them members of the royal family and three Lieutenant Governors—Wallace, Ross and Pearkes. It was replaced by the Order of British Columbia in 1989. In 1968 Wallace became a freeman of the City of Vancouver. He died on November 12, 1982, in Palm Desert, California. He was eighty-eight years old.

Clarence Wallace was the third BC Lieutenant Governor to have served in the First World War, and although he had not worked directly for C.D. Howe's Department of Munitions and Supply in the Second World War as Woodward and Banks had done, his shipyard completed contracts for that department. For his wartime role he had been designated a Commander of the Order of the British Empire (CBE) in 1946. However, his most memorable impact on this province came in 1952 when a shifting political landscape and a very close election required him to exercise the Lieutenant Governor's powers with the goal of achieving political stability.

Frank Mackenzie Ross (1955–60)

Frank Mackenzie Ross, who followed Clarence Wallace as Lieutenant Governor of BC, was born in northern Scotland in 1891, the son of Grace and David Ross, a civil servant who owned land, raised sheep and studied Gaelic. At the age of fifteen, Frank Ross was sent to study at the Tain Royal Academy in the ancient town of Tain on the Dornach Firth. He graduated at nineteen, sailed to Canada and secured a position with the Canadian Bank of Commerce, first in Montreal, then Toronto. In 1915 he enlisted with the 48th Highlanders, but once overseas, he was transferred to the Winnipeg Rifles. He was wounded at the Battle of Arras (April 9 to May 16, 1917) and sent to recover at a military hospital in England. There he met Gertrude

Tomalin, a travelling performer who gave readings to entertain the troops. When their paths crossed again in 1923, they married.

After the war Ross had returned to his job at the Bank of Commerce, then, looking for something more challenging, he accepted a position in New Brunswick with the Saint John Drydock and Shipbuilding Company. Within a year he had been promoted to general manager, and by 1926 he owned the company. Ross then expanded his business interests, becoming vice-president of a ship repair company and founding companies to repair and maintain airplane engines. Also in 1926, Ross became president of International Paints Ltd., a British firm that was setting up paint factories in Canada.

During the Second World War, C.D. Howe, minister of Munitions and Supply, recruited Ross to become the director-general of Naval Armaments and Equipment Production. It would be Ross's responsibility to ensure that the Royal Navy received the necessary "shells, naval guns, naval mountings, bombs, depth charges, torpedoes, Asdic gear to detect the presence of submarines,"[214] and other supplies from Canadian manufacturers. It was also Ross's job to convince the British Admiralty that Canada could supply the equipment it would need, then commandeer and coordinate companies across Canada to build the equipment.

In 1940 while Ross was involved in this new venture, his wife, Gertrude, died. In Ottawa the following year, he met Phyllis Gregory Turner, a widow with two children who, during the Second World War, had worked her way up to the highest civil service position held by a woman in Canada. The daughter of a mining engineer, Phyllis Gregory was born in Rossland, BC, in 1903. A strong scholar, she was the only one of her siblings to pursue a higher education. She studied economics, sociology and political science at UBC from 1921 to 1925, went to Bryn Mawr in Pennsylvania on a scholarship for her doctoral studies, and followed this with studies at the London School of Economics and the University of Marburg in Germany. Her graduate research focused on the history of the Doukhobors, Mennonites and Hutterites. In England in 1928 she married journalist Leonard Turner, whose family ran an import-export company, and the couple had three children: John, Michael (who died in infancy) and Brenda. Phyllis was widowed in 1932, and rather than remaining alone with two young children in

Depression-era England, she brought her children back to Canada. By the next fall she had found a job with the Tariff Board in Ottawa, and by 1939 she was chief research economist for the Board.

When Frank Ross met her in 1941, she was the economic advisor and administrator of Fats and Oils for the Wartime Prices and Trade Board, a job that made her responsible for ensuring that

During the Second World War, Phyllis Gregory Turner, a widowed mother of two, held important positions in the federal civil service. She married Frank Mackenzie Ross in April 1945 and while chatelaine devoted her time to furnishing and designing the interior of the new Government House. In 1961, she was appointed as the first female university chancellor in the British Commonwealth, at the University of British Columbia.

Image courtesy of Government House of British Columbia Archives.

Canada had an adequate supply of animal, fish and vegetable oils as well as glycerine for explosive production. She also represented Canada at the Combined Food Board in Washington. As she was the family breadwinner and worked long hours, she hired a housekeeper to look after her children, but she entertained colleagues at her home with singalongs and discussions of current events. Her son John recalls "As we grew older, we knew she was something special because of the people who used to come home to dinner or to a cocktail party."[215] A great supporter of post-secondary education, she helped found Carleton University in Ottawa in 1942 and became a member of its board of governors; in 1942–43 she served as president of the University Women's Club of Ottawa.

Frank Ross and Phyllis Gregory Turner married in April 1945 and moved to Vancouver where they bought a mansion in West Point Grey. From there, he commuted to Ottawa to assist Howe with postwar reconstruction of the Canadian economy. For her wartime service, Phyllis Ross was appointed a Commander of the Order of the British Empire and received an honorary degree from UBC where she had earned her first degree in 1921. From 1951 to 1954 she served as a member of the senate of the University of British Columbia.

As a hobby and investment, Frank Ross enjoyed farming and ranching, and he began raising Welsh ponies on a small farm in Cloverdale, within a short drive of Vancouver. Then in 1951 he partnered with Colonel Victor Spencer, a son of department store founder David Spencer, to purchase the Douglas Lake Cattle Company, the largest cattle ranch in the Commonwealth. While they enjoyed staying at the ranch and bringing guests to visit, Ross and Spencer also expected the ranch to make a profit, which they felt could be achieved by raising more calves while reducing spending on infrastructure and buildings and selling off the timber to local logging operations. Although the land could hold more cattle, their budget constraints limited how well the ranch could be maintained. In this way Ross and Spencer "gradually learned what other ranchers already knew well, that the ranching business, which is so dependent on variable factors, brings poor returns for dollars invested. The joys of owning and improving such a superb spread as Douglas Lake, of riding through the wide range as dawn breaks, passed them by."[216] In 1959 they sold the ranch to Charles N.

Woodward and John West. Woodward was the thirty-six-year-old president of Woodward's Stores Limited and son of former Lieutenant Governor William Culham Woodward. In 1956 Ross and Spencer provided support to the UBC rowing team, which had qualified for the Olympics in Melbourne, Australia: Spencer purchased the rowing shells, and Ross covered the team's expenses. The crew of four—known as the "Cinderella Crew"—won the gold medal.

In 1955 Frank Ross was appointed Lieutenant Governor of British Columbia and he, Phyllis and her daughter Brenda moved to Government House in Victoria. (By 1952 Phyllis's son, John Turner, had completed a political science degree at UBC and earned a law degree at Oxford as a Rhodes Scholar.) In their new roles, Frank and Phyllis Ross reached out to British Columbians beyond the capital by taking Government House to the people: "Staff members accompanied them to various centres, and receptions, dinners, luncheons and teas were given just as they were in Victoria, even to the use of silver, china and other accessories brought from Government House."[217]

This ability to re-create Government House elsewhere was put to good use after April 15, 1957, when the vice-regal mansion caught fire and burned to the ground. The evening before, they had celebrated Frank's sixtieth birthday with a special dinner. At 1:00 a.m., a maid had smelled smoke and alerted the night watchman, who could not find the source of the smoke. At 4:00 a.m. the cook, Chow Wing Suey, woke and found a storage room on fire. He alerted the residents and Government House was evacuated. Everyone escaped unharmed, but the house and all its contents were lost. Only the port cochère and entranceway were left standing.

Government House had to be replaced, but public opinion was divided on whether the new building should be of traditional or contemporary design. Ultimately the structure was similar to the former building, but the exterior was constructed of stone, concrete and metal, materials that would resist fire. The interior, apart from meeting the province's current structural guidelines, was based on the Maclure-Rattenbury plans for the previous house. The new building was designed by the Department of Public Works, while C.D. Campbell, deputy minister of Public Works and chief provincial architect, oversaw construction. Although some concern about the cost of replacing the building had been expressed, Premier

W.A.C. Bennett is reputed to have stated, "Do it and don't tell me how much it costs." In the end, it cost about $1.5 million.[218]

While the new Government House was under construction, Frank and Phyllis Ross moved into the vice-regal suite at the Empress Hotel, and from here they played a significant role in the furnishing of the new building. Previously, Lieutenant Governors had brought their own furniture and removed it when they left, though over time some had donated furnishings with the result that the collection that had accumulated in the mansion before the fire was quite diverse. The Rosses decided to provide Government House with a full set of furniture and décor, and to this end they toured England and Scotland in the late spring of 1957, seeking antiques and commissioning furniture to suit the space and function of the house. In total they purchased "114 pieces including the complete furnishings for the dining room and several tables, sets of chairs, cabinets, mirrors and bric-a-brac for the other rooms."[219] As portraits of the former Lieutenant Governors had also been lost in

Government House was destroyed by fire a second time on April 15, 1957.
The vice–regal couple, Frank and Phyllis Ross, toured England and Scotland to purchase furniture for the new Government House, including the dining room table and chairs pictured here.
Image courtesy of Government House of British Columbia Archives.

the fire, Frank Ross commissioned a new set of portraits, which now hang in the entrance hall, while other British Columbians donated furniture and paintings.

Phyllis Turner Ross oversaw the renovations with the kind of dedication and attention to detail that she had displayed in her administrative positions for the federal government. She met with the architects, providing information on the design of the previous interior and advising them on the features that would be necessary to carry out "the social and official functions held at Government House." For example, she explained that they would need "adequate cloakrooms; powder rooms; storage spaces for dishes and furniture for large functions; and improvements in the kitchen and pantry areas." She then worked with the architects to select "all the wallpapers, floor covering, wall tiles, bathroom fixtures"; the colour schemes, "the upholstered furniture, bedroom furniture, mattresses, bedding, curtains, draperies," and the "china, silver, glass and linen and kitchen and pantry equipment." By volunteering as interior decorator, Phyllis Ross estimated that she had saved the provincial government $250,000.[220]

In the summer of 1958 Frank and Phyllis hosted Princess Margaret who had come to BC for the celebrations marking the centennial of the founding of the mainland colony of British Columbia. These events promoted the province's natural resources, heritage and tourism, and the official openings conducted by the princess were part of this promotion of modern industry. She opened a railway bridge across the Peace River and the floating bridge across Okanagan Lake at Kelowna and attended Vancouver's Festival of the Arts and the opening of the National Historic Site at Fort Langley.

Princess Margaret was the celebrity of her day, an unattached twenty-seven-year-old princess, suffering from a broken heart after recently ending her engagement to Group Captain Peter Townsend. By this time Phyllis Ross's son, John Turner, was a lawyer in Montreal, but as the family thought he should help entertain the princess, he flew to Vancouver. His biographer writes that "the princess was delighted to meet a handsome and sophisticated young man her own age. She danced with Turner to the exclusion of other partners [at a ball at HMCS *Discovery* in Vancouver harbour], banished her aides from their table and discouraged all interruptions."[221] The media had a field day. Turner insisted that there was no romantic relationship and the two had simply become friends; he was even invited to her wedding with Antony Armstrong-Jones in 1960. Turner went on to a political career, first elected as a Liberal MP in Montreal in 1962, then appointed minister of Justice by Pierre Trudeau in 1968. After Trudeau's resignation in 1984, Turner won the Liberal leadership and briefly served as prime minister before losing the next election.

Both before and after the fire Frank and Phyllis Ross hosted other members of the British royal family. In the fall of 1955 Princess Mary visited Victoria, the Queen Mother stopped there on her way to Australia, and in July 1959 the Rosses hosted the Queen and Prince Philip on their cross-Canada tour. As historian S.W. Jackman points out, the Rosses were very successful hosts: "He was soon recognized to be a bit old-fashioned in manner but with a courteous approach

The centennial celebration of the founding of the mainland colony of British Columbia included a stagecoach run from Victoria to Barkerville. Here, W.A.C. Bennett (left) and Frank Ross pose in the Centennial Stagecoach in Victoria in May 1958.
Photo by Jim Ryan, courtesy of Royal BC Museum and Archives, E–07414.

at all times and thoroughly kind and generous. She had a style and élan; she was socially adroit and guests were put at their ease."[222] Ross was also popular for his efforts to reach out to British Columbians, attend public functions, visit the elderly and throw parties for children, and the BC public showed its appreciation by awarding him freeman status in the cities of Victoria, Nelson, Dawson Creek and Vancouver. The Native Sons of British Columbia granted him the Good Citizen Award, and the BC Government gave him the Order of the Dogwood.

Frank Ross completed his term on October 13, 1960, and continued to travel and work on his business concerns until his death in Vancouver in 1971. Phyllis Ross served as chancellor of UBC from 1961 to 1966, the first woman to serve as a university chancellor in the British Commonwealth. She died in 1988.

The last of a series of business-oriented Lieutenant Governors, Frank Mackenzie Ross served at a time when, despite the continuing widespread acceptance of the gendered division of labour, there was a woman on the throne and the chatelaine of Government House was a Commander of the Order of the British Empire. In a later era, Phyllis Turner Ross would have been an equally suitable candidate for Lieutenant Governor. Most Canadians were enjoying more material comforts, and the 1958 centennial, in which Ross played a key role, gave British Columbians the opportunity to celebrate their pioneer history as well as their industrial achievements. Arguably Frank and Phyllis Ross's most enduring legacy was their contribution to refurnishing and redecorating the vice-regal estate.

IX

Adapting to Social and Political Changes (1960–88)

THE 1960s AND '70s saw social and cultural transformations with the rise of new movements championing the rights of women, francophones, workers, gays, lesbians and Indigenous people, and all these transformations inevitably affected the nature of the office of Lieutenant Governor.

Indigenous groups who were pressing the state for recognition of title and Aboriginal rights had been encouraged by lawyer Thomas Berger's success in defending the hunting rights of two Nanaimo men based on the Douglas treaties; as a result, in 1969 Nisga'a elders hired Berger to argue on their behalf that "Nisga'a title to their lands had never been lawfully extinguished through treaty or by any other means."[223] The case went all the way to the Supreme Court of Canada, which acknowledged the existence of Aboriginal title and forever changed the relationship between government and Indigenous people in this province. In response, some BC Lieutenant Governors in this period made it a priority to meet with First Nations and listen to their concerns. However, while the federal government began negotiating land claims with First Nations in the mid-1970s, British Columbia's government did not take part in these negotiations until 1990.

This was also a politically challenging time to be the vice-regal representative in BC. In 1972, after twenty years of Social Credit governments, the political situation in British Columbia changed radically when the first socialist government was elected. Among the many initiatives introduced by NDP Premier Dave Barrett were an increase in the minimum wage, the protection of agricultural land, an increase in parks and wilderness areas and the introduction of a royalty on mineral production. Then in 1975 the political situation tilted again when three Liberal MLAs crossed the floor to join the Social Credit, giving Bill Bennett the numbers and the credibility to win the election that December.

At the same time the situation was changing dramatically on the federal scene. In 1982 the government redefined Canada's relationship with Great Britain and the Crown by patriating the Constitution, previously known as the British North America Act, while at the same time entrenching a Charter of Rights and Freedoms in the Constitution. Prior to the Constitution Act of 1982, only the British government could amend the Canadian Constitution; now Canada could make changes without approval from Britain, but this fact raised alarm bells for Indigenous people who did not want their historic relationship with the Crown to be altered. Interestingly, however, the 1982 Constitution also provided protection for the office of Lieutenant Governor since it states that making any changes to this office "would require a resolution by the federal House of Commons, Senate, and every Legislative Assembly in the country."[224]

During this period personal wealth became slightly less important as a prerequisite for the job of Lieutenant Governor of BC. The men appointed at this time did not own their own companies, although they often served on boards of directors, and since most of the appointees were taking a pay cut in order to accept the position, the expectation that they would pay for expenses such as Government House staff salaries would soon come to an end.

George Randolph Pearkes (1960–68)

George Randolph Pearkes was born in Watford, Hertfordshire, on February 26, 1888, the son of a department store owner. He had two siblings, Edward (Ted) and Hilda. From the age of eight, Pearkes was sent to the Berkhamsted School where he learned the British middle class values of "hard work, discipline, team spirit and fair play."[225] Shortly after graduation in May 1906, Pearkes left for Canada to learn agricultural skills at a farm near Red Deer, Alberta, which was owned by the headmaster of Berkhamsted.

After learning some farming basics at what neighbours called the "Baby Farm," Pearkes went to work for a nearby farmer who raised purebred horses and cattle. In 1909 Pearkes, now aged twenty-one, rode 112 kilometres (70 mi) west to Rocky Mountain House, found a section of land with river frontage and trees, then returned to Red Deer, where he registered a homestead claim. Before returning to his homestead, he purchased a team of horses, a cow, two pigs, a few chickens, a tent, stove, some provisions and tools, but he found there were multiple challenges for a single man starting a homestead from scratch—building fences to contain his animals, clearing the land before crops could be planted, building a shelter and cooking his own meals. Fortunately the following year his brother Ted, who had followed him to Canada to work at the Berkhamsted Farm, took up the adjoining homestead, and the brothers built a two-room cabin they could share on Ted's property. Then, while Ted worked the land and tended the animals, George earned income off the farm by digging coal, freighting supplies for railroad construction and assisting a survey party.

All this time, the brothers had been sending their mother optimistic letters about their farms, and encouraged by the portrait they painted of homesteading in the west, Mrs. Pearkes, who had separated from their father, and her daughter, Hilda, left England to join them in Canada. The farm was a shock to Mrs. Pearkes, and to create a more satisfactory living environment, she paid for a new, larger farmhouse to be built on George's section. She and Hilda then rolled up their sleeves to pitch in with cooking, cleaning and sewing. However, working as an axeman with a survey crew north of Fort McMurray in 1911 gave Pearkes some time to think about his career plans. The northern landscape certainly appealed to him, but while he now owned a 160-acre (65-ha) homestead, he did not see himself as a farmer for the long term. Instead, he joined the Royal North West Mounted Police (RNWMP), underwent six weeks of training in Regina then volunteered for a post in the Yukon. To get there, he took the train to Vancouver and sailed north through the Inside Passage. By this time the rest of his family had also tired of homesteading and moved to the West Coast.

As a Mountie in the Yukon one of his assignments was acting as a border guard at the White Pass summit, checking the trains for wanted men and stopping men he saw walking beside the tracks to question them. He was told not to allow prostitutes into the Yukon, but because he was too embarrassed to ask women any personal questions, he would board the train and walk through the coaches, glaring at the few women passengers. In winter Pearkes patrolled the area near Carcross, "showing the flag," checking on the well-being of remote trappers and prospectors, and helping to draft the occasional legal document. Not quite satisfied with his life as a member of the RNWMP, Pearkes was contemplating studying law when the course of his life changed once again with Britain's declaration of war in August 1914. The RNWMP was reluctant to lose valuable members, but Pearkes found a way out by saying he needed to check on his neglected homestead.

In February 1915 Pearkes headed south to Victoria, visited his mother and sister, and joined the 2nd Canadian Mounted Rifles (CMR) where he soon held the rank of lance corporal. Training at Willows Beach in Victoria consisted of long marches, rifle practice, attending lectures and taking care of the horses. In reaction to the sinking of the *Lusitania* on May 7, 1915, and the loss in that sinking of former CMR member Lieutenant James Dunsmuir, fights broke out in Victoria and crowds attacked business establishments owned by or associated with German-Canadians. Pearkes was a member of the squadron called out to keep the peace and guard stores from looters.

The 2nd CMR left Victoria for overseas service in early June, arriving in Britain almost three weeks later. In these early days of the war, Pearkes felt strongly that he was fighting for England, his homeland. "I can't say that I ever thought much at that time about fighting for Canada or fighting for democracy," he later told biographer Reginald Roy. "We were fighting for England."[226] Over the summer the 2nd CMR trained at the Shorncliffe army camp in Kent; they rarely had access to horses, but they practised marching, musketry, map reading, what to do in the case of a gas attack and how to build improvised bombs. Their training was designed to prepare men to defend a trench position, but there was little training on how to take a trench held by the enemy.

On September 22 the 2nd CMR sailed for France and was assigned to a quiet but muddy section of the trenches near Messines. In the late fall Pearkes was pulled out of the line to take a course at the 2nd Army Bombing School on offensive fighting and trench raids. He did well in the course and was kept on as an instructor until the early spring of 1916 when he rejoined the 2nd CMR at the Ypres Salient to carry out bombing and counter-bombing attacks. He was wounded there when a German grenade exploded nearby, leaving him with shrapnel in his head and left arm; he spent a week at the Canadian General Hospital in Etaples, then was discharged to command the bombers again. He was hospitalized again after a fragment of a bomb hit close to his eye; the medical staff wanted him to return to England, but Pearkes insisted on going back to the front. In August he was appointed to train bombers for the 8th Canadian Infantry Brigade, and shortly afterwards the brigade was sent to provide relief at the Battle of the Somme; there Pearkes played a key role in closing off the German tunnel network at Moquet Farm. At the end of September he was promoted to officer in command of "C" company, 5th CMR. On October 1–2 the 5th CMR was involved in the taking of Regina Trench, but the Germans took it back before reinforcements could arrive. By this time Pearkes's energy and leadership skills had earned the support of his men, and one NCO later recalled:

> As a commander and leader of men he proved to me he had no fear whatsoever, and I would follow him anywhere . . . I felt safe with him. He was also a generous officer by giving money as prizes in sports and to Section NCOs for the best warfare

training while out for a rest. He has offered to carry a man's pack while the man rode his horse on a route march from one town to another . . . This was the kind of an officer he was.[227]

In April 1917 the 5th CMR formed part of the Canadian attackers on Vimy Ridge, and in October they moved to the muddy wasteland of Passchendaele. During an attack on the morning of October 30, Pearkes was hit in the thigh by shrapnel but, undeterred, he kept advancing. Later he recalled that the mud there had been both a blessing and a curse:

> The mud saved many from the enemy's artillery fire because the shells buried themselves in the mud . . . [which] deadened the effect of the explosion and the spread of fragments from the shell . . . [but] I'm certain there were men who . . . wounded, fell into the shell holes and were drowned. If you got in, you just couldn't climb out by yourself . . . because the sides all kept oozing down if you reached out to help yourself.[228]

As Major Pearkes and "C" Company advanced toward their goal, Vapour Farm, the company that was supposed to protect their flank was delayed in hand-to-hand combat, so that when "C" Company reached their goal, only about three dozen men were left. However, these men, along with stragglers from adjacent companies, managed to take both Vapour and Source farms, and Pearkes sent a carrier pigeon message back to report on the group's progress. They held their precarious position until nightfall when the thirty-five men remaining were relieved by a group of two hundred from other British Columbia companies. By this time Pearkes had gone without sleep for two days, and his thigh wound had caused his leg to go numb. For his leadership in this attack he was awarded the Victoria Cross. How he regarded this award was evident in a speech he gave in London in 1929 when he said on behalf of overseas Victoria Cross holders: "The Cross was never gained without the sacrifice of gallant lives . . . We are simply the lucky ones . . . There aren't enough VCs to go round, and the man who gets one is lucky, for there are tens of thousands as gallant as he."[229]

Shortly after he returned to his unit, Pearkes was promoted to senior major in the 116th Battalion, and whenever his troops were away from the front line, he made sure they were trained in mobile warfare, but he also made time for sports and entertainment as well. In July 1918 the Canadian Corps was moved secretly from the front to provide support for Australian and British forces in an attack planned for August 8. The companies under Pearkes took the Bade Trenches, sending German soldiers to the rear as prisoners. From there Pearkes's 116th battalion advanced with several companies towards Hamon Wood, and the Germans were forced to fall back to the trench system of 1916. As a result of his battalion's success in this attack, Pearkes was awarded the Distinguished Service Order.

One of Pearkes's worst injuries occurred in Guemappe, a small village behind enemy lines, where he was hit in the side, exposing a section of his intestines. He received a blood transfusion from another soldier while he underwent immediate surgery, and six weeks later he was transferred to a hospital in London. About a week after his transfer, the armistice was signed, and Pearkes witnessed Londoners' joyful celebrations. When he was well enough, he returned to France to resume command of the 116th Battalion and oversee the slow process of demobilization. Then, rather than go back to his homestead or the police, Pearkes elected to stay in the army, and he was selected to study with other Canadian officers at the British Staff College at Camberley, Surrey.

Back in Canada in January 1920 Pearkes was stationed in Calgary as General Staff Officer II (GSO II) with the Princess Patricia's Canadian Light Infantry. His job there was to renew the Non-Permanent Active Militia, but it was difficult to gain new recruits when men were anxious to forget the war and return to civilian life. While stationed in Calgary, Pearkes started a Boy Scout troop, taking them camping on the Kananaskis River and enlisting his army colleagues to give the boys lessons in rifle shooting, first aid and music. In 1922 Governor General Baron Byng of Vimy, who had commanded the Canadian Corps in the attack on Vimy in April 1917, toured Alberta, and Pearkes was appointed his temporary aide-de-camp. He followed this in December with a temporary posting as Byng's ADC in Ottawa where the two would occasionally go on afternoon walks and discuss current affairs.

By 1924 Pearkes was based in Winnipeg, and he took leave to visit his mother and sister in Sidney, where they now owned a dairy farm. While attending an Anglican Church service there, he met his wife-to-be, Constance Blytha Copeman, and over the next few

After volunteering in the First World War and earning a Victoria Cross and a
Distinguished Service Order, George Randolph Pearkes chose to stay in the army.
He was based in Winnipeg in 1924 when he went on leave to visit his mother and
sister in Sidney, BC, where he met his wife, Constance Blytha Copeman. The two
are shown here at the time of their engagement.
Image courtesy of University of Victoria Archives and Special Collections, ACC 91–55 Box 5.1.

days he made sure to attend all of the social events that she did.
Blytha was born in 1902 in Cochrane, Alberta, her parents having
emigrated from Norfolk, England, to run a cattle ranch there. Her
father now operated a real estate business in Sidney. Blytha accepted
Pearkes's proposal just nine days after they met; they were married
in Esquimalt in August 1925 and returned to Winnipeg.

In April 1928, just a month after their daughter, Priscilla Edith,
was born, the army transferred Pearkes back to Esquimalt to serve
under the command of Brigadier General A.G.L. McNaughton,
the man destined to command the 1st Canadian Infantry Division
in the Second World War before becoming minister of National
Defence. Pearkes helped organize a central training camp at Vernon,

focusing on training soldiers for the realities of battle, and in 1929 he set up the first combined operations exercise in BC, a practice coastal attack on Maple Bay. Next Pearkes was sent to be GSO I at the Royal Military College in Kingston and, while stationed there, their second child, John, was born. In 1933, at the end of his stint at RMC, Pearkes took his family to England where he attended a refresher staff-training course. On his return to Canada, he was appointed director of Military Training and Staff Duties in Ottawa. Sadly, in 1935 his daughter, Priscilla Edith, died as the result of an infection caught in the hospital at birth, which brought on a series of weakening illnesses.

In contrast to the international militarization that occurred in the mid-1930s, Canada's armed forces were relatively underfunded and underequipped, the result of the isolationist position held by Prime Minister Mackenzie King, who hesitated to offend any of the European powers. He was, however, ignoring the growing turmoil in the world. In October 1935 Italian forces attacked Abyssinia. Early in 1936 German troops occupied the Rhineland, and in July of that year the Spanish Civil War erupted. The Second Sino-Japanese war broke out a year later.

In 1937 Pearkes and his family returned to England so he could attend the Imperial Defence College, and their time in London coincided with the coronation of George VI on May 12, 1937. Blytha was presented at court, thanks to Alice Massey, the wife of Vincent Massey, who was Canada's High Commissioner to the United Kingdom and who would become Canada's first Canadian-born Governor General in 1952. After his course Pearkes spent a few weeks observing British army manoeuvres with modern weapons and vehicles, exercises that highlighted for him the gap between Canadian and British training.

The Pearkes family's next stop was Calgary, where Blytha took up her husband's former hobby by leading a troop of Girl Scouts. During the visit of King George and Queen Elizabeth to Canada in the spring of 1939, Pearkes prepped Alberta MLAs on how to address the king and queen and sat next to Her Majesty at a dinner given by Premier William Aberhart. "I remember her asking Mr. Aberhart to explain what Social Credit was," Pearkes recalled in a 1977 interview. "I don't know how successful he was in selling the idea."[230] The royal visit highlighted the role of the militia, whose presence at many of the engagements helped to increase enlistment.

Soon after Canada declared war on September 10, 1939, Pearkes was appointed commander of the 2nd Canadian Infantry Brigade, which included western units. They embarked for Britain in December and were stationed in the Aldershot-Farnborough area where Pearkes put them through rigorous physical training while they awaited their weapons and vehicles. Then in February 1940 Pearkes came down with spinal meningitis, and Blytha and John moved to England to be close by while he recovered.

After the fall of France, German advances across Europe made it difficult to establish Allied troops on the Continent. On August 19, 1942, an Allied raid took place on the port of Dieppe, France, consisting of mostly Canadian infantry, supported by the Royal Navy, the Royal Air Force and a Canadian armoured regiment. Pearkes was convinced that this raid was not a good idea and was glad that his division did not have to take part. Although he would have supported small-scale raids, he later explained that:

> if there was any large scale raid it would take up so much equipment, it would require so many men and [employ] so much equipment and artillery support if it was going to be effective, that it wasn't worth doing until the real invasion came about. It was only wasting effort. If we withdrew after a couple of days, we would only give the Germans an opportunity to laugh at us and say here was an invasion which failed. I was never in favour of it.[231]

To this day Canadian military historians debate the wisdom and lessons of the Dieppe raid in which 4,963 Canadian soldiers took part; 907 were killed, 2,460 were wounded and 1,946 were taken prisoner by German forces.

Less than two weeks after the raid, Pearkes was on his way back to Canada to take charge of West Coast defences. Anti-Japanese hysteria had been building since the attack on Pearl Harbor in December 1941 as British Columbians were worried that their coast was also vulnerable to attack; some people even feared that Japanese-Canadian fishermen might collaborate with the Japanese navy. In February 1942 the federal government passed an order-in-council authorizing the removal of all "persons of Japanese racial origin" from a 100-mile (322-km)-wide "protected" area on the West Coast.

Pearkes's new Pacific Command covered BC, Alberta, the Yukon and part of the Northwest Territories. Defending this area were about 15,000 reserve soldiers of the Pacific Coast Militia Rangers plus approximately 35,000 regular force soldiers of whom 65 per cent had been conscripted under the National Resources Mobilization Act (NRMA) of June 1940 to serve only in home defence. Despite this restriction, Pearkes wanted to train all the soldiers under his command for possible engagement with Japanese forces, either in British Columbia or in Asia, so with assistance from the Alpine Club of Canada he established a mountain and jungle warfare school, helped start a Japanese language school and organized the training of Chinese-Canadian soldiers in the Okanagan for special operations in Southeast Asia. He also sought to put an end to the Japanese occupation of the Aleutian Islands, an action that had to be coordinated with American military leaders and approved by the Canadian government. In addition, he wanted the definition of "home defence" to be broadened to include Alaska so he could send NRMA men there. In mid-August 1942 American and Canadian forces did land on Kiska in the Aleutians and found it deserted: the Japanese had abandoned it in late July.

In 1943 and 1944 there was a new push to recruit men for active service and convert NRMA recruits into regular soldiers available for duty overseas, but when Pearkes tried to persuade his men to volunteer, he met resistance; he blamed this on a lack of patriotism. He was, however, convinced conscription could be imposed with minimal opposition. He told a reporter:

> Our job is reclaiming lost citizens to Canada . . . boys who have grown up for twenty years without any spirit of patriotism . . . and our reward will be an increasing number who volunteer to join their comrades in storming the bastion of Europe.[232]

Meanwhile, there was trouble brewing in Ottawa as Colonel J.L. Ralston, the minister of National Defence, was pushing for conscription for overseas duty while Mackenzie King was still trying to avoid it. The prime minister's solution to the problem was to replace Ralston with Brigadier General McNaughton, but the new minister had few new ideas to offer for gaining voluntary recruits. Finally, in November 1944 the government passed an order-in-council conscripting sixteen thousand NRMA personnel for overseas service. Announcement of this partial conscription led to protests in military camps throughout British Columbia, and in Terrace NRMA conscripts armed themselves and marched into the town, although actual violence was avoided. Discipline came in the form of withholding pay and transferring some of the BC troops to eastern Canada. Following these incidents, Pearkes asked to be relieved of his command, partly because his efforts to train men for service in Asia were being undermined by the removal of these soldiers for service in Europe and partly because his loyalty had been called into question over the issue of recruitment. His request was granted, and in February 1945 he retired as a major-general, thirty years after joining the Canadian Mounted Rifles, a unit of the Canadian Expeditionary Force.

Soon after he retired, Pearkes was approached to run federally for the newly renamed Progressive Conservative party. Since he was only fifty-seven and saw this as an opportunity to assist returning veterans, he agreed. In June 1945 he ran as a candidate for Nanaimo (a riding that at the time included Esquimalt, Saanich and the Gulf Islands) and, in a close race against the CCF candidate, won the seat. However, Mackenzie King's Liberals were returned with a minority government, and Pearkes found himself on the Opposition benches. Some of the causes he supported in his early years in Parliament included increasing the Old Age Pension, providing more funding for student veterans, and helping returning soldiers who were purchasing homes through the Veterans Land Act. He also lobbied on behalf of disenfranchised groups, pointing out the deplorable state of First Nations reserves in Nanaimo, and supported the Chinese Canadian bid for the franchise, an issue that had been brought to his attention by his special operations soldiers during the war. On the topic of Canadians of Japanese descent, however, Pearkes likely reflected popular sentiment in his riding when he argued that they should not be allowed to return to the coast.

Pearkes was re-elected in 1953 and again in June 1957 when the Progressive Conservatives under John Diefenbaker came to power with a minority government, and he was appointed minister of National Defence. These were the Cold War years, and construction was wrapping up on the Distant Early Warning (DEW) line, the third and most northerly of the chains of early warning radar stations in Canada, which were intended to warn of impending raids by Soviet-manned bombers. One of his first actions was to secure

Prime Minister Diefenbaker's approval for Canada's participation in the North Atlantic Air Defence Command (NORAD), which integrated US and Canadian air-defence forces under a joint command in Colorado Springs. That Diefenbaker signed this agreement so quickly raised some public criticism because of the perceived loss of Canadian sovereignty.

Diefenbaker's government made a number of controversial decisions regarding defence technology in these years. In 1950 the Liberal government had asked the A.V. Roe Company to develop a supersonic jet aircraft capable of intercepting Soviet bombers flying over the Canadian north. The company's Avro Arrow turned out to be an expensive project, but it made use of the skills of many Canadian scientists and engineers in its development. By the mid-1950s, however, senior military officers outside of the air force were questioning the impact of the Arrow on the overall defence budget, and after the Soviets launched the first man-made satellite in October 1957, it was clear that the USSR had the capability to launch a ballistic missile at North America—which the Arrow was not designed to intercept. To help cut the Arrow's costs, Pearkes tried to secure an American commitment to purchase some of the completed planes, but when he was unsuccessful, Diefenbaker announced on February 20, 1959, that the Arrow program would be cancelled and Canada would acquire American-made Bomarc anti-aircraft missiles. Fifty-six of these missiles were deployed in Ontario and Quebec, but the Canadian public was not told until 1960 that, to be operative, they had to be fitted with nuclear warheads; the news caused a debate over whether Canada should have nuclear weapons on its territory. Although Pearkes supported the acquisition of nuclear weapons, the Conservative government was divided on the issue, and Diefenbaker's decision not to accept them led in part to the Conservative defeat in the 1963 election.

Pearkes, however, had left federal politics in 1960, and in October of that year he accepted the prime minister's offer of the Lieutenant Governorship of British Columbia. Having spent most of his career in the armed forces before moving into politics, at seventy-two he was a man of modest means and could not afford to provide the customary lavish entertainments of the position. What he could offer was his time, more so than many of his predecessors who had continued to manage businesses on the side. He began his posting by increasing access to events at Government House, especially for groups visiting from beyond the capital. He later explained:

> I felt that these are people who are tax–payers in the province and that they have a desire to see Government House, and there is no reason why they shouldn't. The expense of giving them tea and biscuits is not great, and it satisfies a group of people who have come in from all over the province or from further afield.[233]

George Randolph and Blytha Pearkes hosted a variety of events over the year including a New Year's Day levee, a state dinner and state ball early in the year, and a summer garden party. At Hallowe'en they handed out candy to neighbourhood children, and at Christmas they hosted a Christmas party for the children of the Protestant orphanage. Pearkes was enthusiastic about travelling the province and meeting as many British Columbians as he could. Visiting Indigenous communities was particularly important to him, and he refused to be deterred by the limitations of the provincial highway system. His private secretary, Commander Gar Dixon, recalled that Pearkes travelled,

> in a dugout canoe. He was in seaplanes, up and down rivers by riverboat. He visited the Babine Lake and the Indians at its northern end via an old flat–bottomed riverboat. He came down the Mackenzie by river barge.[234]

In October 1963 when Pearkes took a float plane to the Nisga'a community of Gingolx (Kincolith), almost a century had passed since the last representative of the Crown, Governor Seymour, had visited in 1869. Local children lined the wharf waving homemade paper Union Jacks, as Pearkes's plane got stuck on a sandbar, possibly the same one that grounded the captain's boat when Seymour visited.[235] Like previous Lieutenant Governors, Pearkes also travelled on naval ships to visit British Columbians living along the coast, and Indigenous communities residing in Nanaimo, Clayoquot Sound and the Cowichan Valley acknowledged his efforts to come to them by naming him an honorary chief, while the Nisga'a made him a hereditary chief. He received several honorary degrees and was appointed an honorary colonel of the British Columbia Dragoons, formerly the Canadian Mounted Rifles, which he had joined in 1915.

As Pearkes's five-year term as Lieutenant Governor was drawing

George Randolph Pearkes (left), seen here with premier W.A.C. Bennett, was a popular Lieutenant Governor who travelled extensively to visit communities throughout the province. At the request of Prime Minister Lester B. Pearson, Pearkes agreed to extend his term by three years, until 1968.
Image courtesy of University of Victoria Library and Archives, ACC 83–188 Box 1.5.7.

to a close, Liberal prime minister Lester B. Pearson asked him to extend his term into 1968 in order to preside over Canada's centennial celebrations in BC. As a result, the next two years were extremely busy ones for Pearkes and his wife. In 1967 Government House became the stopping place for global leaders and members of royal families, including Queen Juliana of the Netherlands, Emperor Haile Selassie of Ethiopia, Prince and Princess Takamatsu of Japan and Prince Rainier III and Princess Grace of Monaco. In addition to receiving more honorary memberships and being made a freeman of several BC cities, Pearkes served as the grand president of the Royal Canadian Legion from 1966 to 1976. He was also made a Companion of the Order of Canada in 1967, the year this award was initiated, and in 1968 he was granted the provincial Order of the Dogwood, created in 1966.

Major-General George Randolph Pearkes lived out his retirement years in Victoria and died there on May 30, 1984; he was ninety-six years old. His wife, Blytha, died in 1995. Pearkes' legacy is still visible today as several institutions have been named after him, including a Victoria treatment centre for children with cerebral palsy (renamed the Children's Health Foundation of Vancouver Island in 2012) and the G.R. Pearkes Recreation Centre in Saanich. Pearkes's personal priorities shifted the direction of the office of the Lieutenant Governor in British Columbia. Although he had been a veteran of two world wars as well as a federal politician, as his predecessors Woodward, Banks, Wallace and Ross had been, he had not been associated with C.D. Howe's Department of Munitions and Supply as they were, and he was also not as wealthy, which meant he had to approach the responsibilities of the office in a less expensive and more down-to-earth manner. This he managed to do successfully for an extended term of eight years.

John Robert Nicholson (1968–73)

John Robert (Jack) Nicholson was born on December 1, 1901, in the small town of Newcastle, New Brunswick, the son of Isabelle and Robert Nicholson, a doctor. Growing up, he was a member of the Boy Scouts and cadets, and at fifteen, having won the Max Aitken Scholarship, he enrolled at Dalhousie University in Halifax. He got his first taste of politics when he participated in the university's mock parliament, and in 1921 he volunteered to work on Mackenzie King's election campaign. By the spring of 1923 Nicholson had completed a law degree and, after he was called to the bar, headed west for British Columbia where by January of the following year he had also qualified to practise law.

That summer he returned to Halifax long enough to marry Charlotte Jean Annand, a fellow student at Dalhousie and a granddaughter of a former premier of Nova Scotia. The couple settled in Vancouver where Nicholson had become a partner in the firm of Locke, Lane, Nicholson and Sheppard. For the next seven years he worked on criminal cases before switching to civil law. One of his earliest cases involved a Chinese man held in custody by authority of the minister of Justice while awaiting deportation. Nicholson, however, discovered that the minister of Justice did not have the right to hold a person for immigration purposes, and that only the minister of Immigration could do so, and he applied for habeas corpus to release the man from unlawful confinement. He was successful and his client was freed. As Nicholson later recalled,

I got tremendous publicity out of that not just in British Columbia but throughout the whole of Canada, and within a matter of weeks I was getting telephone calls from people who were in trouble with the Immigration authorities not only from Victoria and elsewhere in British Columbia, but from Calgary, from Winnipeg, even from Toronto. I never looked back. I was very fortunate.[236]

During the Second World War, Nicholson—although already forty years old—signed up with the Reserve Army and became captain of a BC regiment. He expected to go overseas, but in the late summer of 1941 C.D. Howe, the minister of munitions and supplies, asked him to take on the job of deputy controller of supplies for Canada, working under Controller Alan Williamson. With the bombing of Pearl Harbor in December 1941 and Japan's invasion of Malaya and Burma, Canada no longer had a source of raw rubber, and Nicholson was given the task of promoting the North American production of synthetic rubber. Canada had acquired the formula for producing it thanks to an American scientist who had managed to obtain a German recipe in 1939. Since then, both American and Canadian scientists had been experimenting with different materials and combinations to produce rubber on the scale required for the war effort. Nicholson began by helping to establish a Crown corporation called Polymer in Sarnia, Ontario, which would make rubber from oil. By 1943 Polymer was manufacturing the first rubber made from Canadian styrene and American butadiene by using oil accessed via a pipeline from Louisiana and large quantities of water from Lake Huron. This rubber had a wide range of uses, including tires and airplane and automobile parts. After the war, Nicholson stayed on with the Polymer Corporation, eventually becoming executive vice-president.

Nicholson's work for Polymer and the Department of Munitions and Supply gave him business experience and resulted in an offer to manage a utilities company in Brazil. The opportunity came through Henry Borden, a legal advisor in the Department of Munitions and Supply; he and Nicholson had first met as law students at Dalhousie. After the war Borden had become the chief executive of Brazilian Traction Light and Power Co. Ltd. (Brascan), a utilities company with a majority Canadian ownership, and in 1951 he offered Nicholson the job of chief executive officer. At that time Brascan was a multi-purpose utility company, providing 70 per cent of Brazil's hydroelectric power; the company also ran the gas works and street railways in Rio, Sao Paulo and Santos and supplied two-thirds of the country's telephone service.

When Jack and Jean Nicholson arrived in Brazil in the early 1950s, the Brazilian government was in flux, led by five presidents within five years. Much of Nicholson's work, therefore, involved diplomacy conducted through formal entertaining, and he recalled,

> We entertained two of the presidents of Brazil while we were there, Vargas and Café Filho, his successor. Not in our house but in our summer place—the company's summer place in the mountains about fifty miles [80 km] from Rio. In return, Jean and I were entertained at Catete Palace, where the president does his entertaining.

When queried why Brazilian Traction could extract foreign exchange from Brazil and other companies could not, one Brazilian official had called the company "an octopus . . . but such a friendly octopus." Nicholson referenced this remark when he said in an interview years later that he "was the representative of the 'friendly octopus' and that's the job we had. It was a public relations job to a large extent."[237]

After five years in Brazil, Nicholson and his wife returned to British Columbia where he spent the next three years practising law. One of his most significant cases during that time was his defence of logging operator Wick Gray in the famous Sommers case. In 1955 the BC Liberals had accused Robert Sommers, the Social Credit minister of Lands and Forests, of accepting money from BC Forest Products in exchange for a Forest Management Licence. The issue resulted in several court cases and ultimately both Sommers and Gray received prison sentences, although BC Forest Products was acquitted. Although he lost his case, Nicholson's involvement marked the start of his association with the province's forest industry, and in 1960 he became the first president of the Council of Forest Industries, a position he held for two years. Nicholson explained:

> We had the BC Lumber Manufacturers' Association, we had the BC Loggers' Association, we had a Plywood Manufacturers' Association, we had the Pulp and Paper Manufacturers, but there

was no team play between the units, and they felt, large and small, that they should have a central organization, and being a lawyer with knowledge of that field, I was asked by the heads of several of the companies to accept the responsibility.[238]

Nicholson often lobbied on behalf of the Council of Forest Industries in Ottawa where he found it difficult to convince Conservative prime minister John Diefenbaker to bring about legislation that favoured BC's forest industry. When he expressed his frustration to his old boss in Munitions and Supplies, Howe chided him:

What right have you got to complain? When you got back from Brazil, I suggested that you should get into politics; instead you went back to the practice of law and until you are prepared to do something about it, you shouldn't be too critical of others who are at least trying to do their best.[239]

Nicholson entered politics in 1962 after the Liberal Party asked for his help in the lead-up to the June election. Although he was initially recruited to be campaign chairman for BC, he found himself nominated to represent Vancouver Centre. He won the seat against Conservative incumbent Douglas Jung, Canada's first Chinese Canadian MP. A veteran of the Second World War and a lawyer, Jung had worked hard to represent the interests of the significant Chinese Canadian population in this riding, but Nicholson also had important Chinese Canadian contacts and advertised himself in the *Chinatown News* as a "long-time friend of the Chinese Canadian Community."[240] Diefenbaker's Conservatives won that election—although with a minority—and Nicholson had to wait for the election the following spring when Lester B. Pearson's Liberals formed the government. Over the next five years he held a number of significant portfolios, beginning with minister of Forests, although Pearson first checked with him to see if there was "likely to be an embarrassment" since he had represented some of the larger forest firms in BC. "I said, I didn't think so, but he had to make that decision."[241] As postmaster general in 1964, Nicholson oversaw the issuance of a "peace stamp," and he recalled that:

It was one of the first coloured stamps that were issued. Before that all our stamps had been the head of the reigning sovereign, but I started with the peace stamp and followed it with stamps showing the flowers of the different provinces. I got a message back from the Pope congratulating me on this move to initiate the peace stamp.[242]

After being re-elected in November 1965, Nicholson served briefly as minister of Citizenship and Immigration before he was shifted to the Ministry of Labour where he served until 1968. He found his time in that post the "toughest years of my five years in government" because,

regardless of what your intentions and your wishes are and since I believe in the right to strike [and] I believe in [a] hard bargaining process between employer and employee, but where you have in the federal field of responsibilities essential services such as railways, airlines, dockworkers on both coasts, radio, TV [that] were all fields of federal responsibility, I, as the minister, was in trouble continuously . . . In the year 1966 I had at least one major strike going every single day of the year.[243]

While serving as postmaster general, John Robert Nicholson broke with tradition in April 1964 by issuing a stamp signifying "Peace on Earth." The stamp showed how Canada, as a middle power during the Cold War, sought to represent itself as a peace–seeking and peace–keeping nation.
Image courtesy of Canadian Postage Stamps.

As a negotiator, Nicholson put pressure on both employers and employees, trying to create compromises that would work. He remembered the position as "challenging" although he confessed it "certainly had its human side or rather many human sides."[244] He admired Pearson, who led two minority governments yet managed to pass "a lot of important legislation during that time, due in no small measure to Pearson's ability to compromise and to provide leadership."[245] When Pearson retired in 1968, Nicholson resigned.

Jack Nicholson was appointed to the vice-regal position of BC on July 2, 1968, and he later recalled those years in the late 1960s and early 1970s as a "difficult time" to be Lieutenant Governor. The low point came at the opening of the Legislature in January 1971, when the BC Federation of Labour and the Victoria Low Income Group organized a protest of about two thousand demonstrators who booed the premier, the Lieutenant Governor and the elected officials. From Nicholson's point of view, the crowd on the Legislature lawns looked like "what [he] had seen from the pictures of the Scarlet Pimpernel and the hags in the days of the French Revolution."[246] While Nicholson was reading the throne speech, about three hundred protesters entered the Legislative Buildings and were removed by the RCMP. Student newspapers reporting on the event criticized Nicholson's appointed status and his aloofness, and noted that protesters had shouted at him, "What section of the people do you represent?" The photos they published were captioned with statements such as: "These kids and unemployed workers are one thing, but this old clown in the brocade is WEIRD!" and "Lieutenant-Governor tips his hat to the poor."[247] There was some concern that the protesters might try to crash the Government House ball that evening where the invited guests included the teenage daughters of judges and cabinet ministers and their escorts from Royal Roads Military College and militia units as well as the university. As a precautionary measure the RCMP stationed men on the grounds, while other members of the force danced in uniform at the ball.

In June 1971 Victoria was the site of a federal/provincial constitutional conference where the premiers and Prime Minister Pierre Trudeau, who was hosted at Government House by the Nicholsons, met to discuss the patriation of the Constitution and the Fulton-Favreau formula that would allow for constitutional amendments. Commenting on the attendees from Atlantic Canada, Nicholson recalled that "it was almost like an old home week for graduate students of Dalhousie. It was a fun party—a real fun party."[248]

The Nicholsons held large luncheons and dinners several times a month at Government House, and Jean Nicholson took responsibility for all the menu planning, even for large dinners. Jack Nicholson recalled that he "never knew anyone that didn't congratulate her on the job she did. I don't know what I would have done without her. She made a great contribution."[249] When Governor General Roland Michener and his wife, Norah, old friends of the Nicholsons, stayed at Government House for four days, there were three

A lawyer and former member of Parliament for the Liberal Party, John Robert Nicholson was appointed Lieutenant Governor in 1968, which he recalled as a "difficult time" to hold the position. He is pictured here with his wife, Jean Nicholson, who, like other chatelaines, played an essential role in planning events at Government House.
Image courtesy of Royal BC Museum and Archives, I–32364.

lunches and three state dinners. Royal visitors included Prince Philip who came to BC in 1969 to review the operation of the Duke of Edinburgh's Awards, which he had established in 1956 to promote volunteering, skill building and physical exercise in young people, and in 1971 the Queen, Prince Philip and Princess Anne visited to help celebrate British Columbia's centennial as a province. Nicholson met them in Vancouver and sailed with them and the Governor General on the royal yacht to Victoria. In 1972, as had by then become customary for vice-regal representatives, Nicholson and his wife went to London and paid their respects to the Queen.

Like his immediate predecessors, Nicholson recognized the importance of visiting communities throughout British Columbia and explaining the role of the Queen's representative. In each community, he visited the hospitals, legion halls and schools. He had one particularly memorable interaction in the spring of 1969 when he travelled on a naval vessel to Stewart, BC. The school there did not have a large hall, so Nicholson gave a similar speech in each classroom. He recalled telling grade one students,

> what a pleasure it was to be lieutenant–governor of a province like British Columbia, that it was a beautiful province so rich in resources. Look at the copper that you've got here. Look at our sea with its richness of fish; look at our forests. We are so fortunate to be living in this province . . . I said I'd already been to the Kootenays and that I'd been up [to] the Columbia River Valley and I had been in the Cariboo. It was all a great experience and then I said now that I have said this, rather than make a long speech, you can ask any questions you like. A little child, a red–headed fellow, a cute youngster, his name was Mickey, he put his hand up and he said, "Sir," he said, "how did you get your job?" He had his eye on it. "How did you get the job?" I'll never forget that day.[250]

Nicholson's term concluded on February 13, 1973, five months after British Columbia's first NDP government was elected, ending two decades of Social Credit rule. Then, just as tensions were developing between the forest industry and the new government, which was intent on designating new wilderness areas in BC, the industry, remembering Nicholson's earlier support, appointed him a director of Crestbrook Forest Industries and followed this in 1974 with a directorship of Weyerhaeuser Canada.

John Robert "Jack" Nicholson died in Vancouver on October 8, 1983. He was eighty-one years old. He had enjoyed a diverse career in positions that promoted growth and development—the production of artificial rubber, hydroelectric power and forest products—all of them enterprises that meshed well with the values of W.A.C. Bennett's Social Credit government. While earlier in his career he had helped to promote rights, peace and conciliation through his work as an immigration lawyer, postmaster general and minister of Labour in the Pearson government, he found it somewhat unsettling to serve as Lieutenant Governor in a time of change and protest.

Walter Stewart Owen (1973–78)

Walter Stewart Owen's father, Walter Owen, Sr., left Leicester, England, in 1889 when he was just sixteen to join an older brother who had a stump ranch in the Okanagan. He later enlisted in the provincial police and was posted to Atlin in northwestern British Columbia, the site of a gold rush in the late 1890s. It was there he met Janet Ann Dick who in 1899 followed her gold-miner father to Atlin. Walter Owen and Janet Dick were married in Skagway in 1901, and their son, Walter Stewart Owen, was born in the Atlin jail on January 26, 1904, with Dr. Henry Esson Young, the MLA for Atlin, as the attending physician. Although at one point Walter Owen Sr. tried working as a realtor in Vancouver, he spent most of his working years in the provincial police, moving his family from Atlin to Prince Rupert and finally to Vancouver where he became second in command. Later he was hired as a warden at Oakalla Prison Farm in Burnaby.

As a youth, Walter Stewart Owen joined the Older Boys' Parliament, an organization founded in Ontario in 1917 by Boer War veteran Taylor Statten and supported by Canada's Protestant churches; its primary object was the training of young men in civic affairs. Owen was recruited through his church and the football team he managed as part of the Sunday School League, and in 1924 he became premier of the first Older Boys' Parliament in BC. Through his involvement with this organization, he attended the world YMCA meeting in Helsingfors (Helsinki), Finland, in 1926, an event that he said had a "tremendous influence" on his life "because I had to get up and speak and think on my feet." After the international meeting he went on a speaking tour in British Columbia, "along the Grand Trunk Pacific, and I spoke in every church in that area, I think, and all kinds of churches, too." He recalled that it was a "good thing" because it gave him "a lot of credit . . . for being a good, clean, wholesome fellow, and that helps you as you go through life."[251]

After high school Owen worked at a sawmill in Powell River, but with his mother's encouragement to become a lawyer, he enrolled at the University of British Columbia; his plans changed again, however, after a conversation with Bob Smith, a lawyer and the son of Mary Ellen Smith, the first female MLA in BC and the first female cabinet minister in the British Empire. Bob Smith was working at the courthouse where Walter Owen's father brought prisoners from

Oakalla for trial, and when the younger Owen showed up there one evening to meet his father, Smith asked him about his career plans. Owen explained that he hoped to study law, and Smith responded: "What are you going to university for? I have two degrees and they're not worth a damn to me . . . You don't want to go to university. Come into my office and be a student."[252] Given that UBC did not have a law school until 1945, articling with an established lawyer was still an accepted way to enter the profession. Smith agreed to provide a generous monthly stipend, and in September 1922 Owen began articling with Mayers, Stockton and Smith. Just over a year later he transferred to a firm that included Sir Charles Hibbert Tupper and his son Reginald Tupper to continue his articles. At the same time he took classes at the old Vancouver Law School. "We had lectures all during the week in fall and winter season," he later explained, "and they were all after work, and all the lecturers were lecturing without pay and were members of the profession."[253] Owen did his final year of articling with Lawrence Hunter before being called to the bar in January 1928, after which he stayed on with Hunter for another three or four years as a partner.

Owen's first case as a criminal lawyer involved the defence of a seventeen-year-old boy who had stolen a car and killed an elderly man while speeding down Pender Street in Vancouver. Most of the jury wanted to convict the defendant, but one jurist did not support a conviction. As Owen learned later, her reason had nothing to do with the evidence; she supported an acquittal because she did not want to destroy the first case of a young lawyer just starting out. He immediately realized the advantages of the jury system—especially for the defence.

Thanks to his participation in the Older Boys' Parliament, Owen got an early start in politics. Many years later, when he was asked when he got involved with the Liberal Party, he answered, "Oh, I was always a Liberal . . ." In fact, in 1924 at the same time that he had been premier of the Older Boys' Parliament, he had also been president of the Young Liberals of British Columbia and helped lawyer Gordon McGregor Sloan "reorganize the Liberals in Point Grey." Despite Sloan's backing out of the campaign after a quarrel with lawyer (and later Vancouver mayor) Gerald McGeer, Owen had continued to work with the party. He served as campaign manager in Point Grey in the elections of 1924 and 1928 and nominated Ian

Mackenzie in the 1930 federal election. By Owen's own recollection, he was "fairly influential as a Young Liberal."[254]

On November 8, 1929, Walter Owen married Jean Margaret Dowler. She had been born in Victoria in 1906, though both of her parents—accountant and food broker Ernest David Dowler and Margaret Rankin Dowler—had been born in Glasgow. Walter and Jean Owen had four children: David, Philip, Margaret and Daphne; Philip would serve as mayor of Vancouver from 1993 to 2002.

In 1933 BC's government changed from Conservative to Liberal, and the position of Crown prosecutor became available because in those days the incumbents in such politically plummy posts changed whenever the party in power changed. Thus, at age twenty-nine Owen was appointed county court prosecutor in Vancouver. He spent the next nine years in this part-time, though increasingly demanding role, but in 1942 he resigned in order to devote his time to private practice with the firm of Campney, Owen and Murphy, and he was appointed King's Counsel in 1945.

Much of Owen's work at this time was on behalf of employers in negotiations with labour unions, and he was not above exploiting the public's fear of communism. As he recalled years later,

> I . . . made quite a few speeches about the Communist infiltration in the unions and in industrial activity in British Columbia, and I made considerable hay. I didn't get any denials or corrections from them, so I continued to attack them and speak to service clubs, and that sort of thing.[255]

At one point he advised the Bank of Montreal to fire an employee who was attempting to organize its workers into a union. When the man accused the bank of firing him for union activities, the courts dismissed the case on appeal in favour of the bank. Following that case, the Canadian Bankers' Association sought Owen's advice on "how to successfully resist unionization."[256]

Like J.R. Nicholson, Owen's predecessor in the office of Lieutenant Governor, Owen worked on the high-profile Sommers case in 1957–58, a case in which the Social Credit minister of Lands and Forests, Robert Sommers, was accused of accepting money for granting a Forest Management Licence. BC Forest Products hired Owen to defend the company against the charge that it had provided the bribe. In an interview Owen explained:

They were charged with paying his [Sommers's] rail fare to New York from Toronto. The way that arose, as I recall the evidence, was that they asked him to stay over an extra day or two and he agreed, so they said they'd change the tickets for him, and they would bill him for the difference; that was said to be a bribe, but I think that was a mistake more than anything else and they were charged.[257]

BC Forest Products was acquitted.

Shortly after the trial ended, Owen was elected president of the Canadian Bar Association for 1958–59. He left Campney, Owen & Murphy to set up his own law practice in 1969. At the same time he was serving as a director for Greyhound Bus Lines, Monsanto and Imperial Life Assurance as well as companies involved in forestry, construction, mining, communications, finance and oil. But he also took the time to become involved in several community organizations, such as the YMCA, the Salvation Army and an association for children with intellectual disabilities.

Owen's wife, Jean, died on May 25, 1970. Two years later he married Shirley Woodward Grauer, daughter of Ernest A. Woodward, who owned one of the first private grain elevators in Vancouver, and widow of A.E. (Dal) Grauer, president of the BC Electric Co. and BC Power Corporation. Shirley was an active supporter of the arts in Vancouver, serving as director on the Vancouver Library Board, the Community Arts Council and the Playhouse Theatre Company.

When Owen was first approached in late 1972 about becoming BC's Lieutenant Governor, he was in his late sixties, had just established a new law firm in which he was the senior partner—Owen, Bird and McDonald—and was newly married. Although reluctant to take on another new venture, he nevertheless agreed to consider it. When Prime Minister Pierre Trudeau phoned a few months later to confirm the offer, Owen was hosting a cocktail party to celebrate the opening of Eaton's new store in Vancouver. He recalled:

Just as the phone bell rang, the doorbell rang too, and this was my guests coming. I rushed past them upstairs and left them for half an hour while I talked to the prime minister, and I couldn't explain to them when I came back why I was so rude because it was all very hush–hush.[258]

Owen accepted the position and began his term on February 13, 1973, just five months after the NDP was elected to government in BC, and it is just possible that Trudeau may have chosen the Liberal Owen as a counterbalance to the young socialist government. Prior to his appointment, Owen had not met Trudeau, "except in a mob" although he did know the former Liberal MP James Sinclair, the prime minister's father-in-law, who by the early 1970s was the deputy chairman of Canada Cement Lafarge Ltd. In any case, when Premier Dave Barrett was informed—though not consulted in advance—about the choice of the new Lieutenant Governor, his diplomatic response was that he was "very pleased . . . I don't believe I've ever met the man but I'm looking forward to it. I'm sure we can work together well."[259] Certainly, the contrast between the elected

A lawyer who earned a reputation for advising companies on how to challenge unionization, Walter Stewart Owen may have been selected by Prime Minister Pierre Trudeau as a counterbalance to the New Democratic Party government that had just been elected in BC a few months prior.
Image courtesy of Royal BC Museum and Archives, I–32367.

government and the Crown's new representative did not go unnoticed, and journalist Sean Griffin of the *Vancouver Sun* commented:

> As if the office of lieutenant–governor in British Columbia weren't anachronism enough, Prime Minister Trudeau has appointed to that position a man who is the incarnation of everything that the voters in BC rejected in the last election.

He added that Owen, having been born in a jail, was portrayed as having a rags-to-riches story, but that "as far as many trade unionists are concerned, those who were struggling to organize in the 1940s, Owen would have done a great service to British Columbia if he had simply stayed there."[260]

Although Walter Owen may have been ideologically opposed to the NDP on many issues, one NDP initiative that he seemed to appreciate in his role as host of Government House was that the rules relating to the serving of alcohol had relaxed. W.A.C. Bennett, a teetotaller, had been opposed to serving hard liquor at Government House; after his own government had been sworn in in 1952, Bennett had advised his MLAs at a party in his hotel suite that "Anybody can drink what they like tonight—as long as it's tea, coffee or Ovaltine."[261] Two decades later, the NDP had, according to Owen, "allotted $10,000 for liquor in their first budget."[262]

Accepting a position with a salary of just $18,000 came at a cost to Owen, but he later confessed that "I didn't have to do the things I did [as Lieutenant Governor]. I did them because I liked them, and so I had a much more enjoyable time."[263] Contemplating their move to Government House, Walter and Shirley Owen decided they would miss having a swimming pool as Walter had been swimming twice a day in their own pool; Shirley Owen told the press, "We might build one, but then, of course, the grounds of Government House are open to the public, and we'd have to be careful young children didn't go near it."[264] Owen paid for the new 12.7-metre (42-ft) pool, surrounded by a wall, which was under construction by the fall of 1974; it was built by the Department of Public Works.

Appointed in the midst of the second wave feminist movement, Owen had some catching up to do. The Royal Commission on the Status of Women had published its bestselling report in 1970, and a year later the National Action Committee on the Status of Women had been formed to lobby the government to implement the commission's recommendations on issues such as maternity leave, daycare and birth control. Several newspaper articles introducing the public to the incoming Lieutenant Governor specifically pointed out Owen's less than stellar reputation when it came to women's rights. In particular, at a labour relations hearing in 1951 he had expressed the opinion that "young unmarried women should be discouraged from following business careers," a statement that had made the headlines and earned him the scorn of women's organizations as well as friends such as Tilly Rolston, who would soon be appointed education minister in W.A.C. Bennett's Social Credit government. In 1973 he claimed that he was "being facetious when I was saying that."[265]

During his term as Lieutenant Governor, Owen continued to uphold gendered social conventions while slowly adapting to new standards of equity. On the one hand, Government House still hosted the annual Military Ball in which teenage "debutantes" wearing white formal dresses were presented to society. On the other hand, the BC Older Boys' Parliament, now renamed the BC Youth Parliament, allowed the first female members to join in 1974, appointed a female Lieutenant Governor (Victoria journalist Elizabeth Forbes) and marked the occasion with lunch at Government House.

Distinguished visitors whom Owen hosted included Indira Gandhi, who was prime minister of India from 1966 to 1977 and from 1980 to 1984; her eight-day visit to Canada in June 1973 was interrupted by protests over prisoners held by India in the war over Bangladesh. She spent just an afternoon and an overnight at Government House, but Owen's impression was that "she was a very hard worker and she represented a troubled country . . . They had security par-excellence, you know. She had a hot line to India. But she never rested. She was working all the time."[266]

When King Hussein of Jordan and his wife, Queen Alia, came to Canada in August 1974, their short visit included a stopover in Ottawa, a keynote speech at the Abbotsford International Airshow banquet at the Hotel Vancouver, attendance at the opening day of the airshow, and a brief stay at Government House in Victoria. The king had already survived multiple assassination attempts, so the RCMP had assigned about five hundred officers to provide security for the visit. Owen recalled him as:

one of the most fearless men I've ever met . . . The day he was leaving, the gates of Government House were closed and there were Mounties in every tree and . . . he and I were standing out on the front steps and he was saying good–bye to me and his Queen was, too, and the Mounties sent a message that a Jordanian, recently immigrated to Canada, wanted to see him because they had a baby since they arrived. They wanted him to meet their King.

The King agreed to meet them, but Owen said to him afterwards:

"My God, that was a foolish thing, wasn't it? You didn't know but that he could have a gun in the baby's clothes or a grenade or something."

"Well," [the King] said, "I don't worry about those things."

Yet he had his Prime Minister with him, and [the King] had lost two fingers of his right hand in an attack . . . in London just eight months before.[267]

The Owens travelled to the far corners of the province to meet British Columbians. In May 1974 the Owens flew to Kingcome Inlet in Kwakiutl territory to attend a ceremony at a traditional long-house. In August they visited Walter Owen's birthplace, the town of Atlin. The population had diminished from six thousand during the height of the gold rush in 1899 to just 350, but these were all people who enjoyed the wilderness lifestyle and were willing to put in the effort to extract the remaining gold. The vice-regal couple also went to Fernie in the Kootenay region where Owen explained that his role as Lieutenant Governor was to "make sure the MLAs behave them-selves,"[268] and they toured central BC from Fort St. James to Burns Lake. Owen also made shorter trips, touring a historic church and inspecting cadets in the Comox Valley, opening a Chinese memorial garden in Nanaimo, and joining Premier Bill Bennett and federal Sport and Fitness minister Iona Campagnolo at the opening of a "Participark" complete with exercise stations in Port Coquitlam. Closer to home, Walter and Shirley Owen were occasionally hosted by Victoria realtor and philanthropist Eric Charman at his house north of Elk Lake, and he recalled that the Lieutenant Governor,

Walter Owen married Shirley Woodward Grauer in 1972, shortly before he accepted the position of Lieutenant Governor. During his term, Walter and Shirley Owen built a pool at Government House, toured the province and hosted distinguished international visitors such as Indian prime minister Indira Gandhi and King Hussein and Queen Alia of Jordan.

Image courtesy of Government House of British Columbia Archives.

dressed in a black jacket and pinstriped pants, would ask "to walk through the barn and the chicken houses because the farmyard smells reminded him of his childhood in Northern BC."[269]

In 1975, halfway through Owen's term as Lieutenant Governor, Dave Barrett called an election, although it was almost two years before the end of the NDP's mandate. By this time the Social Credit Party had a new leader, W.A.C. Bennett's son, Bill Bennett, and had gained four seats after four Vancouver Liberal MLAs had defected.

In the election of December 22, 1975, the NDP retained around 39 per cent of the vote, while Social Credit formed the new government with just over 49 per cent of the vote. The Liberal Party had elected just one MLA, and in February Trudeau visited BC to meet with Liberal Party members to find out why British Columbians were rejecting the party at the provincial level. He also attended a reception at Government House, a place that was normally above politics, but on this occasion the state ball reflected the continuing tensions between the government and the Opposition.

In Owen's final year as Lieutenant Governor he hosted seventeen-year-old Prince Andrew, Duke of York, who spent a few days on the West Coast in July 1977, including a day fishing in the waters off Sooke with Owen's granddaughter, Lise Owen, for company, along with police protection. The newspaper reported that the prince arrived at the Pedder Bay Marina before 7 a.m., wearing a Cowichan sweater and carrying a bowl of Government House cherries. His fishing trip was followed by a tour of Pearson College and the Sooke Forest Products mill.

After his term as Lieutenant Governor ended on May 18, 1978, Owen retired to Vancouver. He died there on January 14, 1981, age eighty years. Shirley Owen died on July 6, 1982. In his will, Owen left a bequest of $5,000 to the Youth Parliament to serve as the basis for the Walter S. Owen Fund, which still assists with travel and operating expenses.

As an anti-communist lawyer who had done well for himself financially through directorships of various finance and resource companies, Owen had certainly not been a close ally of the NDP, nor was he popular among those who supported labour or women's rights. Yet he had accepted the position of Lieutenant Governor with a positive attitude, and he was flexible enough to be able to cooperate with his provincial advisors, whether they were NDP or—by December 1975—the Social Credit.

Henry Pybus Bell-Irving (1978–83)

The patriarch of the British Columbia branch of the Bell-Irving family, Henry Ogle Bell-Irving (1856–1931), was born in Scotland and trained as an engineer in Germany before coming to Canada in 1882 to work for the CPR as a surveyor. In 1891 he became a founding partner in the Anglo-BC Packing Company, which bought up canneries along the coast and on the Fraser River to become the largest exporter of canned salmon in BC. Bell-Irving and his wife, Marie Ysabel del Carmen Beattie, had six sons and four daughters. Their first son, Henry Beattie, was born in 1887, and he and Annie Hylda "Nan" Pybus were the parents of Henry Pybus Bell-Irving, born in Vancouver on January 21, 1913. They nicknamed their son "Budge" because of the shape he made when Nan was pregnant with him, and the nickname remained with him throughout his life.

Henry Pybus Bell-Irving's grandfather was an influential figure in his upbringing. He taught him how to shoot on the family-owned Pasley Island just west of Bowen Island, paid for the boy to attend Shawnigan Lake School on Vancouver Island from 1925 to 1927 and sponsored his high school education at Loretto School, Scotland's oldest boarding school. Henry Pybus Bell-Irving was the eighth member of his family to attend Loretto, where he was enrolled in 1927 at age fourteen. (The only other North American student at the school at the time was Gordon Winter who, by coincidence, served as Lieutenant Governor of Newfoundland from 1974 to 1981.) While at Loretto, Henry participated in the Officers' Training Corps. He spent his summer holidays with his Scottish relatives, who had an estate near Lockerbie where he learned fly-fishing and helped with the otter hunts, and his Christmas holidays at a ski resort in Switzerland with his grandfather and a young aunt.

Having completed his education at Loretto, Henry Bell-Irving returned to Vancouver in 1931 and was hired by his family's Anglo-BC Packing Company to work at the Arrandale Cannery on the Nass River, north of Prince Rupert. When he wasn't needed in the first-aid room or at the gas station on the wharf, he molded lead weights for use at the bottom of gillnets. Work at the cannery was structured according to ethnicity and gender: the crew included Indigenous and Japanese fishers, a small group of Euro-Canadian cannery workers, Chinese men who tended the equipment at the cannery, and Indigenous and Japanese women who filled the cans with salmon.

Music enlivened quiet moments on the Nass. With his private school education, Bell-Irving appreciated classical music and had brought his own gramophone records and played them until the cannery foreman tossed them into the river. With his own collection gone, Bell-Irving enjoyed listening to the Nisga'a Arrandale Brass Band playing Gilbert and Sullivan on the dock on weekends in good weather. The band members had ordered their instruments from the T. Eaton catalogue and taught themselves how to play.

Although Bell-Irving considered studying aeronautical engineering at the University of Toronto, in order to stay closer to home he enrolled in Commerce at the University of British Columbia. It was in the UBC bookstore that he met his future wife, Nancy Symes, who was recruiting new members for the UBC Players Club, which was preparing for a tour of the province, and Bell-Irving joined them to help backstage. But while his studies at Loretto prepared him to do well at UBC, he stayed for just one year. As he explained to his biographer, Raymond Eagle:

> This first year had not given me the spark of enthusiasm to carry on into more interesting studies and an eventual degree. Again, this would have been an appropriate time for some wise consultation as to my future, but it did not occur to me to seek it. After only two terms I decided to "call it a day" and go out to work.[270]

He went back to the Nass River, this time as skipper and engineer of the *Daisy Leaf*, a packer that collected salmon from the gillnetters, which were mostly two-man, sail-powered, 27-foot (8-m) -long Columbia River boats with a small covered space for the off-duty man to sleep. They drifted overnight with their nets set, and each morning Bell-Irving met them to collect the fish. At the end of the summer he returned to Vancouver where he worked at a series of short-term jobs, including booking passengers and cargo for his father's shipping company and selling lumber for the Alberta Pacific Timber Co. In 1933 after a chance conversation with the commanding officer of the Seaforth Highlanders, he applied for a commission, and by July of that year he was a second lieutenant. Two years later, to earn a second pip, he took a course with the Princess Patricia's Canadian Light Infantry in Esquimalt.

Henry Bell-Irving met Nancy Symes again at a bridge party in Shaughnessy and invited her to Pasley Island for a weekend of canoeing and fishing. The pair became close, but when Symes completed her degree at UBC in 1934 she went to Newnham, a women's college at Cambridge, to study modern history. That October Bell-Irving landed a job in administration at H.R. MacMillan Export on West Hastings Street in Vancouver, a company that would soon become BC's foremost exporter of lumber.

When Symes returned to Vancouver in the summer of 1935, Bell-Irving had to compete for her attentions with a medical student. When she took the train east en route back to England at the end of the summer, she had not decided between them, but at Broadview, Saskatchewan, she got off the train and returned to Vancouver to give Bell-Irving another chance. He thought it would be feasible to support the two of them on an income of $100 per month, but MacMillan would not give him a raise, so he left to work for the family company, H. Bell-Irving and Co., led by his Uncle Richard who was willing to give him a wage of $100. Unknown to Henry at the time, $25 of this amount came directly from his uncle's pocket. Henry Bell-Irving and Nancy Symes were married in Vancouver on April 8, 1937, and spent their honeymoon in Carmel, California. Back in Vancouver he maintained his membership with the Seaforth Highlanders, a commitment that involved summer training camps in Saanich and Vernon. In July 1939 Henry and Nancy enjoyed a sailing holiday from Pasley Island north to Comox and back in a 16-foot (5 m), International-Class dinghy, their last adventure together before the war.

The Seaforth Highlanders of Canada were mobilized on September 1, 1939, the day that Hitler marched his forces into Poland, and Henry, after obtaining leave from H. Bell-Irving & Co., was appointed to command the No. 4 Carrier platoon. The Seaforths were included in the 2nd Canadian Infantry Brigade, commanded by Brigadier George Pearkes, and on six hours' notice on November 11 Henry left for Britain for small arms training. Nancy went with him, and during the spring of 1940 she stayed with Brigadier and Mrs. Pearkes in Surrey while Henry's battalion trained in various locations to become an anti-invasion force. In July 1940 Henry was offered an instructor's job but, not having had battle experience, he was reluctant to train other men. Nevertheless, he was promoted to captain with "A" Company.

On July 28, 1943, the Seaforth Highlanders, Princess Patricia's Canadian Light Infantry and the Edmonton Regiment boarded the *Circassia* in Glasgow, headed for Sicily. After two weeks on the left flank of the 8th Army, the 1st Canadian Division was poised to take the town of Leonforte, southwest of Mount Etna, which they believed was unoccupied. Bell-Irving's "A" Company was in the lead of the advance on this town when they came under heavy fire, and though the Seaforths managed to capture the town, they suffered seventy-six casualties. "A" Company's next task was to take Mount Fronte; again under heavy fire, Bell-Irving and two of his platoons scaled a sheer 90-metre (300-ft) cliff while a third platoon distracted the Germans from the west. The company then held their commanding position and, when reinforcements arrived the next morning, they secured the hill and dispersed the German troops. For his successful initiative, Henry Bell-Irving was awarded a Distinguished Service Order, promoted to lieutenant colonel and ordered back to the UK where he was briefly in charge of the Canadian Officer Cadet Training Unit. He then returned to Italy where he commanded the Loyal Edmonton regiment on the Gothic and Rimini lines.

In the spring of 1945 Bell-Irving led troops over the River Ijssel, a branch of the Rhine in the Netherlands, putting himself in danger by taking a forward position. On May 5 Germany surrendered control of the Netherlands, and on the morning of May 7 a battalion of the Princess Patricia's Canadian Light Infantry drove through Amsterdam on its way to secure a cache of weapons and ammunition. The Seaforth Highlanders, along with the Princess Louise's Dragoon Guards, arrived in Amsterdam later that morning to garrison the city and oversee the removal of German troops. Lieutenant Colonel Bell-Irving, who led the contingent, remembered, "There must have been half a million people throwing beautiful flowers at us. An old lady, handing me a bunch of roses, said from the very bottom of her soul, 'Thank God, at last you have come.'"[271]

At the end of the war when Henry and Nancy returned to Canada, he became the North American sales agent for a British company, Lines Brothers Toys; he had met Walter Lines, the company's director, when billeted at his home during the war. In Canada he travelled to the headquarters of various department stores to show them the toys and baby equipment produced by Lines Brothers, then helped set up a Lines manufacturing plant on the Lachine Canal in Montreal. Nancy travelled with him to help with logistics in presentations to department store buyers before she returned to Vancouver where their first son, Henry Symes "Hal" Bell-Irving, was born prematurely in November 1947. He spent the first few weeks of his life in an incubator. Since they had lost their first baby to miscarriage and a second at three days old, they were very grateful for this son after ten years of marriage, and Henry wrote:

> We have been fairly enterprising in our first ten years of life together. With our God–given son to crown it all, we are both being pretty enterprising now. It is our way of life and we'll go places together—we three.[272]

They later had two more sons, Roderick and Donald.

Henry next moved into real estate sales and was hired by the family-run Bell-Irving Insurance Agencies Ltd. He started by knocking on doors to ask people if they were interested in selling, then took a course from the American Appraisal Institute in Seattle and started making appraisals in expropriation cases. By the mid-1950s he had created an independent real estate branch for the family company, which he called Bell-Irving Realty Ltd. Then, to standardize the qualifications of realtors in BC, he worked with lawyer Irwin Davis to found the Real Estate Agents' Licensing Board, and in 1958, largely based on his recommendations, the University of BC established a real estate course. That year—the same year the BC Real Estate Act was passed—he also became president of the Vancouver Real Estate Board.

In the 1970s Henry Bell-Irving gained experience representing the interests of realtors to government. In 1972 he became the first president of the Canadian Real Estate Association and in 1974 the president of the Vancouver Board of Trade, a position his grandfather had held almost eighty years earlier. He held both of these positions during the time the New Democratic Party governed British Columbia, from 1972 to 1975. As an avowed advocate of free enterprise, he opposed the NDP's new mining regulations, but he was before his time in appreciating the value of the NDP's proposed Land Commission Act, which would create denser urban housing and protect Fraser Valley farmland. In an interview with the *Journal of Commerce*, he said:

> Over the years we have become accustomed to the single family dwelling with a garden in front, behind and on both sides. This has been the standard, and one that the population in the main wants to preserve. It is becoming more and more evident that we cannot afford this. We must learn to live closer together

in high–rise apartments and terraced housing with party walls, which may be under condominium or corporate ownership with leases.[273]

Just before he retired at age sixty-five in 1978, Henry Pybus Bell-Irving's name was put forward as a potential Lieutenant Governor for British Columbia, and Prime Minister Pierre Trudeau phoned to ask if he would like to move to Victoria. He was sworn in on May 18, 1978. Four days later he and Nancy rode in the annual Victoria Day Parade.

Bell-Irving had the advantage, like Dunsmuir, Barnard, Woodward and Wallace before him, to be descended from a very

The grandson of Henry Ogle Bell–Irving, an engineer who made his fortune through investment in salmon canneries, Henry Pybus Bell–Irving had a successful career in real estate before becoming Lieutenant Governor.
Image courtesy of Royal BC Museum and Archives, I–32362.

221

successful family and therefore had deep roots and good connections in the province. However, as the grandson, rather than the son, of a wealthy businessman, he had not inherited the financial security they had, though he had done well on his own in his final career, real estate. To maintain the traditions of hosting at Government House and travelling the province, initially he was required to contribute his salary and even some of his own personal funds, as had those who came before him. But thanks to an intervention by his private secretary, Michael Roberts, provincial funding was increased, and by the end of his term Bell-Irving no longer had to subsidize the office.

Two memorable tours brought Henry Bell-Irving back to Nisga'a territory where, as a young man, he had worked at the Arrandale Cannery. A land tour in May 1979 included stops in the Nisga'a villages of Kincolith, Aiyansh and Canyon City. In Kincolith the residents told him that they wanted a road connection to other Nisga'a communities, and he urged them to "be careful not to lose their ancient civilization, which he had been privileged to see as a young man." In Terrace he was the centre of a special ceremony held by Chiefs James Gosnell, Rod Robinson and Percy Tate illustrating the beginnings of time and the origins of the world. Bell-Irving was brought into the centre of the circle and clothed in a ceremonial blanket, skirt, leggings, a cedar bark chief's collar and a cedar bark headdress symbolizing unity. He recalled:

> The story was told of the beginning—the coming of light, the coming of the water [the Nass] and, finally, the rock at the mouth of the river—the "heart" of the river. Then Chief James Gosnell invested me with the name COOV LISIMS, meaning The Rock.[274]

On the Lieutenant Governor's spring cruise in 1980 the Nisga'a Tribal Council met him at the Nass Estuary, a challenging passageway for a ship as large as the HMCS *Yukon*. The Lieutenant Governor wore his Nisga'a cloak over his Windsor uniform to show his respect for the people, and he listened while they expressed their need for more representation on the hospital board and a study of the potential pollution that a new mine in the area might cause. It would be more than a decade before the provincial government began to negotiate with the federal government to provide the Nisga'a with more control over their lands and resources, but the Nisga'a Treaty, when it did come into effect in 2000, was the first modern treaty signed in British Columbia.

Bell-Irving was particularly interested in promoting opportunities for youth, and on that same cruise on the HMCS *Yukon* in 1980, he asked Michael Roberts to recruit an equal number of young people who had won the Duke of Edinburgh's Gold Award and youth in crisis in Victoria, hoping that the latter might learn about the "possibilities that might be open to them." Roberts recalled:

> Once they got on the ship, they were all put in identical black coveralls, so that nobody knew who anybody was . . . And it worked out pretty well. The ship's crew was not easy on any of them. They were basically there to work, not just to have fun.[275]

Henry Bell-Irving took his constitutional role very seriously. Although by this time the Lieutenant Governor rarely withheld consent for bills, he wanted to understand what he was signing and did not want to just give "rubber-stamp" approval. He asked for copies of bills in advance so that he could review them and asked to speak with ministers if anything was unclear. Roberts, who called him "one of the major mentors in my life," recalled that Bell-Irving,

> had a particular interest in wanting to understand fully what he might be called upon to do in the event of either a constitutional impasse or crisis. He read all the material he could find that enabled him to better understand the complexities and talked to constitutional experts to broaden his knowledge of the office. He never opened his mouth until he was sure of what he was saying, to avoid speaking from a position of ignorance on a topic or a situation.[276]

Bell-Irving met with other Canadian Lieutenant Governors at national meetings and at the Commonwealth Games in Edmonton in 1978. There they discussed the appropriate non-constitutional aspects of their role and the limits to their political involvement, "agreeing on suitable subjects for their speeches and how to best define what were political and non-political subjects."[277] Bell-Irving, however, did occasionally overstep these bounds. For example, in his 1978 Christmas message he referred to the potential separation of Quebec from Canada and told his listeners: "I would be happy if you shared my desire to tell the people of Quebec that we really want them to stay with us by signing the 'People to People' petition soon to be circulated."[278] MLA Rafe Mair thought this statement was too political. The media also criticized some of the remarks Bell-Irving made in his 1979 New Year's speech, but he resented efforts by provincial politicians to limit his statements and wrote that the cabinet did not "want me involving myself in such 'political' matters as the continuity of Canadian unity, federal-provincial relations, etc. Nothing or nobody will quash my interest and involvement in the future of our country, regardless of criticism."[279]

Henry Pybus Bell-Irving served as Lieutenant Governor until July 15, 1983. During his term the Dutch honoured him with a new variety of tulip named the Bell-Irving tulip, and in 1985 he was awarded the Order of Canada. Following his retirement from office, he stayed involved with the Seaforths until his honourable discharge in 1990, supported forest and stream conservation in the North Shore Mountains and volunteered with the Scout movement and the Disabled Sailing Association of BC. In 1997, a few months after they celebrated their sixtieth wedding anniversary, Nancy

During Bell–Irving's term as Lieutenant Governor, the Dutch named a new variety of tulip after him in commemoration of his service in the Netherlands during the Second World War.
Image courtesy of Royal BC Museum and Archives, I–67876.

Bell-Irving passed away after a long illness. In 2001 Henry Bell-Irving married for the second time, but he died on September 21, 2002, at the age of eighty-nine.

Henry Pybus Bell-Irving was the second BC Lieutenant Governor to have served overseas in the Second World War—the first being George Randolph Pearkes—but he was distinct from the set of vice-regal representatives who preceded him in that he did not have clear ties to Ottawa and had not had a political career. He was, therefore, an unusually non-partisan choice, and this distance from party politics it gave him the ability to see several sides of an issue, not take his constitutional role lightly and speak out in support of Canadian unity. While his caution and critical perspective may have made it difficult for Bill Bennett's Social Credit government to gain approval for legislation simply and quickly, Henry Bell-Irving carried out his role with dignity and integrity, maintaining a distinct separation between the elected government and the Crown.

Robert Gordon Rogers (1983–88)

The son of George and Eva Rogers, Robert Gordon "Bob" Rogers was born in Westmount, Quebec, on August 19, 1919, and raised as a Roman Catholic. When he was ten years old, his father, who worked for the telephone company, moved the family to Toronto, so the boy spent his formative years there during the Depression. His father could not afford to send his three sons to private schools, but he enrolled Robert at the University of Toronto Schools, a merit-based secondary school associated with the Faculty of Education at the University of Toronto. His grades were good though not exceptional throughout his years there, but he became class captain, played hockey and football well and worked his way up through the ranks of the school's cadet corps; at fifteen he won the gold medal in rifle training, and the year he graduated he was the cadet corps commanding officer. In the summer holidays he went to camp, and when he had gained the necessary skills, he earned some extra cash in the summers working as a guide in northern Ontario, an experience that sparked an interest in promoting outdoor life for young people.

After graduating from high school in 1938, Rogers took a year off to work, "driving a fish truck from Owen Sound down to Windsor" and working in the mail-order department of Simpsons. He started an engineering degree at the University of Toronto in the fall of

1939 just as war was breaking out in Europe. After his two older brothers volunteered for the army and air force, his "heart wasn't in the University,"[280] and in 1940 when the Canadian Armoured Corps recruiters came to the university looking for engineering students, he applied. With his previous experience in the cadets, he was accepted into the Corps as a second lieutenant. By December 1940 he was training at Camp Borden, and in 1941 he began officer training. Just twenty-one years old, Rogers was now in charge of about thirty new volunteers age eighteen to thirty-two, but his experience in cadets and as a guide had given him confidence and leadership skills: "When you are under stress, as you are in the bush, the same principles apply," he told historian Reginald Roy many decades later when the two met to record a series of interviews. "There was never any problem with discipline . . . The troops did what you told them to do or asked them to do."[281]

In June 1941 Rogers married Elizabeth Jane Hargrave. The daughter of Ralph and Doreen Hargrave, she was born in Toronto in 1919, and as a young woman had studied at the Toronto Conservatory of Music. Robert took his bride on a canoe trip for their honeymoon, since "that was my idea of really living . . . She wasn't quite so thrilled but she went along with it, God bless her, up in [the] northern Ontario bush."[282]

In November 1941 Rogers and his troop sailed from Halifax to Liverpool on board a Cunard liner, but while he had a well-appointed cabin and his own steward, on the first night out his men were in hammocks in the hold with nothing to eat but hard tack. To avoid a riot, he raided the dining room and took his men biscuits, cake and fruit. For the rest of the voyage, due to a lack of hammocks, many of the soldiers slept on the deck. On arrival in Liverpool, they were loaded aboard trains for Aldershot. From the fall of 1941 to the summer of 1942 Rogers went through intensive training on the use of armoured equipment, guns and motorcycles, and took signals and gunnery courses, and in the spring of 1942 his troop finally got access to General Lee tanks. Jane was also in Britain during the war, serving with the Red Cross, and she and Robert met whenever he had leave.

Rogers was a member of the armoured division that landed on the beaches on D-Day, June 6, 1944. Later that summer he was sent back to Canada via New York on the *Queen Mary* but spent the voyage in the sick bay, ill with dysentery. Jane arrived in Toronto a few weeks later, pregnant with their first child; she had to wait until the second trimester to receive permission to travel home. As Rogers recalled, she returned "with a group of Red Cross girls who all were pregnant, by the way." Some of them would face motherhood on their own, since "many had unfortunately lost their husbands, some with me in my regiment." The typical scenario of wives welcoming husbands home was reversed when he met Jane in Toronto: "I greeted her on arrival in Union Station . . . with the press there to take pictures of me welcoming my wife home from overseas. There was a picture in the *Toronto Star* which I still have in my scrapbook."[283] Their son, John, was born in February 1945. When the war in Europe ended on May 8, 1945, Rogers was working for the military in Ottawa. "Like everybody else I well remember the day . . . and very shortly thereafter the war ended for me [since] I was a . . . civilian soldier . . . and my mind immediately turned" to postwar life.[284]

There were incentives to go back to school since the Canadian government would fund veterans' education, but he was eager to get on with a career: "There were so many things I wanted to do and I saw so many opportunities in Canada."[285] With his ability to read blueprints and his enviable people skills, he was soon hired by Norman Smith who operated a subsidiary of the US company Philip Carey Manufacturing Corporation, owners of an asbestos mine and fibreglass plant in Quebec. Rogers's new job was selling fibreglass insulation, "which was just brand new coming onto the market, 85% magnesia, which is industrial insulation, and asbestos. We were basically in the asbestos and magnesia business."[286] Rogers and Smith put in bids to supply insulation to Toronto construction projects, especially manufacturing plants. As Rogers later explained, "Everybody's business is booming, and they all have money and they want to upgrade their plants."[287]

The Rogers family was living the postwar dream. They bought a three-bedroom house in the Kingsway, an affluent neighbourhood in Etobicoke, and a brand new Ford. Robert often travelled for his work, so for the most part Jane was responsible for the home and, by then, two young children. Smith's company continued to grow and gain successful bids, but at the same time it was spending money as fast as it made it, and Rogers, who by now owned 10 per cent of the business, was nervous about the company constantly owing money to the bank. In late 1947 he took a new job as sales manager of the insulation division at Philip Carey, and he, Jane and their two children moved to a small farm in the Eastern Townships near Montreal; Jane was expecting their third baby.

Rogers was now situated at an important juncture in the postwar economy, selling a product that was essential to Canada's booming construction and oil and gas industries. The country's first major postwar discovery of oil had occurred in Leduc, Alberta, earlier that year, and to deliver this oil to market, the first leg of the Interprovincial Pipeline was soon under construction from Edmonton to the Great Lakes. Pipeline construction, Rogers explained, created a new market for asbestos insulation:

> If you are familiar with the oil business, you know that, before you put any pipes into the ground, you wrap it with anti–frozen material, which is made of asbestos, by the way, saturated in asphalt. Knowing something about the market, I very quickly found that this was potential business, and [on] my first order, I think my commission was better than my salary for the month.[288]

Concerns about the safety of asbestos were rare in this period of economic growth. Miners, however, had begun to raise the issue of health hazards from being exposed to asbestos fibres on the job, and in February 1949 miners in the town of Asbestos, Quebec, went on strike, calling for an increase in wages to a dollar an hour, a pension plan and action to address the lung disease caused by breathing in asbestos dust. The strike spread to the other major asbestos mines in the province, and Rogers observed, "This was really the start of the revolution in Quebec."[289]

The Philip Carey mine in East Broughton was not immediately affected by the strike as it was located about 80 to 100 kilometres (50 to 60 mi) away from the other mines, but organizers soon came to East Broughton to try to convince the miners to walk off the job. At that point the manager called Rogers to warn him that "rabble rousers" had turned up at the work site. Rogers hopped in his car and drove the three hours from Montreal to East Broughton where he found "three men there with beards trying to talk our miners into going on strike." The mine manager had brought in the local priest to try to convince the workers not to strike, and Rogers recalled:

In those days the church was all dominant . . . [so] there was quite a confrontation. Well, it turned out—and I didn't realize it at the time who I was talking to—but it was the three wise men, Messieurs Pelletier, Marchand and Trudeau. At that time [Trudeau] was working as a writer for *Cité Libre* . . . To finish that story, my men never did go on strike. The priest prevailed on them and they kept working for the duration of the strike, which was very prolonged. We were shipping dust really because any asbestos fibre you get at all was better than none . . . we were literally the only asbestos mine in Quebec operating. And Quebec was then supplying a large part of the world's asbestos.[290]

In June 1950 Rogers's career path took a new turn after he received a phone call from Hollis Martin, the vice-president of Dominion Tar and Chemical (Domtar). As the result of that call, Rogers started a new job as vice-president of Alexander Murray Ltd., a Domtar subsidiary that sold building materials. In his new job, he would submit a brief to the Domtar executive level whenever he had a proposal to build or purchase something:

I think I can say I never got turned down for anything, which is exciting in itself. In those days, to ask for X million dollars to build a plant or renovate a plant or buy a company, and money was always there. It was great fun. We just expanded like topsy.[291]

While working for Domtar, Rogers remained based in Montreal but spent most of his time travelling Canada and internationally since Alexander Murray also distributed building materials that were made by other companies. At the same time, he was taking business management courses in New York to upgrade his skills. In 1954 he was transferred within the company to become president of a new acquisition, Brantford Roofing of Ontario, but discovering that it was top-heavy with office staff, many of whom were friends or relatives of the owners, he paid them off and ran the plant with just a manager and one engineer. After building a second Brantford Roofing plant in Montreal, he pointed out to Domtar that Brantford was now competing with Alexander Murray; the two were then merged as Murray Brantford, with Rogers as vice-president, based in Montreal.

In 1960, when Rogers was forty years old, he was approached by a headhunter seeking a manager for Crown Zellerbach, one of three major forest companies then operating in western Canada. Initially he was not interested, but the headhunter did not give up, and on Rogers's next work visit to Vancouver, Pinky Galloway, president of Crown Zellerbach's Canadian subsidiary, gave Rogers a tour of the company's timber holdings, flying him in a Grumman Goose over "their thousands of acres of beautiful timber land" on Vancouver Island. He was also given a tour of the company's Elk Falls mill, which had been built in the early 1950s. Impressed, Rogers was tempted to take the job, though reluctant to leave the life he had in Quebec, but Galloway eventually convinced him to move across the country by offering to transfer his pension and giving him the opportunity to take over as president when Galloway retired. In September 1960 Bob and Jane and their two daughters, Susan and Patty, who were then thirteen and twelve, moved out to Vancouver where he started work as vice-president of Crown Zellerbach's building materials division. Their son, John, stayed in Quebec as he was about to enter his last year at Bishops College School.

As vice-president of building materials, Rogers's task was to reorganize, improve efficiency and reduce operating costs. He selected new managers and sent them to take management and business courses, "so we could at least talk the same language." Then he and the new management team made cuts:

> First thing we did was shut down the shingle mill. We got out of the shingle business because we were wasting good cedar that could have been used for other purposes. We got out of the presto log business because that was good fibre that we could sell to the pulp mill at market price and this was losing money anyway. We cut the crew down from about 1,500 to about 1,000 in the first year at Fraser Mills.[292]

Crown Zellerbach owned a number of lumberyards across the Prairies, most of which were small operations employing between one and four men. Since it was no longer profitable to ship lumber east of the Rockies, Rogers visited each of these yards and sold off those that were not making money. In 1962 he became executive vice-president responsible for all marketing, and in August 1964 he was promoted to president and chief executive officer. He had just turned forty-five.

Jane Rogers played an essential role in the social side of managing this major company. Every week she and Bob hosted parties in Vancouver or attended events in towns where Crown Zellerbach was a major employer, and he credited these social events with creating a sense of community within the company and even reducing labour conflict. Being president of Crown Zellerbach had its perks since he and Jane hosted international dignitaries, and on one occasion Queen Elizabeth stayed at the company's fishing lodge in Comox. However, a management position of this kind also entailed sacrifices in the Rogers's family life, as they seldom saw their children, who were all attending boarding schools.

When Rogers was not reducing inefficiencies in his own company, he was involved in streamlining cooperation within the BC forest industry.

> When I came out [to BC], I found out that we belonged to something called the BCLMA [BC Lumber Manufacturers' Association], the PMBC [Plywood Manufacturers of BC], the Red Cedar Shingle Bureau and so on . . . For every business you were in you had an association. And I found myself going to association meetings every day of the week . . . And some of us—and I take some credit because I was one of the main pushes in this—we said, "Look, this isn't good enough . . . Why don't we pool all these organizations together? They are controlled basically by the same four large companies and a lot of little ones anyway." So in the early '60s we formed something called the Council of Forest Industries (COFI).[293]

The aims of COFI were to lobby governments, promote the BC forest industry abroad and secure favourable trade arrangements. The organization's first president was John Robert Nicholson, who would be appointed BC Lieutenant Governor in 1968.

Seaboard Lumber Company, owned by a consortium of about fifteen lumber companies, marketed Crown Zellerbach's wood products around the Pacific Rim, while a consortium called Canover (Canadian Overseas Sales Company) marketed the company's newsprint and paper products. As chairman of these marketing consortia at various times, Rogers visited their offices in Tokyo, London, Australia and elsewhere to familiarize himself with their operations. As BC companies had limited opportunities to sell in Europe, the provincial government had always realized the importance of the Pacific Rim market, but it wasn't until the mid-1960s that the federal government began to promote sales in this market. In 1964 the federal government, noting Rogers' experience representing Crown Zellerbach in Asia, asked him to join a trade mission to Japan. As a result, in the years that followed he was often called upon to provide advice to Ottawa on international trade development.

By the late 1960s the remote coastal town of Ocean Falls, purchased by Crown Zellerbach in 1946, had turned into a liability. Even though the pulp and paper mill there was operating at full capacity and selling everything it produced, it was costing too much to run. When established in 1916, the entire operation had run on locally produced hydro power, but the majority of the power was now coming from an oil-powered generator. The decision was made to phase out the mill, a process that would affect about 350 employees and their families as well as federal and provincial service providers. To avoid creating a ghost town, Rogers tried to find an alternate purpose for it, proposing to federal cabinet ministers that it could be transformed into a penitentiary or rehabilitation centre, but there were no takers, and he began the shutdown in 1968 with the closure of the kraft and sulphite factories. A few years later the company received permission from the provincial government to divert logs from its Ocean Falls tree farm licence for use at its mill at Elk Falls, near Campbell River. Then, at a shareholders' meeting in Vancouver in April 1972, Rogers announced that Ocean Falls would be completely phased out by March 1973. The details of the shutdown, including a timeline and compensation and relocation packages, were explained to employees at Ocean Falls that same afternoon.

However, on August 30, 1972, British Columbia elected its first NDP government, and despite the closure being already in progress, the new government changed Ocean Falls's fate—for a time—when it bought it from Crown Zellerbach for a million dollars just two weeks before all operations were destined to be turned off. But the NDP soon learned what Crown Zellerbach already knew—that it was too costly to operate; however, Social Credit, which formed a new government in 1975, kept the mill running for another five years, finally closing it down in 1980.

When the NDP had come to power in 1972, American-owned Crown Zellerbach had postponed plans to build new mills in BC and waited three years for the re-election of the Social Credit before restarting its capital program. Rogers remembered:

> I had the pleasure of going over [to Victoria] and meeting with the premier, and I said, "Mr. Premier, I want you to know first that tomorrow we are announcing a $250 million program." Well, was the premier ever happy because that was the sort of news he was looking for.[294]

Committed to overseeing the company's rebuilding process, Rogers stayed on for several years past his planned retirement date. By 1982, however, Crown Zellerbach was in financial trouble and looking for a buyer, and just before he retired in August of that year, Rogers helped arrange the sale of the company to Fletcher Challenge of New Zealand. At the start of his retirement, Bob and Jane Rogers went on an extended vacation to France. Rogers, however, was not quite ready to put up his feet and relax, and in 1982–83 he took on the job of chairman of the Canada Harbour Place Corporation in Vancouver.

Back in 1968 Bob Rogers had been reading a biography of Pierre Trudeau when he realized that Trudeau had been one of the three "rabble-rousers" who visited the mine in East Broughton. Shortly after that realization Trudeau, now prime minister, had invited Rogers to dinner at 24 Sussex Drive. "At that time," Rogers recalled, "I wasn't very fond of Mr. Trudeau, of course, because those memories still prevailed." But he was soon won over. Trudeau greeted Rogers and his other guests personally at the door.

> By the end of the dinner he had us eating out of his hand, of course. So I reminded him, and he laughed and said, "Well, [there's been] a lot of . . . water over the dam since then," but it was hard for me to see that man who had tried to shut our mine down as the same man who had just been elected by a large majority as our prime minister. And he remembered it—he didn't remember me any more than I remembered him—but he remembered the incident.[295]

In the years after that second meeting, Rogers had often advised the federal government on international trade, and in July 1983 it was Pierre Trudeau who phoned to ask him to become British Columbia's next Lieutenant Governor. At that time Bill Bennett and the Social Credit Party formed BC's government, and critics of Rogers's appointment pointed out that he did not meet the requirements for neutrality. *The Globe and Mail*, for example, called him a "long-time Liberal Party member and New Democratic Party-basher—albeit a polite one." In his own defence, Rogers stated that "I have no politics anymore."[296] Like many Lieutenant Governors before him, and some since, accepting the position meant a pay cut and out-of-pocket costs beyond what would be covered by his annual salary of $35,000 and $18,000 for travel and other expenses.

Bob Rogers was sworn in as Lieutenant Governor on July 15, 1983, and he soon developed a reputation as the essence of dignified statesmanship though with a comfortable conviviality that put people at ease. He and Jane were in favour of making Government House more accessible and friendly to the general public, and they ended the annual garden party that had grown to about four thousand guests who spent much of their time in a lineup waiting to shake hands with the vice-regal couple. Instead, they began hosting

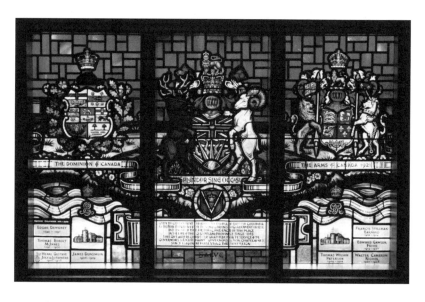

The Government House Foundation, established in 1988 by Robert Gordon Rogers to raise funds to preserve and enhance Government House, has played an important role in supporting the legacy projects of Lieutenant Governors. The first project supported by the foundation was the creation of this stained glass window above the main staircase.

Image courtesy of Government House of British Columbia Archives.

smaller events, such as tea dances, as well as parties for children that were inspired by their seven young grandsons. Rogers also commissioned his private secretary, Michael Roberts, to write a pamphlet explaining the role of the Lieutenant Governor to hand out to the thousands of schoolchildren who visited Government House.

In 1988 Rogers established the Government House Foundation, which to this day raises funds to preserve and enhance Government House. The foundation's first project was the spectacular stained glass window above the main staircase, which was the brainchild of Jane Rogers. It was designed by stained glass artist Christopher Wallis, and the images in the window represent the province's landscape and flora, Indigenous and colonial heritage, as well as the Crown and Lieutenant Governor. With funding from the BC Building Corporation, Jane Rogers also took the initiative to redecorate the royal suite, little changed since the house was constructed in 1959.

She also started a number of projects to connect Government House to the broader public, organizing a group of volunteer "flower ladies" to create bouquets from flowers growing in the gardens and greenhouses, a group that still plays an essential role at Government House today. She invited students from the University of Victoria to conduct tours of the house, while volunteers from the Horticultural Centre of the Pacific took care of the vegetable gardens, donating the produce to Mustard Seed, a food bank in Victoria.

Rogers concluded his term as Lieutenant Governor in 1988 and was appointed to the Order of British Columbia in 1990. He served as Chancellor of the University of Victoria from 1991 to 1996, and with his vast experience in business, he helped the university organize its first capital campaign in 1991. During his term as chancellor, the university played an important role in hosting the 1994 Commonwealth Games.

In their retirement years Robert and Jane Rogers divided their time between their farm in the Eastern Townships of Quebec, their waterfront home north of Nanaimo, and Vancouver and Victoria. Robert Gordon Rogers died on May 21, 2010; he was ninety-one. Jane Rogers died a year later.

Bob Rogers had developed a number of skills that eased his transition into the position of Lieutenant Governor: he had travelled widely, he and Jane had years of experience hosting events and visiting BC

During his term as Lieutenant Governor from 1983 to 1988, Robert Gordon Rogers and his wife, Jane, sought to beautify Government House and make it more accessible to the public.

Image courtesy of Government House of British Columbia Archives.

communities; he had boosted British Columbia abroad; and he was known to and trusted by the federal government. But they also established new trends during their time in Government House, such as staging smaller, more accessible events, and after they started the Government House Foundation, which raised money and provided financial support for the stained glass window proposed by Jane, it became customary for Lieutenant Governors to design personal legacy projects assisted by the Government House Foundation.

X

Diverse Identities and Priority Projects (1988–2018)

THE NEXT FIVE Lieutenant Governors who were appointed, unlike the twenty-four who served before them, reflected more of the diversity in British Columbia's population: women and men, Indigenous people and visible minorities. However, BC was the ninth province to have a female Lieutenant Governor, and although it was the first in Canada to have an Asian Canadian Lieutenant Governor, it was not until 2007—thirty-three years after Cree leader Ralph Steinhauer was appointed in Alberta—that an Indigenous person was asked to take this post in BC.

From 1986 to 2001 BC's politics were beset by scandal and conflict of interest, and four premiers resigned between 1991 and 2017, with the result that Lieutenant Governors in this period had to be prepared to act in what historian Christopher McCreery has described as their "constitutional fire-extinguisher role."[297] But they kept the lines of communication open by continuing to hold private meetings with the premiers to discuss political and constitutional matters.

During this time the ceremonial role of the Lieutenant Governors also expanded, partly due to efforts by these incumbents to create projects that recognized the achievements and nurtured the potential of a broader range of British Columbians. Robert Gordon Rogers established the Government House Foundation and those who followed him each created a "legacy project" to improve Government House or promote particular issues in the province as a whole. As former private secretary Herbert LeRoy has explained, accomplishing legacy goals was expedited by identifying priorities at the beginning of a Lieutenant Governor's term. These projects included redesigning the Government House gardens, improving wheelchair access to the grounds, creating new awards, promoting literacy and engaging youth in environmental stewardship. In addition, each new Lieutenant Governor endeavoured to maintain the projects that were set in motion before his or her term, creating a sense of continuity and making a greater impact among diverse communities in the province.

David See-Chai Lam (1988–95)

Born in Hong Kong on July 25, 1923, David See-Chai Lam grew up in a wealthy household in Kowloon, the mainland part of the British colony of Hong Kong. The family was Baptist as his paternal grandfather, Lam Siu-Fun, had embraced the new faith while studying at the Ling Tung Baptist Mission. His first son, Lam Chi Fung, who was David's father, began training to be a doctor, but finding that this did not suit him, left for Hong Kong where, by the early 1930s, he had helped found the Sze Wai Company, which imported and distributed coal from French Indochina. Due to his strong Christian beliefs, Lam Chi Fung gave away part of his earnings in support of the Baptist church and paid for an irrigation system in his hometown. His goals for his own children included a Christian perspective, a good education, a healthy body through exercise, an understanding of Confucian philosophy and a pride in their Chinese origins.

David See Chai Lam, the second of Lam Chi Fung's nine children, took an early interest in gardening and as a young teenager grew vegetables and flowers for sale at his family's property in Kowloon. When Japanese forces invaded Hong Kong on December 8, 1941, David Lam was eighteen years old and in his second term at Lingnan University, which had relocated from Canton to Hong Kong because of the war. For his children's safety Lam Chi Fung decided to send them to the neutral Portuguese colony of Macao, and he put David in charge of the move since his older brother, Daniel, was now in the Philippines.

After the move, David worked briefly for his father, maintaining contact with coal distribution stations, until his father sent him back to school where he thought his son would be safer. The staff, instructors and students of Lingnan University had moved again, however, this time to northern Guangdong province, and to get there Lam, a small group of students and a guide had to travel through Japanese-held territory. When they arrived, they found that the students and faculty had built much of their rural campus themselves out of split, woven and whitewashed bamboo. About a year and a half later, as Japanese forces neared the area, Lam set off for Hong Kong again via the coastal city of Zhanjiang, this time with his young uncle who was a fellow student. In Zhanjiang they took passage on a 45-foot (14-m) motor vessel, the *Sin Gin Maru*. After fending off a pirate attack, the crew found what they thought was a safe cove for shelter, but the anchor chain broke and the ship crashed into the rocks. The two young men swam ashore where they received aid from a fisherman and his wife, and Lam then helped convince the crew of a Japanese naval supply vessel to transport the *Sin Gin Maru*'s survivors to Hong Kong in its cargo hold. In Hong Kong only one ticket was available for the ferry to Macao, so Lam and his uncle found space instead on a small sailing vessel. Again, luck was with the two young men as the ferry was attacked by an American warplane and sunk half an hour out of the harbour, with the loss of hundreds of lives.

Before the end of the war Lam made some good investments that would allow him to complete his university degree and go to the United States to study. Meanwhile, friends planned to send a load of salt to Macao, and thinking that Lam with his investment know-how would bring their venture good luck, they loaned him the money to invest in one-third of the shares. When the salt did not arrive in Macao, it was assumed that the shipment had been lost; the ship, however, had only been delayed while undergoing repairs for storm damage. In the interval the price of salt had risen from $33 to $90 per 60-kilogram (133-lb.) sack, leaving Lam with an excellent return. He invested this money in old Hong Kong dollars rather than the new ones printed by the Japanese, thinking it would be more likely that the British would recognize the face value of the old notes. Fortunately for him, at the end of the war Britain accepted both old and new notes at face value.

The Lam family moved back to Hong Kong where Lam invested some of his new savings in mortgages. Then, in 1947, having finally completed his bachelor of arts degree at Lingnan, he went to the United States to take a master's in business administration at Temple University in Philadelphia. To make friends there, he stayed in a dormitory with seventeen other students rather than take a single room. He completed his MBA in the spring of 1948 and was accepted into the doctoral program in economics at New York University, but in 1950 when his progress there was too slow, he returned to Hong Kong.

By then the defeat of the Nationalist forces and victory of the Communists in mainland China had caused a refugee crisis in Hong Kong, and as a result of the Korean War, the United States had placed an embargo on trade from China, which had a negative impact on Hong Kong's role as a middleman. Nevertheless, the construction of new housing and local manufacturing for export were doing well, and the Lam family partnered with the Cheng brothers to found Chiap Hua Manufactory, which salvaged scrap metal from wartime ships to make it into lanterns, thermos flasks and window and door frames. David Lam went to work as a sub-manager for the Ka Wah Bank, an institution in which his father had a majority share, and brought it more attention by moving it out of its small office into a new, specially constructed building. Over time, the Lam family split the Chiap Hwa manufacturing company with the Cheng family, the Lams keeping the flashlight factory, which became the Raylam Battery Company, a major supplier of flashlights and batteries to an American firm, Ray-O-Vac; this development took Lam to Bangkok to establish a new factory.

David Lam had known Dorothy Tan since their childhood.

Their fathers had gone to school together, and David had attended Lingnan University with her older siblings, but Dorothy and David did not start dating until 1952 when they met again at a ball given by the governor of Hong Kong in honour of the visiting Duke of Kent. She was one of ten female students invited to the ball from the University of Hong Kong, and he was invited due to his reputation as a businessman. Soon after Dorothy graduated, they married. When she moved into David's family home with his parents and siblings, it became her responsibility to manage the servants and food budget and host guests, partly because this was the traditional role of a daughter-in-law and partly because her mother-in-law was recovering from a stroke. When they had children, however, Dorothy and David Lam purchased land and built a new house where David enjoyed working in the garden, planting "hundreds of rose bushes, Chinese sweet oranges, papayas and bougainvillea, a bamboo grove and dozens of flowers and vegetables."[298] The young Lam family lived comfortably: they had a boat, hired servants and owned two cars. Meanwhile, in addition to his responsibilities as a bank manager, David aided in the construction of a Baptist hospital to serve refugees and others on limited incomes.

By the early 1960s David Lam was becoming frustrated with the limitations inherent in the family business. His father had set it up as a private company so all decisions were made by consensus and shares could only be sold within the family. As he explained to biographer Reginald Roy:

> The worst thing that can happen is to own shares as a minority shareholder in a private company because there is no market for them. While I was working for the company, I was willing to work for almost nothing to build it up. When it was built up, I could not turn my shares into cash.[299]

By 1961 David and Dorothy Lam were considering leaving Hong Kong, and they took a long trip to Australia, New Zealand, the United States and Canada to look at immigration possibilities. Lam was seeking a "democratic country with the freedom to use one's own initiative . . . one that had a good record of tolerance and was free of the excesses of racism."[300] They found Vancouver the most appealing but put the idea on hold while they wrapped up business responsibilities in Hong Kong.

At that time, however, Canada had limits on Chinese immigration, and it was not until 1967 that acceptance to this country was changed to a points system based on education, skills and capital, all of which made it easier for Hong Kong residents such as the Lams to immigrate here. Indeed, they became part of the new wave of urban, well-educated, English-speaking Chinese who arrived in Canada from 1967 onwards. David and Dorothy Lam and their three daughters, Deborah, Daphne and Doreen, arrived in Vancouver on May 29, 1967.

From his investments and interests in companies outside the family business, Lam had saved some capital, which allowed the family to buy a house and cover expenses for a few months, but he could not find a managerial position at a level similar to what he had left in Hong Kong and lacked the funds to start his own business. Then, recognizing the opportunities in real estate, he started working for Newcombe Realty while taking courses on real estate appraisal at the University of British Columbia. Initially he sold houses but soon found his niche as a matchmaker—identifying commercial real estate with potential for development or improvement and matching it with an interested buyer or group of buyers, many of them Hong Kong investors. And it turned out that he had arrived at the right time because in the 1970s there was a boom in Vancouver real estate. In 1975 Lam's commission from a major real estate deal brokered with Bob Lee for the sale of the Baxter and Board of Trade buildings on behalf of brothers C.K. Lau and Geoffrey Lau gave him the chance to found his own company, Canadian International Properties. By this time he was also advising clients on properties outside the province, and in 1977 his own company purchased the Insurance Exchange Building in San Francisco. In Vancouver, because of restrictions on developing residential units, he continued to focus on commercial properties such as shopping centres.

By the late 1970s Lam had started to wrap up his business involvements, and he retired in 1982 at age sixty. In his retirement he was generous with both his time and money, supporting causes such as education and intercultural understanding as he saw "giving as an obligation of good citizenship."[301] Likely as a result of his Baptist upbringing and the example set by his grandfather, Lam had for decades kept aside 10 per cent of his earnings for charity in a separate account, and from this account in 1982 the Lams founded the Floribunda Philanthropic Society and followed that in 1985 with the David and Dorothy Lam Foundation. Some of the many causes these foundations supported included the Baptist Church, hospitals, music, theatre and service groups. Blake Bromley, a Vancouver tax lawyer who helped Lam establish his foundations, commented that Lam gave in two distinct ways: "David the Christian is a reactive, emotive giver. David the philanthropist is a proactive, strategic giver."[302] And Lam explained that:

> In reactive giving, you react to requests. In creative giving, you go out and ask yourself, "Why isn't something done? What would it take to have it done?" And you start planning on it and getting people together and working on it. It is a lot of work, but it is also very exciting because you are creating something from nothing. And you only play a part by putting in a certain amount of money as a challenge to all parties to fulfil and complete the project.[303]

Through his foundation, Lam provided the money to create a Faculty of Commerce Research Library at UBC as an incentive to other donors to provide funds for the larger Management Research Centre that would house the library. When the David See Chai Lam Management Library was opened in 1985, he acknowledged the good fortune he had enjoyed as an immigrant to Canada:

> Very few countries offer the opportunities for success which enable an immigrant without capital to accumulate enough money to put something back into the community . . . My contribution to this library is but a small payment to the debt of gratitude which I owe.[304]

The Lams also endowed two chairs at UBC, one in multicultural education and the other in special education, and because of his love of gardens, he funded improvements to UBC's Asian Gardens and was a key contributor to the Dr. Sun Yat-sen Classical Garden in Vancouver's Chinatown. The Lam Foundation also funded the Chinese Studies Program at Regent College, the Centre for Asia-Pacific Initiatives, the Institute for Dispute Resolution and the Centre on Aging at the University of Victoria, and the Centre for International Communications and other initiatives at Simon Fraser University.

Lam had become an admirer of the work of Dr. Howard Petch, president of the University of Victoria from 1975 to 1990, and as a retirement gift decided to fund the construction of a fountain in front of the library. Although he had imagined a small fountain with a few goldfish, the university's architects came up with a plan for a large fountain with water falling over rocks and tree-shaded areas surrounding it. Lam agreed with the plan but asked the provincial government to match his donation. The fountain, now a favourite location for students to meet, study and have lunch, was dedicated in June 1990. In recognition of his support of post-secondary education generally, Lam has received honorary doctorates from several major universities in BC, and in 1988 he became a member of the Order of Canada.

David Lam was always active in promoting intercultural understanding and harmony, speaking out against racism and encouraging newcomers to learn about Canadian culture. He urged his audiences to overcome their fear of difference and seek not just a common ground with individuals of different cultural backgrounds but "the higher ground of enjoyment, learning and enrichment." To inform newcomers about Canadian society, he proposed and then played a role in a Chinese-language video made for the Asia-Pacific Initiative; the video was also shown to Hong Kong residents when they were granted Canadian visas. He played an important role in promoting the first dragon boat races in Vancouver, and when the Chinese Cultural Centre organized dragon boat races for Expo 86, he proposed inviting teams from other countries to take part. In its early years he also helped fund the annual Dragon Boat Festival in False Creek, and his daughter Doreen Lau recalls that Lam saw the festival as the ultimate event for "showcasing what multiculturalism means"[305] with teams coming together to work toward a common goal, while meeting people from different cultures.

In 1988, the same year Lam received his Order of Canada, Social Credit premier Bill Vander Zalm asked if he could nominate him for the position of BC's Lieutenant Governor. Initially Lam turned down the nomination as both he and Dorothy felt that it would be an intimidating responsibility. Besides, he was busy and happy with his lifestyle. Then, after taking some time to think and pray about it, he agreed to the nomination, and he took office on September 9, 1988. In some ways, his appointment was surprising since he was the first Chinese Canadian Lieutenant Governor in Canada, yet it also affirmed the growing value placed on multiculturalism in BC.

Canadian writer Peter Newman commented that before Lam, Lieutenant Governors had been British, usually Anglican, and "were probably raised on porridge. This self-perpetuating daisy-chain was abruptly snapped with the appointment of British Columbia's twenty-fifth lieutenant-governor, David See Chai Lam."[306] And his private secretary, Michael Roberts, later observed that Lam had much to offer:

> He was a Baptist by religion but a Confucian by philosophy. Culturally he was Chinese–born, but he was educated extremely well in the West . . . so he had these four different points that lent him a particular perspective.[307]

When planning how to carry out the ceremonial and promotional aspects of the office of Lieutenant Governor, Lam "wanted to bring messages of good will, compassion and understanding, to be a vice-regal cheerleader for the province and to make his office and himself better known."[308] He was determined to travel the whole province and meet as many British Columbians as he could, though without placing too much of a financial burden on community organizations to host him. So when the Union of British Columbia Municipalities met for a conference in Victoria in the late 1980s, he invited the mayors' spouses to Government House. He told them he wanted to go to their communities, and he explained how this could be done at very little cost to them: he would pay for his own transportation, and he would attend morning and afternoon events—speaking at a school, speaking on local radio, seeing the sights and going to the city hall. He insisted that they take the idea back to their spouses and invite him to visit. As Lieutenant Governors before him had done, he also travelled with the Royal Canadian Navy to visit communities along the coast. Private secretary Michael Roberts remembers that David Lam was "exceptionally busy. There were some days when he attended eight events . . . He really felt he had a calling to do this."[309] On one cruise on the HMCS *Huron* he brought along two helicopters so he could reach communities that were inaccessible to the 5,000-ton, 430-foot-long destroyer.

In the 1980s provincial retrenchment policies had reduced funding to Government House and gardens, and to maintain the Government House budget, employees now had to pay for their own lunches and coffee, and the chauffeur was paid for the time he spent driving rather than for an eight-hour day. In spite of the cutbacks, Lam was determined that his major legacy to Government House would be the revitalization of the gardens and making them more accessible to the general public, and he accomplished this through

David See–Chai Lam came to the position of Lieutenant Governor with a great love of gardens. He planted a new rose garden at Government House, then, with advice from local gardeners, established a popular volunteer gardener program, the Friends of the Government House Gardens Society. In this photo, David and Dorothy Lam stand among the tulips at Government House.

Image courtesy of Government House of British Columbia Archives.

generous donations and the work of hundreds of volunteers. After the unusually cold first winter of his stay devastated the rose garden planted by Robert and Jane Rogers, he rescued what was left of it and planted another more protected rose garden. Then he invited three expert Victoria gardeners—Elizabeth Kerfoot, George Radford and Phoebe Noble—to come for tea and discuss his idea for a volunteer gardener program. A subsequent article in the *Times Colonist* attracted numerous volunteers, resulting in the formation of the Friends of the Government House Gardens Society, to which he donated his salary for the purchase of plants and equipment. When neighbours saw the work that was being done, they also donated money for the gardens as did Lam's friends from Hong Kong, some of whom came to visit Government House. Today the Friends of Government House Gardens Society has a membership of over four hundred; about half of them volunteer in the gardens while others help with the archives, administration and organizing events. Altogether they maintain seventeen gardens on fourteen of the 36 acres (14 ha) that comprise the grounds at Government House.

David Lam came closest to having to exercise the Lieutenant Governor's constitutional prerogative to dismiss a premier and select a new one when Premier Bill Vander Zalm was caught in a conflict of interest in 1990. It had become routine for the premier or an MLA to ask the Lieutenant Governor to host a group at Government House with the funding for the event coming from that MLA's budget, and in this way the estate was used for a variety of functions at limited expense to the government. Thus, Lam was not overly surprised when in late August 1990 the premier asked if he would host a luncheon for a group of investors from Taiwan. Lam agreed but only learned the names of the guests when the press reported in early September that Vander Zalm was discussing the possible sale of Fantasy Gardens, his property in Richmond, to a Taiwanese investor by the name of Tan Yu. Lam then found out that the guest list for the luncheon included Tan Yu, his daughter and Vancouver realtor Faye Leung, along with the premier. Just days later, Vander Zalm sold his property to Tan Yu, and almost immediately Faye Leung began complaining that the sale commission she had expected to receive had not been forthcoming. Vander Zalm was subsequently accused of conflict of interest for using Government House for his private benefit. While the provincial conflict of interest commissioner was writing his report, Lam consulted constitutional experts and worked with his private secretary, Michael Roberts, to outline his possible options. The commissioner's report found that Vander Zalm had not actually committed a criminal act, although he had overstepped his own guidelines and misused his position to gain the invitation to Government House. Fortunately, Lam was saved having to act as Vander Zalm resigned, and the Social Credit caucus selected a new leader, Rita Johnson.

An election later in 1990 brought the NDP under Michael Harcourt to government. Unlike his predecessors, Harcourt arranged for the swearing-in ceremony of his government to be held in the auditorium of the University of Victoria, rather than at Government House, in order to open the event to a larger audience. At the ceremony Lam shared a short lesson from Confucius who said that government needs three things: food for the population, a military to protect them and the confidence of the people, the most important being the confidence of the people. It was an ambiguous lesson, Lam later recalled. For some in the audience, he said,

> I could be giving the New Democratic Party government a reminder that they must have the people's trust. To some, I was criticizing Vander Zalm because he lost the people's trust. I said no more.[310]

At the opening of the Legislature a year later, a crowd of people, dissatisfied with Harcourt's environmental record, broke into the Legislative Buildings and tried to enter the chamber where Lam was giving his speech. Although shaken by the event, Lam reflected that he was glad that he lived in a democratic country where the police could assert control without resorting to violence.

It was already customary for Lieutenant Governors to travel to London to be introduced to the Queen, though not to make official visits overseas for other reasons. This changed in the late 1980s and 1990s as some Lieutenant Governors began to take part in goodwill missions. David Lam was used to speaking to audiences in Canada on the issue of intercultural harmony, but with his connections to Hong Kong and China, he was also an ideal candidate to strengthen Canada's ties in the Pacific Rim. Early in his term, he hosted Wan Li, the chairman of the National People's Congress of China, and as the meeting went well, the Chinese government invited Lam to pay an official visit. Unfortunately, the Chinese government's crackdown on protesters in Tiananmen Square occurred shortly after the invitation was extended, and Lam could not accept. With the support of both federal and provincial governments, however, he did make an official visit to Hong Kong in November 1989. Indeed, the BC government saw this as an opportunity for Lam to promote British Columbia and attract investment. Then in 1992, as relations thawed between China and Canada, the Canadian government gave approval for David and Dorothy Lam to accept an invitation to make an unofficial visit to Beijing. Even though he was there as a private individual, his hosts arranged for Lam to meet with Chairman Jiang Zemin, the general secretary of the Chinese Communist party. In May 1993 His Excellency Zhu Rongji, vice-premier of the People's Republic of China, visited Vancouver and held a short meeting with

David Lam was a thoughtful and diplomatic Lieutenant Governor who promoted intercultural harmony and carefully navigated a potential constitutional crisis. When Queen Elizabeth and Prince Philip stayed with the Lams during the Commonwealth Games in Victoria in 1994, the Queen made Lam a commander of the Royal Victorian Order. Here, Queen Elizabeth and David Lam follow piper John Mager through the grounds at Government House.
Image courtesy of Government House of British Columbia Archives.

Lam at the Waterfront Centre Hotel, where both parties discussed their desire to improve relations between Canada and China.

David Lam's time in Government House was extended beyond the usual five years so that he would be in office until after the Commonwealth Games, which were held in Victoria in the summer of 1994. During the games, Queen Elizabeth and Prince Philip stayed with the Lams and officially opened the new Government House gardens. Although some guests preferred their privacy, the Queen had breakfast with the Lams in their private dining room.

Endless attention to detail was required to give citizens the opportunity to meet the Queen while she was there, and Michael Roberts reports that on one memorable day, August 18, 1994, Government House had seven events before noon:

> Many of them were in the same room but with different players, so you had to have people arrive at certain times and be held in different areas in Government House, and attended to by an aide–de–camp, and when one event was completed, those involved in a following event would be moved to the room just vacated, while the Queen, who was involved in all these events, moved to an adjacent room to participate in the next event.[311]

Prime Minister Jean Chrétien seemed to be in no rush to replace him, but at a concert at the University of Victoria, the Queen spoke to Chrétien on Lam's behalf, and it was decided that he would complete his term in April 1995. At the end of her visit to Government House, the Queen made Lam a commander of the Royal Victorian Order and appointed Michael Roberts a lieutenant of the same order. David Lam was only the second Lieutenant Governor to be awarded this honour, after John Hendrie in Ontario in 1908.

Following his term as Lieutenant Governor, one of Lam's goals was to "make Vancouver the cherry capital of the West Coast." In June 2010 he donated one hundred flowering cherry trees to David Lam Park in Vancouver. Not only are they beautiful in bloom, but Lam saw them as a model for responsible living: "The cherry tree keeps its promise to burst forth with blossoms, doing its best to use every part of itself. When it is finished, every blossom can shed like snow, having delivered fully."[312]

David and Dorothy Lam were both awarded the Order of British Columbia in 1995 for their philanthropic efforts. Dorothy Lam died two years later, in 1997. David See Chai Lam died in 2010 at the age of eighty-seven. The next year his family gave another three thousand trees to the Vancouver Cherry Tree Festival Society, which was marking Vancouver's 125th anniversary. The trees were sold to city residents at just above cost, with the proceeds supporting the society.

David Lam's appointment clearly demonstrated that British Columbia's Lieutenant Governors would no longer be drawn only from a pool of white, male candidates and placed a new emphasis on representing and engaging with the province's multicultural society. As Lieutenant Governor, he had promoted intercultural communication and understanding among citizens and introduced a new facet to the job by playing a role in trans-Pacific diplomacy.

Garde Basil Gardom (1995–2001)

Garde Basil Gardom was born in Banff, Alberta, on July 17, 1924. His father was Basil Gardom who was born in Leamington, England, and had come to Canada in 1893 to homestead in the Deep Creek area near Enderby, BC, but in 1897, at age twenty-two, he left Canada to join the South African Mounted Constabulary and fight in the Boer War. On his return he joined the BC Provincial Police force and was assigned to police the area from Enderby to Penticton on horseback. Around 1906 he married Helen Munro and they had a daughter. The next year, when he was accompanying a prisoner to Kamloops, the prisoner escaped, and Gardom lost his job, despite the efforts of the Enderby council and petitions in his favour. Gardom left town and headed for the Fraser Valley where he bought a dairy farm in Dewdney. His next career was with the Canadian Pacific Railway, and by 1918 he had become the company's superintendent of construction and repair for all non-railway construction work in western Canada.

It is unclear what became of Gardom's first family, but he met Garde's mother, Welsh-born Gabrielle Gwladys Bell, at Lake Louise in the early 1920s. Their blond-haired son, Garde Basil Gardom, drew the attention of the Stoney people when, at the age of three, he sat in the saddle in front of his father for the ride from Lake Louise to Moraine Lake. The Stoney people gave the little boy the name Okee Mow Nootska (Little White-Haired Chief).

In July 1928 Basil Gardom left the CPR and moved his family to the Dewdney farm where, until he was eight, Garde was home-schooled by his mother, and Basil Gardom wrote in his memoirs that "Gabrielle provided him with a much better and more mature education [than local schooling could provide], even a little French." Farm life could be dangerous for children, and on one occasion, when Garde was running in the cow barn, he fell onto the tip of a pitchfork and had to be taken to hospital in Vancouver. Later, he almost drowned in the Nicomen Slough while saving his dog, and Basil Gardom's prescription for the boy on that occasion was "a drink of whiskey and a long sleep."[313]

In the mid-1930s the family moved to Vancouver, and Garde finished his elementary schooling at Prince of Wales before moving on to Point Grey Junior High and graduating from Magee Secondary. At Point Grey while playing lacrosse, another player accidently checked him in the back of the neck and fractured a disc, forcing him to wear a brace for the next year and a half. Although his lacrosse injury precluded further contact sports, while a student at UBC he managed the basketball team. He graduated with his LLB in 1949 and articled at the law firm of Campbell Brazier to lawyer A.T.R. Campbell, QC, and was called to the bar on December 7, 1949. He stayed with Campbell Brazier another two years, and one of his first successes was suing the CPR for blocking culverts on the farm his father had owned in Dewdney. When he was not practising law, Gardom was skiing or playing tennis or squash.

Garde Gardom was already a lawyer when he met Helen Mackenzie, who was still at university. She was the daughter of Eileen and Bill Mackenzie, who owned British Columbia Bridge and Dredging. After boarding school in Vancouver, she had attended Sault-au-Récollet in Montreal followed by UBC and a year of university in London, England. After graduation, she first worked for her father, then started her own company specializing in temporary secretarial assistance; most of her clients were lawyers, including Garde Gardom. Helen and Garde were married in 1956, and their family would come to include four daughters and one son. One of their shared passions was tennis, and in 1965 they won the Haggart Cup for married mixed doubles.

Garde Gardom was first elected to the provincial Legislature as a Liberal in 1966 in the two-seat riding of Vancouver-Point Grey, defeating W.A.C. Bennett's Social Credit attorney-general, Robert Bonner. Gardom's running mate in that election, Dr. Patrick McGeer, was a fraternity brother who had also belonged to the UBC basketball team. The election returned Social Credit to power, the New Democratic Party headed by Robert Strachan was the official Opposition, and the Liberals held just six seats. BC historians Geoff Meggs and Rod Mickleburgh point out that since 1952 "government administration [had] remained unchanged . . . [and] all significant decisions were made by Bennett alone." The rules of procedure in the Legislature were even more stagnant, having a similar form since 1920: "There was no Question Period. There was no *Hansard* record of debate. If time ran short at the end of a session, Bennett simply continued debate around the clock until the opposition members sagged with exhaustion."[314] While all of the provinces had been slow to follow the example of the federal House of Commons, which had been keeping a *Hansard* report, a verbatim record of the debates in Parliament, since 1880, British Columbia, according to

Before serving as Lieutenant Governor, Garde Gardom was a lawyer with twenty years of experience as an MLA, first with the Liberal Party, then with the Social Credit.

Image courtesy of Royal BC Museum and Archives, I–32468.

Gardom, was "the land of the legislative hush-hush."[315] But thanks to the pressure he applied, BC started reporting debates in the provincial Legislature after 1970 and provided a full public report after 1972.

Gardom was re-elected in Vancouver Point Grey in 1969 and again in 1972 when the New Democratic Party under Dave Barrett came to power and introduced a range of legislation that would modernize and change the face of the province. Supporters of the other parties, however, feared the NDP's socialist leanings and the dramatic changes they were making. As Barrett explained in his memoirs, in 1975 there was "a concerted effort from all sectors of the business community to try to get rid of us in the next election. A group of businessmen formed the 21 Club to raise money for a revitalized Social Credit party."[316] All members of the Liberal and Conservative parties were under pressure to cross the floor to the Social Credit side, and in the spring of 1975 Alan Williams, McGeer and Gardom resigned from the Liberal Party, then sat as independents until September when they joined the Social Credit Party. As they were recognized as moderate, intelligent and professional, their move made it much easier for Bill Bennett to win the election of December 1975.

In the new government Garde Gardom became attorney general, a position he held from 1975 to 1979, and one of the most important initiatives he supported was raising public awareness of the dangers of drinking and driving, especially since the legal drinking age had recently been lowered, and driving under the influence was not considered a serious crime. As a lawyer, he had seen "these horribly injured people, permanently maimed by a drunken driver whom society did not consider a criminal. The penalties were inadequate."[317] He organized a coordinated effort by a number of government agencies, including schools and the Insurance Corporation of British Columbia, in order to change long-standing attitudes and make drinking and driving unacceptable. The resulting CounterAttack program included roadblocks, breath testing by the BAT Mobile (Breath-Alcohol Testing Mobile Units), suspension of driving privileges and education in schools and in the media. The dissemination of the message was so successful that "soon children were telling their parents not to drink and drive."[318] Overall, "British Columbia had, by the early 1980s, some of the toughest drinking and driving laws in North America." Additional support for the CounterAttack program and its message came from the formation in 1981 of the BC chapter of Mothers Against Drinking and Driving (MADD), which "pushed for stronger legislation, stricter enforcement and the elimination of drinking and driving as socially acceptable behaviour."[319]

Among the other progressive bills Gardom introduced to the BC Legislature was the Good Samaritan Act, which protects bystanders from liability charges if they help a person injured in an accident. He was also instrumental in creating the Office of the BC Ombudsman (now Ombudsperson) to provide the public with independent and impartial investigations of complaints about unfair actions by provincial or local governments. (Two decades later, when serving as Lieutenant Governor, Gardom proclaimed October 1–8, 1999, as "Ombudsman Week" to bring attention to the services that the office offered.)

As attorney general, Gardom helped resolve long-standing tensions between the province and its Doukhobor residents. Since 1908 the members of this Russian pacifist religious sect had lived in southeastern British Columbia where they asked only that they be allowed to live communally, be exempt from military service and avoid government interference in their lives. At first, in order to acquire new agricultural settlers, the province had accepted the first two terms, but tensions had arisen when Doukhobors refused to send their children to public schools or register births and deaths. When the province insisted on schooling the children, the most radical faction of the Doukhobors responded with acts of arson and nude protests. By the 1960s and '70s a stalemate existed, and while the Doukhobors had asked several attorneys general to establish a commission of inquiry, it was Gardom who accepted the challenge. The authors of the report he commissioned, Gregory Cran and Hugh Herbison, recommended that the government change its tactic from dealing with the issue in the criminal justice system to developing "an improved social climate in which protest and depredation would not flourish." To implement the plan, in Cranbrook on November 13, 1979, Gardom announced the creation of the Kootenay Committee on Intergroup Relations, but he did not oversee the outcomes of this fresh approach as just ten days later the premier placed him in a new position.

While attorney general, Gardom had also helped articulate BC's position on Canadian unity. In 1976, after Quebec voters elected a government headed by the Parti Québécois, which called for a more independent Quebec within Canada, other provinces were inspired to call for more autonomy and more control over their resources. BC Premier Bill Bennett appointed Rafe Mair and Garde Gardom to co-chair a cabinet committee on the Constitution, with the result that British Columbia joined with other provinces to insist that the provinces must consent to any amendment to the Constitution. To represent the province in these negotiations, on November 23, 1979, a Ministry of Intergovernmental Relations was created with Gardom as the new minister.

Meanwhile, by the early 1980s the federal government had negotiated modern treaties with Indigenous peoples in Quebec, Yukon and the Northwest Territories whereby they agreed to give up their Aboriginal title to broad territories in exchange for compensation, hunting and fishing rights and the ownership of much smaller areas of land. First Nations in British Columbia, however, faced a provincial government that was unwilling to acknowledge Aboriginal title. In his study of Aboriginal politics in BC, Paul Tennant observed that the problem lay in the fact that "Social Credit sees free and enterprising individuals as the key element in society and rejects the notion that individuals should receive rights or benefits because they belong to a particular group."[320] Consistent with this philosophy, Gardom and other Social Credit MLAs opposed the possibility that treaties might impede on economic land uses such as fishing, forestry and tourism and argued that Crown land "should be controlled for the benefit of *all* British Columbians."[321] Such an argument did not take into account that Aboriginal rights to most of the land in the province had not been extinguished through treaties.

As part of his intergovernmental affairs portfolio, Gardom was responsible for official visits to Expo 86, Vancouver's international exposition celebrating advances in transportation and communication. His role involved coordinating and hosting the visits of royalty, world leaders and dignitaries, among whom were Prince Harald and Princess Sonja of Norway, the prime minister of the United Kingdom, Vice-President George H.W. Bush of the United States and former Canadian prime minister Pierre Trudeau, but the most important personage would be the member of the royal family who opened the event. On the Queen's visit to Vancouver in 1984, she had attended a ground-breaking ceremony for Expo and offered to return to open the fair two years later, but Bill Bennett had another plan in mind: "He loved his queen dearly, but he didn't want her to open Expo. He wanted the Prince and Princess of Wales. They were a hot property, especially Diana. But how do you uninvite the queen?" After some delicate negotiations by Stu Hodgson, who had been invited to the prince's wedding and was then in charge of building the SkyTrain, Prince Charles offered to relieve his mother of the task of opening the fair. Although no one knows what motivated the Queen, Bill Bennett's biographer, Bob Plecas, speculates: "Not only gracious but smart, the queen, aware that the Prince and Princess of Wales were doing so much to restore people's confidence in the future of the monarchy, wisely agreed." Planned in advance in minute detail, every aspect of the royal visit "was timed, scripted, practiced and followed."[322] Through his responsibility for official visits such as this one, Gardom gained experience hosting international dignitaries as well as intimate knowledge of the protocol that guides such events, skills that he would apply as Lieutenant Governor.

Gardom left politics in October 1986, having served as an MLA for twenty years. In June 1987 he and Helen moved to London where he took up the role of BC's agent-general, a position he held until 1992. His role there was to promote BC businesses in Britain and Europe, and Helen Gardom recalled travelling all over Britain and back and forth to their office in Dusseldorf, Germany. They hosted parties for such British Columbia groups as rugby players and students, and receptions for those interested in buying BC products, and Gardom's success was demonstrated by the increase of "exports of manufactured goods from British Columbia from $10 million in 1986 to $125 million by the time he finished his term."[323]

After three years as agent-general, Garde Gardom was asked to become BC's Lieutenant Governor, starting in April 1995. As well as all his experience in politics and Expo and as agent-general, he had the most essential quality for success as a Lieutenant Governor: he loved interacting with the public. As his daughter, Karen, recalled, her father was "very loud and gregarious and outgoing and boisterous. You heard him and saw him when he came into a room."[324] He combined an appreciation for protocol with an approachable and down-to-earth style.

When the Gardoms moved into Government House, they kept their family close, inviting them to stay and celebrating holidays together. As Gardom's colleague, Social Credit politician Grace McCarthy, observed, Gardom "enjoyed people and people enjoyed him. And he was an exceptionally good father and grandfather."[325]

The Gardoms worked at Government House as a team. Helen's responsibilities as chatelaine included acting as patron for a number of organizations and giving speeches. At the citizenship ceremonies at Government House, Garde would give a speech in English, and Helen would follow with a speech in French, thanks to her schooling in Montreal. She met with the chef once a week to go over menus; in one case, she wanted a special dish to be prepared, but Government House did not have the necessary china to serve it on, and she went out and purchased it so the chef could make that dish. She also became involved in redecorating Government House, re-covering the furniture and bringing in new artwork, including

Garde Gardom came to the position of Lieutenant Governor as an experienced ambassador for British Columbia: he was responsible for official visits to Expo 86 and served as BC's agent–general in London from 1987 to 1992.
Photo by Bruce Stotesbury, courtesy of Victoria Times Colonist.

pieces by Emily Carr and E.J. Hughes, which she borrowed from the Art Gallery of Greater Victoria and the Maltwood Gallery at the University of Victoria.

Gardom's term overlapped with the careers of five premiers. The first, Mike Harcourt, took political responsibility for another MLA's use of the proceeds of a charity bingo to fund the NDP Party and resigned in February 1996. The next leader of the NDP, Glen Clark, won a narrow victory in the election that May. Criticized for over-spending on "fast ferries," Clark resigned in August 1999 when it became public knowledge that he was under police investigation (he was later cleared). At the request of the NDP caucus, Gardom then appointed Dan Miller as interim leader, and he was replaced at the NDP provincial leadership convention in February 2000 by Ujjal Dosanjh, Canada's first South Asian premier.

A few days later, in a speech delivered at the swearing-in cere-mony for Dosanjh's cabinet, Gardom quoted Captain George Vancouver. In 1792 while sailing along the coast of what would become British Columbia, Vancouver wrote in his journal that "the serenity of the climate, the innumerable pleasing landscapes and the abundant fertility that unassisted nature puts forth requires only to be enriched by man to render it the most lovely country that could be imagined." Chief Joe Mathias and Grand Chief Edward John, sitting in the front row as representatives of the First Nations Summit, could not believe that the Lieutenant Governor would repeat a sentiment that suggested the Northwest Coast had been an empty land that only needed the presence of Europeans. Once the ceremony was over, the two men expressed their concern to Gardom, who replied that "his statements were not insulting."[326] As he had been speaking as the Lieutenant Governor, however, his words received much publicity, and given the important relationship between First Nations and the Crown, the First Nations Summit wrote him an open letter explaining their grievance and requesting an apology. They pointed out that despite the legal recognition of Aboriginal title in the Constitution, "the Crown continues to deny the very existence of Aboriginal rights and Aboriginal title. So the significance of the office of the lieutenant-governor, representing as it does the Crown, is not lost on us."[327]

Ujjal Dosanjh's government lasted until the election of June 2001, when the Liberals led by Gordon Campbell took seventy-seven seats, leaving the NDP with only two. According to BC legislation, to have official Opposition status, a party must have at least four elected representatives, and taking a legal—yet petty—position, Campbell refused to recognize the NDP as the Opposition, thus denying the party funding for such things as office services. But having an Opposition party, however small, is an essential component of the Westminster system, and Gardom upheld this democratic tradition by a small but significant gesture when he delivered the speech from the throne at the opening of the new Legislature. On his way into the Legislative Chamber he stopped to shake hands with the premier, and after delivering the speech from the throne, he stopped to shake hands with Joy MacPhail, leader of the NDP. Although Gardom had shaken hands with the leader of the Opposition before, Vaughn Palmer of the *Vancouver Sun* pointed out that,

> in this instance the gesture went well beyond mere courtesy. In a stroke, the vice–regal representative had conferred all due recognition on MacPhail. Campbell and his small–minded cohort could say what they liked. Henceforth, she was the leader of Her Majesty's Loyal Opposition. One could not have asked for a more dramatic illustration of the virtues of an office that is intended to rise above the worst excesses of partisan politics. And Garde Gardom, bless him, did it with a handshake.[328]

Gardom's legacy to Government House was the construction of wheelchair accessible paths. Before his term, it had been difficult for those in wheelchairs or with a stroller to access the gardens. With Gardom's support, the Government House Foundation raised funds to build and upgrade pathways and also make a public washroom accessible to visitors using wheelchairs.

Garde Basil Gardom completed his term on September 25, 2001. A year later he was awarded the Order of British Columbia. In 2010 the 4-H livestock auction at the Pacific National Exhibition was dedicated to Garde and Helen Gardom who had been buying animals every year from the auction and donating them to the Salvation Army. Garde Gardom died on June 18, 2013, in Vancouver at the age of eighty-eight.

"Garde Gardom, the large, boisterous, hail-fellow-well-met former Liberal," Bob Plecas wrote, "was well connected in Ottawa and well-liked by his peers across Canada, [but] his larger-than-life personality hid a very shrewd legal mind that focused on constitutional issues."[329] When it came to minorities, in some cases he acted as a force for reconciliation, for example on the issue of Doukhobor protests, but in the case of Aboriginal title, he focused on what he saw as the potential negative repercussions of negotiating land claims. As Lieutenant Governor, he was outgoing and enthusiastic, but he could also be quietly influential, for example when he upheld the democratic tradition of an official Opposition with a simple handshake.

Iona Victoria Campagnolo (2001–7)

Iona Victoria Hardy was born in Vancouver on October 18, 1932, to Rosamond and Kenneth Hardy. Soon after her birth, the family returned to Galiano Island where her grandfather, Finlay Murcheson, had settled in 1882. In 1940 her father was hired as chief of maintenance at the North Pacific Cannery on the Skeena River, and her family moved north to make their home near Prince Rupert. She recalls "a remarkable childhood living beside one of the world's great rivers . . . The Skeena River . . . forms the current of my personal landscape."[330] Two months after the bombing of Pearl Harbor on December 7, 1941, the federal government ordered all persons of Japanese descent living on the West Coast to leave their homes, businesses, farms and fishing boats and move east to internment camps or work sites east of the Rockies. Campagnolo, whose classmates and friends were almost all Indigenous or Japanese British Columbians, recalls that "I was a child when the Japanese were taken. I still remember my brother and I standing beside the train tracks, crying our eyes out, you know . . . And we didn't understand it."[331] Before she reached her teens, Campagnolo started her first job, working at the salmon cannery for forty-two cents an hour.

In 1952 when she was just nineteen, Iona Hardy followed the somewhat traditional life pathway for Canadian women of that era by marrying Louis Campagnolo and shortly thereafter becoming the mother of two daughters, Gianna and Jennifer. When the Campagnolos separated and divorced more than twenty years later, Iona kept her married name. Her role as a mother and her concern over her daughters' education soon drew her into Prince Rupert politics, and in 1966 she was elected to the school board where she served for six years as Chairman of the Board. She followed that with a term on city council, and in her role as head of the "Aesthetics Committee" she helped coordinate both vice-regal visits and Queen Elizabeth, Prince Philip and Princess Anne's 1971 visit to Prince Rupert for the city's fiftieth anniversary celebrations.

At the same time, Campagnolo was developing a career as a radio broadcaster, hosting a program on CHTK Radio titled "Ladies First," which won her the BC Broadcaster of the Year Award in 1973. That year she was also made a member of the Order of Canada, thanks to two decades of volunteerism within her community, including her work as director, producer and costume designer for the North Pacific Players theatre company.

Campagnolo entered federal politics in the summer of 1974 when she was elected as a Liberal to represent the riding of Skeena. She told Roy MacGregor of *Canadian Magazine* that:

> When the chance came for me to run, I thought, there are women all over the country seeking a chance to run, and here you have one "on a silver platter." And I decided to take it and run as far as I could with it.[332]

Winning a seat meant travelling regularly between Prince Rupert and Ottawa, often on the Sunday night "red-eye" in order to arrive in Ottawa in time for a shower and a quick change of clothes before going to work. Her first appointment as an MP was parliamentary secretary to the minister of Indian Affairs and Northern Development, Judd Buchanan, and she held this post from 1974 to 1976. It was during this time that Buchanan's department, responding to a number of court cases, including the Calder case involving the Nisga'a and the subsequent increasing recognition of Aboriginal rights in Canada, created an Office of Native Claims. In 1975 the federal government made a precedent-setting agreement with the Cree of northern Quebec and in 1976 started negotiations with the Nisga'a, who were among Campagnolo's constituents.

Campagnolo's next posting was the result of Canada's poor showing in the Summer Olympics of 1976, which Canada hosted in Montreal. Soviet-bloc athletes had dominated the games, while Canada had ranked twenty-seventh on the medal list. This was the first—and only—time that an Olympic host country had not won a single gold medal. This was not altogether unexpected. After the Soviet hockey team had showed its strength during the 1972

ALL SET FOR SNOWSLIDE VICTORY

Sometimes political candidates kiss babies and sometimes political candidates kiss dogs, but in his particular case, Skeena Liberal candidate Iona Campagnolo does both. This 12-week-old St. Bernard, which weighs 25 pounds seems to enjoy the embrace as much as Iona Campagnolo. Also pictured is Teresa Wright, campaign assistant, as the Liberal candidate visited the Kispiox Rodeo on Saturday.

When Iona Campagnolo campaigned as a Liberal candidate for the riding of Skeena in 1974, her previous experience in politics included serving as a member of the school board and as a city councillor in Prince Rupert. In this photo, Campagnolo (right) and her campaign assistant Teresa Wright (left) visit the Kispiox Rodeo in June 1974.

Photo credit: The Honourable Iona Campagnolo fonds, Northern BC Archives, UNBC Accession #2009.6.1.50. Used with permission of Black Press Media.

Summit Series, Canada had sent a fact-finding mission to the Soviet Union to look at the Russians' athletic system. However, it was not until this country's inglorious showing in the 1976 Olympics that the government ramped up its efforts to produce world-class athletes, improve overall physical fitness among the general population and become a respectable player in Cold War international sport competitions. In September 1976 Prime Minister Pierre Trudeau appointed Campagnolo a minister with her own newly created portfolio: Ministry of State for Fitness and Amateur Sport. A new state-organized "Canadian Sport System" incorporated elements of Soviet-bloc training systems, including involving children in a wide variety of physical activities and offering specialized training to those who showed aptitude in certain sports. The result was a dramatic increase in this country's success in international sport competitions, and when Canadian athletes won the most medals at the 1978 Commonwealth Games in Edmonton, they showed their appreciation of Campagnolo and the Canadian government by carrying her on their shoulders into the closing ceremonies.

Along with several other cabinet ministers, Campagnolo lost her seat in the spring 1979 election when the Trudeau Liberals were replaced by a minority government under Conservative Joe Clark. For the next three years she hosted *One of a Kind*, a CBCTV interview program out of Vancouver, before branching out into national and international projects. Working for CUSO (Canadian University Services Overseas Organization), she gave talks and raised over half-a-million dollars in support of Thai-Kampuchean border refugees. She helped organize the "Future's Secretariat" for the secretary of state for External Affairs, a project intended to raise awareness of Canadians' international roles and responsibilities. At the same time she continued her involvement in the Canadian sports scene, helping the Calgary Olympic Development Association prepare and present its successful bid for the 1988 Winter Olympics.

In 1982, however, Campagnolo re-entered the federal political realm as the first woman president of the Liberal Party of Canada. Two years later, with John Turner leading the Liberals, she made a bid to return to Parliament by running in the North Vancouver–Burnaby riding but failed. During the campaign, one small but symbolic event occurred that raised concerns across Canada about Turner's outdated attitudes toward women: he was caught on camera patting the posterior of Liberal Party president Iona Campagnolo. Making light of the incident, she patted him right back, but the damage had been done. There was, however, already tension between them: a few weeks earlier, she had openly expressed her preference for Jean Chrétien as Liberal Party leader when she described him as the "man who came in second but first in our hearts."[333]

Throughout these years Iona Campagnolo maintained her close ties with the Indigenous people in her community, ties that dated back to her childhood at the fish cannery on the Skeena, and she received two Indigenous names. The first, given to her around 1972 by Chief Haq be quot'o, Kenneth Harris of the Tsimshian Nation, was the name Notz-whe-Neah (Mother of the Big Fin), an orca name that was associated with a dance and a song that became her property during her lifetime. In 1977, after she had worked with the Haida people to obtain federal funds to build a small museum at Skidegate, Haida Chief Skidegate, Clarence Dempsey Collinson, gave her the second name, Saan aag X'wha (Person Who Sits High), which referred to a person who sat with the leading chiefs away from the entrance in the cedar longhouse. Campagnolo brought Prime Minister Pierre Trudeau and his family to officiate at the museum's opening ceremonies and it was on that occasion that Trudeau and his three sons received Haida names.[334]

This museum was soon too small for the many artifacts the people wished to preserve and showcase, and it was later replaced by a larger museum called Kay Llnagaay or Sea Lion House.

Campagnolo had also supported the determined efforts of the Nisga'a to achieve sovereignty and a treaty. Even as a child she had observed how they asserted their right to just treatment:

In the spring, each of the different tribal groups would come to the cannery to negotiate the price of salmon with the owners. When the Nisga'a came in their small boats, powered by five horsepower engines, all the way down from the Nass River, in general, they would not come off their boats until they were dressed in black suits, white shirts, black ties. Only then they would come and negotiate the price.[335]

Campagnolo had gone to high school with two young men who would become leaders of the treaty movement, Anglican priest Rod Robinson and school principal Alvin McKay: when she was working in radio in Prince Rupert, a group of Nisga'a leaders had invited her to meet them in town with her tape recorder so they could tell her the list of rights they would be pursuing. Later, as parliamentary secretary to the minister of Indian and Northern Affairs, she had brought Minister Judd Buchanan to the Nisga'a village of Aiyansh on January 26, 1976, for the formal opening of treaty discussions. Another fourteen years passed, however, before the provincial government came to the treaty negotiating table, and ten more years before the Nisga'a Treaty, an agreement signed between the Nisga'a and both federal and provincial governments, came into effect. The celebration of the signing of the treaty took place in

2001, by which time Campagnolo was Lieutenant Governor, and although she had some concerns that attending the celebration of this landmark treaty might contravene the neutrality of her post, she reasoned that her position on this issue was no secret.

Iona Campagnolo began her term as Lieutenant Governor of British Columbia on September 25, 2001. As the first woman to hold this position in BC, she knew she would be "watched very carefully." In a recent interview she reflected on her travels throughout the province while Lieutenant Governor and recalled "the lovely things [she] would hear from young people" when she asked them about their plans for the future, and she concluded that of all the responsibilities she had held during her six-year term her "prime function" had been to help make young people "a confident part of British Columbia."[336] As well, she went to great lengths to familiarize British Columbians with the Lieutenant Governor's role by visiting as many communities in the province as she could.

It was also important for Campagnolo to "British Columbianize" the office in order to "make us proud of what we are and the great good fortune we have to live here." She changed the title of Government House to the Ceremonial Home of All British Columbians to show that all were welcome there, and then began making significant changes to the interior. She redecorated two rooms and had them named after the two architects who had designed the second Government House in 1903: Francis Rattenbury and Samuel Maclure. The Rattenbury Room is located on the second floor and offers a place for the Lieutenant Governor to host small formal dinners. Guests eat at a dining table that was once owned by Rattenbury and is now on loan from the Royal BC Museum. The Maclure room on the ground floor, which is decorated with brown-toned arts-and-crafts furniture and a copper-foil ceiling, is used to host conferences, meetings and informal buffets. She also brought in the artwork of British Columbians from a variety of cultural origins, including Takao Tanabe, Judith Currelly and Ted Harrison, all of them inspired by BC's landscapes, cultures and stories.

When Campagnolo started her term, the names of nineteenth- and twentieth-century Lieutenant Governors were inscribed in the stained glass window over the main staircase, but no spaces had been left to add new names. A conversation that Campagnolo had with the premier, Gordon Campbell, helped secure funding for new windows.

In 2006 a new set of stained glass windows was installed high above the Great Hall. The six sets of three windows represent native flowers from the province's six geographic and climatic regions. For her window, Campagnolo chose the skunk cabbage, *Lysichiton americanus*, partly because it grows in all parts of the province. She had always appreciated the beauty of the skunk cabbage, having won first place in a flower arranging contest as a young girl with a bouquet that included a skunk cabbage: "I took the centre out of it and put a yellow hyacinth in it, and then did a Japanese arrangement."[337]

On her travels throughout the province, Campagnolo collected rocks from each of BC's major rivers and brought them back to the Government House gardens where they were inscribed with the name of their river of origin. She explained that "everybody knows about the Fraser River, not a lot know about all the other rivers that there are."[338] When she left the office, the Friends of Government House Gardens gave Campagnolo her own rock inscribed with "Government House, 2001 to 2007."

Campagnolo also designed a new uniform for herself and had it made by a military tailor at her own expense. The state uniform worn by the male Lieutenant Governors for decades had palm fronds on the cuffs and gold detailing, closely resembling the court uniform of Queen Victoria's colonial ministers. Campagnolo's uniform was made of midnight-blue military weight wool and decorated in silver to represent the moon, a symbol traditionally associated with women. Western red cedar motifs adorn the collar and cuffs. A semi-circle of dogwood flowers represented all British Columbians. Campagnolo's two Indigenous names are also symbolized on the uniform by a Haida eagle designed by Bill Reid and a killer whale designed by Tsimshian/Haida artist Roy Henry Vickers. Campagnolo intended the uniform to symbolize her place in the province and the rich cultural heritage and opportunities available to British Columbians, and she told the press that: "I wear all these symbols proudly in the silver of the moon, as a daughter of this magnificent land which gives to all its citizens the choices necessary to work toward our own best selves."[339] Her uniform now resides in the Royal BC Museum along with the uniform that Thomas Robert McInnes saved from the fire in 1899. Each Christmastime Campagnolo took out of storage the uniform worn by her more recent male

The first woman to serve as Lieutenant Governor in this province, Iona Campagnolo sought to "British Columbianize" the office, bringing the work of diverse regional artists into Government House and designing her own uniform, which included symbols of British Columbia.
Image courtesy of Government House of British Columbia.

predecessors and wore it to read stories to children; after the story-telling, they would all go outside, light the tree and march around it.

As a feminist, Campagnolo sought to equalize the roles of men and women at Government House. A formal ball sponsored by the military had taken place there on and off since the colonial era, and by the time Campagnolo was appointed in 2001, this event had come to be known as the "Debutante Ball." Since she thought it was a sexist and outdated idea to present these "bride-dressed" teenage daughters of members of the military to a representative of the royal family, she negotiated with the military to change the event into a Garrison Ball, to which everyone was invited. And while she was at it, she also renamed the Ball Room the Great Hall.

When it came to choosing her legacy projects, Campagnolo set the bar high for those who would follow her by establishing two award programs that would recognize excellence in the areas of literature and wine-making. Her private secretary, Herbert LeRoy, worked with her and other staff at Government House to decide what these awards would be and how they would be granted, and they determined that the awards should not overlap with any existing competition, they should be open to all people in the province, and they should be judged by experts in the field. The Lieutenant Governor's Award for Literary Excellence came into being in 2003. Awarded as one of the BC Book Prizes, which had been established in 1985, this new award recognizes an individual who has "written a substantial body of literary work throughout their career" and made a significant contribution to the province's literary community. Government House hosts the deliberation by the judges and, every second or third year, the awards ceremony itself. The first award was given in 2004 and the recipient was poet and writer P.K. Page; subsequent winners during Campagnolo's term included Robert Bringhurst, who wrote a study of Bill Reid's sculptures and works on Haida oral history, and Jack Hodgins, an instructor and author of numerous works of fiction set on Vancouver Island.

The other award, the Lieutenant Governor's Awards for Excellence in British Columbia Wines, is given to ten excellent BC wines per year through the BC Wine Institute. Wineries submit sample bottles—one year there were 428 different wines submitted—and these are assessed blind by a panel of judges at Government House. The prizes are usually split between repeat winners and new winners. The Lieutenant Governor then travels to the various wineries to present the awards accompanied by "a bus load of . . . aides-de-camp, staff and consuls general"; the press attend as well. "And the wine cellar at Government House has improved dramatically," LeRoy notes.[340] Even as the Lieutenant Governors who followed Campagnolo have started their own far-reaching legacy projects, they have continued to sponsor the wine and book awards. (Although Steven Point does not drink alcohol himself, he toured the Okanagan to hand out the wine awards and recognize the work of wineries in producing fine-quality products.)

After completing her term on October 1, 2007, Iona Campagnolo moved back to the Comox Valley where she continues to support Indigenous rights and reconciliation, and environmental issues such as salmon sustainability. She also serves as a representative of the Comox Valley Justice Centre, which is dedicated to restorative justice.

Steven Lewis Point, Xwĕ lī qwĕl tĕl (2007–12)

Steven Lewis Point, who was born on July 28, 1951, is a member of the Skowkale First Nation. From his mother's brother, Peter Bolan, he received the hereditary name of Xwĕ lī qwĕl tĕl, which means Speaker of the House. Point's parents, Rena and Roy Edgar Point, had married relatively young, their match decided by the elders. Roy Point had been adopted by his grandmother and her husband, Dan Milo, and they offered the young couple their house and farm as their inheritance. For much of their marriage, Roy worked at logging camps along the Fraser River, at Harrison Lake and on Mount Baker in Washington State while Rena worked on the farm and raised their ten children. She also took in sixteen foster children whom the province asked her to care for. All of the children had specific chores around the farm; Steven's job was to take care of the chickens.

Rena, having been taught the traditional Stó:lō knowledge and skills by her own grandparents, passed this knowledge on to Steven and her other children as she wanted them to grow up understanding their responsibility toward others. She told them how the Stó:lō people had always governed themselves and protected their communities along the river. This training became vital to Steven when there was a riot at his high school in Sardis. As vice-president of the student council, he spoke to the students over the PA system, then went out and reasoned with them and managed to stop the riot. Proud of her son's efforts as a mediator, Rena later observed:

> No one told him this was his duty, but he had an inner, a built-in feeling that, if he could do something to help, then he just had to do it . . . This is the kind of feeling that most of my children have. If they feel they can help someone, anywhere, they do so. It doesn't matter if it is giving food or clothing or listening to hard-time stories or family problems—they're involved in all kinds of things like this.[341]

After Steven Point graduated from high school in 1969, he

went to Vancouver to study at the University of British Columbia. He attended UBC for two years before deciding to return to Chilliwack, but his mother was already convinced that he should consider a career in the law, and she arranged for Andy Thomas, a Chilliwack lawyer, to pick up her son from Vancouver. Thomas took Point to meet a household of hippie law students and gave him a biography of lawyer Clarence Darrow before dropping him off at home.

In Chilliwack, Point married Gwendolyn Rose Felix (Shoysh qwel whet), a member of the Chehalis First Nation, and the couple began their family, which would grow to include four children. Like his father, Steven worked as a logger to support his family, starting out at eighteen on a logging show at Harrison Lake as a rig slinger, hook tender and bucker. He valued his woods experience: "What logging does for you—and I wish this happened more for young men nowadays—is that it teaches you how to work. And it teaches you to appreciate the dollar you make."[342] At the age of twenty-three, he was elected chief by the Skowkale First Nation, and he held this position, with some interruptions, for the next fifteen years; he also served on the executive of the Union of BC Indian Chiefs (UBCIC).

By the 1970s the federal government was negotiating with the provinces over constitutional change, redefining federal and provincial powers and adding a charter of rights to the Constitution as part of a plan to patriate the Constitution from Great Britain and bring it under Canadian control. But Indigenous organizations across Canada were becoming concerned about the effects of patriation on their rights. Those who had signed treaties had done so with the Crown, and those who had not signed treaties—which included most of the First Nations in British Columbia—wanted to protect their rights and titles that were not yet extinguished. Point observed that, when Trudeau wanted "to bring the constitution home . . . Indians said, 'Well, wait a minute, we have a relationship with the Crown, and not with the Canadian government. What about that relationship?'" In 1980–81, George Manuel, a member of the Neskonlith Band, president of the Union of British Columbia Indian Chiefs (UBCIC) and president of the World Council of Indigenous Peoples, led a movement known as the Constitution Express. Activists chartered trains from Vancouver to Ottawa to raise concerns about the impact of the proposed Canadian Constitution on Aboriginal rights. Point noted, "Elders from our own reserve went on the train to argue that we still have a relationship to the Crown, to the Queen."[343] Due to the attention this group raised internationally, the federal government included Section 35 in the Canadian Constitution to recognize Aboriginal rights.

When Steven Point read the Darrow biography given to him by Andy Thomas, he had been inspired by Darrow's efforts to use legal means to improve the lives of children working in coal mines, and this led him to reconsider what he was doing with his own life. One day while looking out over the Chilliwack Valley, it occurred to him that he didn't "have to be doing this for the rest of my life, working in the logging industry. I could actually go back to school and become a lawyer."[344] He knew that a firm grounding in Canadian law would help him in his role as chief and in his work with the Union of BC Indian Chiefs, and he turned for advice to Louise Mandell and Leslie Pinder, two lawyers who were working for UBCIC at the time.

When Point started his law degree at UBC in 1982 he was thirty-one years old. He and Gwen moved into a basement suite in Vancouver with their two children. She was pregnant with their third child at the time. When it became impossible for them to cover their expenses in the city, he stayed on while the family moved back to Chilliwack. While completing his degree, he worked as a researcher for the Union of BC Indian Chiefs, helping to draft George Manuel's speeches, writing up meeting minutes and helping people find documents from Indian Affairs and information in the McKenna-McBride Commission Report. But he also did whatever was needed to make the office run smoothly: "If you had to make photocopies, you made photocopies; if you had to make coffee, you made coffee; if you had to drive stuff all the way up to Kamloops, you did that."[345]

He completed his law degree at UBC in 1985 and articled with the law firm of Mandell Pinder. For Point, working with them was "a great learning experience." Louise Mandell had grown up in a middle-class Jewish family in Toronto, completed a law degree at UBC in the 1970s and was specializing in Aboriginal law. She remembers Point as showing "great curiosity as to how to approach the land question through the vehicle of the law."[346] At Point's call (to the bar) ceremony in 1986,

his community [had] presented him with a gift of a suit, which he wore proudly. Thus began a legal career which, from roots formed in Stó:lō and Canadian legal tradition, reflects an abiding sense of justice and humanity.[347]

After being called to the bar, Point returned to Chilliwack to found a law firm with Karen Pruden Shirley. A Métis woman who had grown up in Winnipeg, Pruden Shirley had also studied law at UBC. When they opened their law practice they did not have much capital but received help from the local Stó:lō community, and Point recalls:

> We didn't have any furniture, we didn't even have a way of painting the building. So the court–workers arrived, and they painted it, and the Indian bands got together, and they bought us desks and chairs for the front and plants, things like that. So, we got a little bit, borrowed a little bit of money from the bank . . . hired a secretary, and we started working.[348]

Their practice was not very lucrative, but they soon built a solid base of clients. In fact, a lawyer from Abbotsford complained to Point that he was losing his Indigenous clients, who told him: "We don't need you anymore, we've got our own lawyer now, Steve Point."[349] Point was the first lawyer from the Stó:lō Nation, and he inspired trust and respect among his people. After three years Point left the firm to work for the Department of Employment and Immigration in Vancouver as a refugee adjudicator; after a year in this post he shifted his energies to teaching law and advising on Aboriginal rights cases. From 1991 to 1994 he was director of the Native Law program at UBC, and he also taught Native Law at the University of Saskatchewan and a course on Stó:lō values at the University College of the Fraser Valley.

During these years Point provided advice on several landmark cases involving Aboriginal rights and title. In particular, he was "passionate and clear about identifying fishing rights as essential to the continuation of the elaborate cultures and economies of the coastal and river First Nations of British Columbia."[350] One of the cases on which he worked was R. v. Sparrow (1990), a case that had originated in 1984 when Ronald Sparrow, a member of the Musqueam Indian Band, was arrested for fishing with a net longer than allowed by the limitations of his food fishing licence. Government regulations at that time stated that Indigenous people only had the right to fish for their food, not to fish for sale, despite the pre-contact importance of their fishery for both consumption and trade. Sparrow was found guilty at the provincial level, but the Musqueam appealed and the Supreme Court of Canada ruled that Sparrow had a right to fish because his right had not been extinguished by treaty before the 1982 Constitution.

Point also worked with Louise Mandell on the case of Dorothy Van der Peet, a member of the Stó:lō Nation, who was charged with selling ten fish illegally in Chilliwack. Like Sparrow, her licence as an Aboriginal person only allowed her to fish for sustenance or ceremonial purposes, not for sale. She argued that Section 35 of the Constitution Act protected her right to sell fish, and Point provided legal aid for the initial case, which was tried in the Surrey courthouse. Every day an elder would pick up Van der Peet and Point and drive them to Surrey. Point cross-examined all the witnesses, gathering all the information they thought would be pertinent, after which "Louise took it over up to County Court and up, all the way to the Supreme Court of Canada."[351] Although the Supreme Court ruled that selling fish was not an Aboriginal right, this case took the argument a step further than the Sparrow ruling in developing criteria for determining Aboriginal rights based on the particular Aboriginal group that was claiming that right. However, the ruling was criticized for portraying Aboriginal rights as static and unchanging, rooted in a particular pre-contact period, and for overlooking the important trade in fish that had taken place along the Fraser River.

Point played a role as well in the Delgamuukw case (1997) by representing the UBCIC when it supported the Gitxsan and Wet'suwet'en in the BC Court of Appeal. As Point recalled, the law office of Mandell Pinder and law professor Michael Jackson requested his assistance on this case as they sometimes did when they had a heavy case load, and Point worked into the early hours of the morning with Jackson, Mandell and Rini Taylor to compose a *factum* to submit to the court. Often the court would simply read the *factum*, but since the UBCIC was raising the issue of sovereignty, they asked Point to present their case to the Court of Appeal. (Point kept the *factum* "just as a souvenir.") Like the cases involving Sparrow and Van der Peet, the Delgamuukw case also went to the Supreme Court of Canada, which accepted oral evidence as proof and held that Aboriginal title, an ancestral right to use and occupy the land, was protected by Section 35 of the Constitution Act. As the BC Treaty Commission explains, this case created a new reality for treaty negotiations:

> The decision confirmed aboriginal title does exist in British Columbia, that it's a right to the land itself—not just the right to hunt, fish or gather—and that when dealing with Crown land, the government must consult with and may have to compensate First Nations whose rights are affected.[352]

During the years that Steven Point was establishing his law career, Gwen Point was developing a career in Indigenous education. She completed a bachelor of education at the University of British Columbia in 1987 through the Indigenous Teacher Education Program and earned a master's of education at the University of Portland in 1998. She worked as a regional coordinator in the Aboriginal Services Branch of the Ministry of Education, Skills and Training from 1997 to 2000 and as manager of the Stó:lō Nation Education Department where her responsibilities included Indigenous culture and language programs. In 2001 she became the Aboriginal Curriculum Coordinator for the University College of the Fraser Valley and four years later was appointed assistant professor, teaching First Nations Studies in the School of Social Work; her courses included Stó:lō Communications and World View and Stó:lō Nation Development. Gwen Point particularly valued her teaching experiences, as she said:

> My grandmother told me that what you know has no value. It's like sand in your hand unless you pass it on to others. I know that teaching the community about the Stó:lō people has made a difference, and I really believe that it is an act of reconciliation. It is helping to create a better understanding of recent history. Every class I would see a shift and transformation in the students.[353]

In addition to serving as chief of the Skowkale Nation and working as a lawyer, in the 1990s Steven Point took on additional positions of leadership and responsibility. In 1997 the nineteen chiefs of the Stó:lō Nation elected him to act as their representative in treaty negotiations. Two years later he accepted an appointment to the provincial court bench, inspired in part by Alfred Scow, the first Indigenous judge in BC. Before 1951, as a way to stall the land-claims process, the Indian Act had barred Indigenous people from hiring lawyers and forced Indigenous people who wished to practice law or other professions to give up their Indian status. This part of the Indian Act was repealed in 1951, allowing Scow—who graduated a decade later—to receive his law degree while maintaining his status. In 1971 he became the first Indigenous person to be appointed a BC provincial court judge, subtly changing the composition of the legal profession and paving the way for other Indigenous people to become lawyers and judges. This was especially important, Point notes, since Indigenous people are over-represented as defendants and prisoners but under-represented in the legal profession. Reflecting on his own role as a judge, he commented that his presence in the justice system could be a subtle force to challenge racism and promote reconciliation:

> What I found out from talking to people such as Aboriginal constables in the Royal Canadian Mounted Police is that change occurred not because they pointed out problems in the system and complained, but simply because they were there. In just the same way, my becoming a judge—just being there—and my background as being chief of my community and speaking on behalf of my community will make a difference.[354]

In 2000, Point's contributions to Canadian law and Indigenous rights were recognized by an honorary Doctorate of Laws degree from the University of the Fraser Valley and a National Aboriginal Achievement Award.

In 2005 Steven Point was invited to become chief commissioner of the British Columbia Treaty Commission, the independent organization that since 1992 has facilitated and overseen the negotiation of treaties in BC between Canada, BC and First Nations. In this new role, as Mandell wrote, he "worked hard to achieve a respectful and honourable reconciliation," dealing with "many of the same old problems in Aboriginal/Crown relations for which no solutions had yet been found."[355] At the same time, the Stó:lō people expressed their continued confidence in Point's leadership by appointing him grand chief.

In 2007 Prime Minister Stephen Harper invited Steven Point to become the Lieutenant Governor of BC. He was surprised by the invitation, and like some others before him, he was initially unsure about accepting; then, as he and Gwen learned more about the position and what was involved, he became even less enthusiastic. He explains that "Canada has not had altogether that positive a relationship with First Nations." Having fought for Indigenous rights for most of his legal career, often in opposition to provincial or federal governments, he decided "it probably wouldn't be a very good idea for me to be representing the Crown. I thought Indian people wouldn't be happy with it either."[356] Gwen Point, however, suggested that it might be good for First Nations generally if an Indigenous person held this respected position. Point's mother, Rena, agreed that if he became Lieutenant Governor, it would be "good for the

Having fought for Indigenous rights throughout his career, Steven Lewis Point, Xwĕ lī qwĕl tĕl, was hesitant to accept a position representing the Crown. His wife, Gwen Point, and mother, Rena Point Bolton, encouraged him with the argument that he could make a positive difference for Indigenous people in BC by holding this respected position.
Image courtesy of Government House of British Columbia Archives.

esteem of our people. We have been invisible for too long. There will be those, a few people, who have negative things to say, but that you find everywhere and in everything."[357]

When Steven Lewis Point began his term as Lieutenant Governor of British Columbia on October 1, 2007, he had already established his priorities and the legacies he wanted to leave, and high on his list were promoting literacy and self-confident, capable youth. Literacy was important to Point partly because of what he had observed as a provincial court judge:

> There's a real correlation between children who are having difficulty in school, who don't do well in school, who end up dropping out of school, who end up getting into trouble. The key, I think, is to help communities realize the value of literacy, the value of a good education. If we can find ways of impressing upon them that literacy is a good thing, then it might help them to stay the course, stay in school.[358]

To promote literacy, he supported the provision of books to First Nations communities in BC because, based on his personal experience, he knew that "a book is a fork in the road. It's a turning place. It's got the power to create a different future."[359] At the time, less than a third of First Nations communities in Canada had a local library, but Point was intrigued to hear that the Lieutenant Governor of Ontario, James Bartleman, was delivering books to isolated communities. He mentioned this fact to his aide-de-camp Bob Blacker, who happened to be a member of the Rotary Club, an organization known for delivering books to foreign countries. When Point asked him whether Rotary ever sent books to Canadian communities, the answer was no, but Blacker arranged for Point to be invited to speak to the Rotarians. They responded enthusiastically to the idea of delivering books to isolated BC communities, and Britco, a Langley company that had manufactured trailers for the 2010 Olympics, offered to donate a trailer that would house a library. The first library was opened in June 2011 by the Tl'esqox community near Williams Lake where the nearest library had been an hour's drive away, and previously the local children had the opportunity to visit it only once a week. The new library was set up in three days, and as Point comments, "That's the only air-conditioned building that community has on the whole reserve."[360]

That first library was such a success, with Rotarians and various companies continuing to make contributions and First Nations communities setting up the site and managing the libraries, that by 2018 the Write to Read Project had built libraries in seventeen BC First Nations communities. Point sees these libraries as a means of bridge building and reconciliation between Indigenous and non-Indigenous communities: "It's connecting these folks, breaking down barriers that should never have been there. And they're coming out to the communities for the first time, saying, 'We want to help.'"[361]

Point also promoted youth literacy through the "Write Me a Story" Program. He began by hiring an illustrator to draw an Indigenous child named Kaia dressed in a Cowichan sweater who is involved in various activities such as fishing or working on a school project. The idea was to invite children to write stories about Kaia, but not knowing how the children would respond, he did a test run with one school in Abbotsford, and it was a runaway success:

> Well, it turns out the teachers just loved this because teachers are constantly trying to think of ways of encouraging the kids to write, to keep them occupied with something interesting and that captures their imagination. So all of a sudden, I started getting envelopes full of stories about Kaia.[362]

The project branched out to other schools, and Point received hundreds—if not thousands—of stories from schools across the province. He read many of them, autographed all of them and returned them to the writers with a small gift of a pencil or a sticker. Whenever possible, he would deliver them to the school himself.

Point also promoted youth development by sponsoring his own Aboriginal cadet corps. As an honorary captain in the navy and himself a former cadet, he became interested when in 2009 Lieutenant (Ret'd) Allan Waddy, the past president of the Cowichan Branch 53 Royal Canadian Legion, told him of helping to establish the first such corps on Christian Island in Ontario in 1981. As, historically, Indigenous youth had been trained in self-defence and, even as teenagers, were expected to be able to survive on their own, Point thought that an organization of this kind was a good fit. He remembered Indigenous youth from his own area of Chilliwack who had joined cadets and experienced a transformation, gaining self-confidence and self-discipline, and although he acknowledges that a cadet program is "not the only avenue . . . you can take to change your life," it can be a good thing for Indigenous youth, especially those whose families experienced poverty and low self-esteem related to multiple generations having attended residential schools. He took the cadet corps idea to the chief of the Cowichan Tribes, suggesting that it might be an organization that would benefit the youth in that community, and the result of that conversation was the formation of an all-Aboriginal cadet corps in Duncan, only the second one in Canada. In March 2011 when he went to the Cowichan Valley to inspect the new cadet corps, known as the Army Cadet Corps 2924 Kowutzun, he told them, "I'm proud of you. You're making history in the Cowichan Valley . . . I expect you to be ambassadors for me. You are my corps."[363]

Point actively promoted reconciliation through his own artistic endeavours as well, carving two canoes while at Government House. The idea for the first came to him when he found a log on the beach that was pointed on both ends, and he carved it on his own time and gave it as a gift to the province. His second project was an ocean-going canoe, a remake of one that had been created for his father's memorial, and he painted it and gave it to the navy. As a legacy to Government House, he had a bandshell constructed for musical events on the grounds, and with Chief Tony Hunt he carved a storyboard for the bandshell retelling a legend told to him by his great-grandfather about the return of the Salmon People to the Fraser River. He even wrote a song, called "British Columbia," which he gave to the province at the end of his term. In 2012 to celebrate the Queen's Diamond Jubilee, Point and the Government House Foundation also commissioned Chief Hunt to carve the *Hosaqami* totem pole, a replica of a pole the Royal Canadian Navy had commissioned Chief Hunt's adopted grandfather, Chief Mungo Martin, to carve in 1959 for presentation to the Royal Navy.

One of the most memorable royal visits to Government House during Steven Point's tenure was that of the Emperor Akihito and the Empress Michiko of Japan in July 2009. It was the emperor's second visit to Government House; in 1953 while travelling to London for the coronation of Queen Elizabeth, he had been the guest of Clarence Wallace. This visit fifty-six years later was a "sentimental journey" marking twenty years since his ascension to the throne and fifty years of marriage to the empress. The emperor, himself a marine biologist, was interested to learn about the trees surrounding Government House, so Point's private secretary, Herbert LeRoy, arranged for his son, a forester, to give him a tour, focusing on dendrology. The empress, an accomplished pianist, "came down on her own to play on the grand piano in the house," LeRoy recalled. "They were very much at home. Very [friendly] people, and they liked to interact with the staff."[364]

Point is a compelling speaker, and he approached the formal speech-making of the Lieutenant Governor's position with a deep knowledge of British Columbia's complex and at times messy past. Dr. Eric Charman, a philanthropist and trustee of the Government House Foundation, "was always impressed with his very touching speeches, speeches that were softly and gently delivered without any written notes."[365] LeRoy confirms that rather than writing speeches in advance, Point would speak from the heart: "He would speak like

Emperor Akihito of Japan (left) and Empress Michiko (not pictured), visited Steven (centre) and Gwen Point (right) in Victoria in July 2009. This was a "sentimental journey" for the emperor since he had stayed at the previous Government House in 1953 on his way to the coronation of Queen Elizabeth.
Image courtesy of Government House of British Columbia Archives.

he didn't know what he was going to say!" Normally, according to LeRoy, all of the Lieutenant Governor's speeches are scripted, and "all the bureaucrats know what's going to happen next." When Point spoke off-script, this made the bureaucrats a bit nervous. Occasionally, Point would subvert protocol entirely, telling LeRoy that he was planning a surprise. This might involve showing up to an event with a drum or "spontaneously getting people in the ballroom to form two large circles, go counter clockwise," and introduce themselves. On one occasion when Prince Charles visited, Point appeared in a headdress and holding a talking stick, which he presented to the prince with a long, unscripted speech. Despite the consternation of the bureaucrats, the prince was "very touched" by the speech.[366]

Steven Point was only sixty-one when he completed his term as Lieutenant Governor on November 2, 2012. Having given up his position on the provincial court bench in 2007 to serve as Lieutenant Governor, he was happy to be re-appointed as a judge in 2014 and accept a position at the courthouse in Abbotsford. He received an honorary Doctorate of Laws degree from the University of Victoria in 2012 and Capilano University in 2017, and an honorary Doctorate of Sacred Letters from St. Mark's College in 2013.

In 2014 after serving for five years as the chatelaine of Government House, Gwen Point was appointed chancellor of the University of the Fraser Valley. The next year she defended her doctoral dissertation at Simon Fraser University, entitled "Intergenerational experiences in aboriginal education: my family story."

The appointment of an Indigenous Lieutenant Governor had been long overdue in BC, but when it came, it signalled a commitment to reconciliation. Since Point had spent much of his career challenging the provincial and federal governments to recognize Aboriginal rights and title, accepting this position had provided him with a fresh way to build bridges between Indigenous and non-Indigenous communities in BC, raise awareness of this province's complex history and promote reconciliation in his own soft-spoken, yet powerful way.

Judith Guichon (2012–18)

Judith Guichon was born Judith Isabel Rea in Montreal in 1947, the youngest of six children. When she was ten years old, her parents, in anticipation of their retirement, bought a farm on the outskirts of Hawkesbury, a city about halfway between Montreal and Ottawa, on the banks of the Ottawa River, and from then on, she spent her weekends and summers there. "I had the best of both worlds," she recalls, "the Montreal Canadiens and the Montreal Symphony during the week, and the cows on the weekend."[367] When her father retired, her parents moved to Hawkesbury year-round, but Judith stayed in Montreal, where for three years she ran a clinic at the Montreal Children's Hospital for children with epilepsy. Then in 1967, wanting to avoid the crowds who would come to Expo, she spent the summer travelling in Europe.

Two years later Rea and two girlfriends took a trip across Canada in their Austin Cambridge, and she recalls they "saw a lot of it through the floorboards of the old car." They stopped to visit relatives along the way—Rea had a sister in Winnipeg and a brother and sister on the West Coast. The trip took them to Vancouver, across to Vancouver Island, then north to the Alaska Highway, which was not yet paved. Their journey of "5,500 miles [8,800 km] without a flat tire" culminated in Whitehorse. "It was wonderful—Whitehorse was a vibrant community—the whole Yukon was still very young, very friendly." But while Whitehorse had many attractions, living expenses were high, and to make ends meet, Rea waitressed, worked at the Bank of Montreal and for the White Pass and Yukon Railway.

All three of the young women from Montreal married men they met in the Yukon. Rea's future husband, Lawrence Guichon, the eldest son of Gerard and Ruth Guichon, ranchers in BC's Nicola Valley, was working in the north as a commercial pilot "doing caribou studies for the first pipeline . . . Up in the Old Crow area and all through the Yukon [with its] beautiful ridges and mountains." They were married in Hawkesbury in 1971, and she took her husband's name. The couple returned to the Yukon and spent their first Christmas together in Inuvik where Lawrence was posted for work. They harvested a miniature Christmas tree, stunted by permafrost, and decorated it with bottle caps.

The Guichons soon returned to Whitehorse, where one morning Lawrence asked, "What do you think about going back to the ranch?" Having grown up around cows, she thought this was a great idea, and in January 1972 they set off for Skagway with another couple, "our dog, their cat," and two pickups "with all our belongings," then took the ferry from Skagway to Prince Rupert. It was a winter of very heavy snows, and when the Guichons finally arrived at the Beaver Ranch in the Nicola Valley, they were met with what Judith Guichon describes as

> the biggest snow year I've ever seen . . . we had our big dog, and she could sit on the snowbank and look in the windows of the big house. And that spring we got stuck everywhere. It was wonderful. Water filled up the water holes. I don't think we've had that kind of snow since.

Lawrence Guichon was descended from a long line of ranchers, starting with his great-grandfather, Joseph Guichon, who was born in Chambéry, France, in 1843. Joseph had arrived in the Cariboo goldfields in March 1864 to join his three older brothers and had at first tried his hand at mining, but like many other would-be miners, he soon realized that provisioning miners and settlers would provide more reliable employment. He began working at ranches in the Ashcroft area, including one owned by a future Lieutenant Governor, Clement Francis Cornwall, then got a job with the legendary packer Jean Caux. In 1868 Joseph Guichon, his brother Laurent and other francophones began developing farms near Mamit Lake. Joseph married Josephine Rey in 1878, and Laurent married Josephine's sister. By 1882 Joseph had established a ranch east of Nicola Lake, the Guichon Cattle Company, which sold beef to CPR construction crews and residents of the growing railway town of Kamloops. They imported the first Hereford cows to the area and built the Quilchena Hotel. When Joseph Guichon died in 1921, the company owned 40,000 acres (16,000 ha) of "deeded land" and held grazing leases on over 500,000 acres (200,000 ha) of Crown land.

Joseph Guichon's eldest son, Lawrence Peter (1879–1963), was instrumental in establishing ranching networks and solving problems related to insects and disease. In 1914 he became one of the founders of the Nicola Stock Breeders' Association, and four years later he joined other ranchers to start the Provincial Bull Sale in Kamloops. In the 1920s Lawrence Peter Guichon and Frank Ward of the Douglas Lake Cattle Company, following the advice of Dominion entomologists, were at the forefront of efforts to minimize a grasshopper invasion. When *brucellosis*, a disease causing cows to abort their calves, hit the province in the 1940s, the Guichons worked with chief veterinarian Dr. Wallace Gunn to establish the Nicola Valley as a disease-free area. In 1953 Lawrence Peter Guichon was awarded an honorary doctorate of science from UBC for his use of "new machinery in agriculture and restoring the sensitive environment of the Nicola Valley grasslands, which had fallen victim to overgrazing."[368]

When Judith and Lawrence arrived at the ranch in the winter of 1972, it was operated by Lawrence's parents, Ruth and Gerard Guichon. The original company had been divided in 1957 between two of Joseph Guichon's grandsons, Guy Rose and Gerard Guichon. The elder Guichons soon set to work teaching the young couple how to run the ranch. The efforts of Lawrence Peter Guichon's son, Gerard, to solve problems faced by Nicola Valley ranchers had extended his influence beyond the region, and that same year Gerard was inducted into the Order of Canada "for his leading role in provincial and national cattle organizations by pursuing changes in national agricultural policy."[369]

The Guichons were among the first ranchers in the area to adopt holistic management, a ranching philosophy developed in Zimbabwe by Allan Savory and his wife, Jody Butterfield. In 1984, after they moved to the United States, they established the Center for Holistic Management, and although radical at the time, their use of grazing animals to restore healthy environments (rather than blaming desertification on overgrazing) have since influenced thousands of ranchers and farmers and received international acclaim. After hearing about this method at a conference of the Alberta Stockgrowers in 1985, Gerard persuaded Lawrence and Judith to attend a week-long course on holistic management directed by Savory and two other instructors.

For the Guichon family, the course "changed how we did everything" because holistic management involved setting long-term goals that considered factors beyond the production of beef such as "quality of life, your forms of production, and the future landscape."[370] The family had already implemented a long-term approach to grasslands management, and now they were inspired to organize courses for other ranchers in the Nicola Valley. They sought the advice of biologists from the Ministry of Environment to help them maintain a healthy habitat for a variety of native species, helped found Holistic Management Canada, and Lawrence became a board member of the international organization based in New Mexico. Since, in addition to planning for the health of the whole landscape, holistic management involves a round-table approach to decision-making, the Guichons brought in educators to teach the consensus model locally. Residents of the Nicola Valley still gather for round table meetings and use this non-confrontational approach to make decisions on such important issues as changes to electoral boundaries or the spreading of bio-solids.

The semi-desert conditions of the Nicola Valley are a challenge to ranchers. There is "little biological breakdown of woody debris and plants. It's chemical breakdown instead, so it's very much harder to enrich your soils as a result." When the Guichons put in the highest bid for a visit from Allan Savory at a fundraising auction, they "invited a whole lot of people and went out on the land with Allan." It had been customary in the region to graze cattle extensively "over large areas over a longer time." Drawing on holistic management practices, the Guichon ranch shifted to more intensive grazing, "having cattle on a smaller area for a short time." Confining cattle to smaller areas resulted in a greater concentration of manure. This attracted a higher number of dung beetles that broke down the manure, and drew bird flocks that fed on the insects; as Guichon explains, "you just get a whole lot of bacterial and biological processes going on as a result."[371] The cattle are herded elsewhere, the manure breaks down, enriching the soil and reducing the carbon footprint, and the grasses grow back in fertile soil. Lawrence also designed a bale miser to increase the efficiency of feeding the cattle. The Guichons patented and produced the bale miser, and Judith demonstrated it at trade shows as far away as Saskatoon. Although the bale misers did not catch on with a broad market, several neighbours still use them.

After the family discovered that it was better for the local ecology to have the cattle grazing on grasslands, the ranch stopped plowing and growing hay. When they need hay, they bring it in. This deposits more nutrients into the soil in the long run, rather than simply exporting nutrients through the cattle. To minimize their use of hay and cut the dollar and fuel cost of hauling it in, they chop it up, which makes it more easily digestible and gives the cattle twice the amount of nutrition from the same amount of hay. Recently, instead of sending their cattle to a packing plant in Alberta, the ranch sold its yearlings to a company in Ashcroft, BC, that will process the meat for retail consumption within the province. When schoolchildren visit the ranch, Judith Guichon tells them, "We're in the business of harvesting sunshine. We use grass, and the cattle are our tools to harvest it and turn it into a product for human consumption."[372]

Raising cattle in semi-arid conditions has sometimes meant trucking water to them, so the Guichon family has long had a special interest in water conservation, and it became an important topic of conversation for the community round table: "We developed what we call WUMP—a water use management plan." Thus, when the January 1977 throne speech announced that the new Social Credit government intended to build a highway from Merritt to Hope through the Coquihalla Pass, ranchers started to become concerned about traffic and water quality. After the first section of the Coquihalla was completed in 1986, it was announced that the Ministry of Transportation and Highways was considering a four-lane connector from Merritt to Kamloops, right through the centre of the Nicola Valley, which would seriously compromise the viability of the ranching industry. Lawrence Guichon played a significant role in redirecting that stretch of highway by flying government officials and engineers along the route the highway would eventually follow. As a result, instead of running through the middle of the range, the Coquihalla runs along the periphery. Meanwhile, the Nicola group continued with their water use plan, using grant money to have studies completed, and submitted a water use proposal to the Ministry of Environment in the hope that their recommendations would be incorporated into an amended Water Act.

Growing up in large families, Judith and Lawrence looked forward to having "at least half a dozen children to run wild on the ranch." When they realized that they could not have children biologically, they applied to adopt. "We'd always wanted a large family and we had plenty of resources and wide open spaces to offer," she explained. "It's impossible to describe the joy and happiness that filled our hearts as we went to the office and met our ten-day-old daughter, Allison. She was and still is perfect in every way." When Allison was almost four, they adopted an infant son, Michael. Two other children joined the family in 1989, a sister and brother aged five and three. As Lieutenant Governor, Guichon drew on her personal experience to speak in support of Adoption Awareness Month in November 2014:

> The adoption process is necessarily long and somewhat cumbersome. We will never be able to make it perfect because we are dealing with humans and all their eccentricities, but the families that it creates, with all their bumps and warts, are the wonderful reward for perseverance. Families today come in all shapes and variations. This is part of our beautiful and growing diversity.[373]

Judith Guichon's environmental concerns extended beyond the conservation of grasslands and water resources to waste reduction, and in the mid-1990s she and a neighbour, veterinarian Jean Lauder, decided that Merritt and the surrounding region should have a recycling service, so they created one. After enlisting other friends and neighbours, the two women went into the schools and put on a skit to educate the children about garbage-free lunches. Guichon recalls that, though the skit greatly embarrassed her own children, it taught local families about the value of reducing waste and recycling, and many parents phoned to ask for more details. About five times a year the group set up a recycling station in town where they collected glass, cardboard, paper and tin cans. They bought a machine to bale cardboard and newspaper and stored it in an old trailer until they could transport it to a market, and they smashed the glass in barrels and delivered it to a buyer in Lumby, BC. This first attempt at recycling in Merritt eventually failed because neighbours of the community centre, where the group smashed the glass, complained about the noise.

The 4-H clubs in Merritt had lapsed in the early 1990s, so Guichon, who had belonged to the 4-H Club in Hawkesbury and raised her own Jersey calf, joined with friends to start a new 4-H club for their own children and children from the nearby Indigenous community The club was primarily focused on raising steers, and activities included a summer camp, leadership classes, public speaking and first aid, with up to forty young members participating in the Pacific Winter Fair in Kamloops. The club ceased operation in 2006, but when Guichon's daughter Allison found herself driving her own daughter all the way to Kamloops for 4-H meetings, she got together with other local parents to start a new club in Merritt, offering young people a chance to develop their skills in raising horses, lambs and chickens, and in public speaking, photography and sewing.

In July 1999 Lawrence Guichon died in a motorcycle accident not far from the ranch. At the time their children were twenty, sixteen, fifteen and thirteen. In the aftermath Judith Guichon said, "For a short time after the accident we were in survival mode. To say that I would not have endured without my children is not overstating the case. The love of my children enabled me to carry on."[374] She continued with the commitments she and her husband had made before his death, acting as a director of the Grasslands Conservation Council of BC and of the Fraser Basin Council of BC. Her advice and experience has also been valuable as a member of the Provincial Task Force on Species at Risk, the Ranching Task Force for BC and the British Columbia Agri-Food Trade Advisory Council. And just before becoming Lieutenant Governor, she served as president of the British Columbia Cattlemen's Association.

The invitation to become Lieutenant Governor came out of the blue, and at first she could not believe that the offer was serious, but it came at an ideal time for her and her family. She had just decided to retire from running the ranch and had helped draft a new management agreement with her two eldest children, but she was unsure how to ease out of her role there. "So when I got the phone call," Guichon says, "I thought this is the best retirement plan I never had." The invitation to become vice-regal representative was confidential until it was formally announced, but Guichon sought the advice of a neighbour who had served as chief of his First Nations community and who worked on the ranch. She asked him, "Can I do anything beneficial?" and he said, "Yes, you can. You can use it to create some positive change." She adds, "So that's why I took it on."[375]

On November 2, 2012, Guichon began her term as Lieutenant Governor supported by her second husband, Bruno Mailloux, an invasive plant specialist. From the beginning of her term one of Guichon's primary goals was to foster and strengthen urban-rural connections in the province. "I think there's a vast and growing disconnect between urban and rural," she explained. "There's very little understanding of where the resources and the wealth come from in order to generate that activity that takes place in Vancouver and Victoria."[376] To improve on this understanding, she set out to visit every valley in the province and was struck by the creativity and ingenuity with which communities confront economic challenges. For example, in Stewart, BC, she was a guest at the September 2015 opening of the $70-million Stewart World Port developed by Ted Pickell of Fort St. John. With the decline of logging and mining activities, the town's population had fallen from two thousand in the early 1990s to just under five hundred residents, but this new facility in Stewart's deep, ice-free harbour would allow shippers from Asia to reduce shipping time by a day and a half in comparison with more southerly ports. With this advantage, the mayor was looking forward to the new port increasing revenue and attracting other industries.

Guichon was also inspired by Tumbler Ridge in the foothills of the Rockies, which was incorporated in 1981 as a company town

Judith Guichon, Lieutenant Governor from 2012 to 2018, took part in the Truth and Reconciliation Commission's BC Reconciliation Week Opening Ceremonies in September 2013. Here, she is pictured with Clément Chartier (left), president of the Métis National Council, and Shawn Atleo, national chief of the Assembly of First Nations.

Image courtesy of Government House of British Columbia.

to house workers at nearby coal mines. With only one mine still operating, the town turned to promoting outdoor recreation and its proximity to Monkman Provincial Park and Kinuseo Falls, a little-known, 60-metre (200-ft) cascade that is higher than Niagara Falls. Then in 2000 two boys who were tubing down Flatbed Creek found depressions in the rock that looked like dinosaur tracks. A palae-ontologist confirmed that they were right, and since then Tumbler Ridge has yielded a rich and varied concentration of dinosaur bones from ankylosaurs, theropods, tyrannosaurs, hadrosaurs and ancient crocodiles, turtles and fish. In June 2015 Guichon attended the opening of the Tumbler Ridge Geopark, a site later designated as the second UNESCO Global Geopark in North America after Stonehammer in New Brunswick.

Guichon enjoyed the many forms of water travel involved in her role as Lieutenant Governor, and in a speech at the SS *Beaver* Medal Presentation, she commented that "this grand adventure has afforded me the opportunity to have a very different relationship with water in so many different vessels."[377] She had set off on her first sea voyage as Lieutenant Governor in April 2014, a four-day coastal tour on the naval vessel HMCS *Calgary*, making stops at Alert Bay, Sointula, Port Hardy, Rivers Inlet and Heriot Bay. Guichon was accompanied by aide-de-camp Bob Blacker, the Rotarian who had helped Steven Point initiate the "Write to Read" program by setting up libraries in remote First Nations communities, and at Rivers Inlet, they joined members of the Wuikinuxv (Oweekeeno) Nation to open a new library.

As part of her exploration of the West Coast she also travelled on the Coast Guard patrol vessel *Tanu*, went day-sailing on the *Oriole* and aboard Royal Canadian Search and Rescue vessels, but she ventured as well 100 metres (330 ft) below the surface of the ocean aboard HMCS *Victoria*, a submarine based in Esquimalt. Reflecting on this trip at a banquet commemorating the centennial of Cana-dian submarines, Guichon told her audience:

Two things amazed me about the operation on board HMCS *Victoria*. Firstly, the quiet, competent manner in which all the 57 or so crew members floated through their tasks in such tight confines without ever seeming to run into one another or be frustrated in any way by the restricted space. It reminded me of a well-rehearsed ballet. The second aspect that struck me was how peaceful and quiet it was down there in that glorious green environment. Certainly on that day in July, 105 metres [345 ft] below the Strait of Georgia, traffic was not an issue.[378]

Guichon also came to her vice-regal role with a commitment to involve young people in conversations about environmental sustainability because it is important that "we make very wise decisions, not just quick decisions." In 2015 she spread the word to schoolchildren and politicians alike about the International Year of Soils with the result that "most of the members of the legislature now know that . . . there are more living organisms in one tablespoon of soil than all the people on earth."[379]

As her legacy project, Guichon chose to create "Stewards of the Future," a project designed to involve high school students in "hands-on activities and real world learning experiences in their communities." The program provides funding, resources and support to "encourage open discussion and gain a better understanding of the issues that affect our natural surroundings."[380] Students participate in place-based, experiential projects that emphasize learning from local experts, giving students the opportunity to interview stakeholders, go on field trips, carry out in-depth research and discuss the results. The program provides funding for field trips, guest speakers and other activities, and students are invited to download a passport containing a list of activities such as attending a community meeting, volunteering with an environmental project, listening to a guest speaker discuss an environmental issue and sharing what they learned from the program. In June 2015 Guichon hosted the first annual "Stewards of the Future Conference" at Pearson College in Metchosin where student participants presented project reports, shared insights and listened to inspiring talks from speakers such as astronaut Dr. Robert Thirsk and J.B. MacKinnon, co-author of *The 100-Mile Diet*.[381] Subsequent conferences took place in 2016 at the University of Northern British Columbia in Prince George and in Gibsons on the Sunshine Coast in 2017.

Another priority program Guichon initiated was "Sing Me a Song." Having played the flute in the Nicola Valley Community Band, she appreciates the value of music in building community spirit, so she invited British Columbians of all ages to compose, record and submit a song that expressed what Canada's 150th anniversary meant to them. Entries were posted on the "Sing Me a Song" YouTube channel and a panel of judges awarded prizes annually based on originality, musicality and spirit.

Early on in her tenure, Guichon also expressed her commitment to engaging British Columbians in conversations about the constitutional monarchy, "a stabilizing factor in our democratic system."[382] When she visits schools, Guichon says, "I lecture the kids about getting involved, and about democracy—democracy is not an armchair sport, and we are very privileged to live in this country."[383] Inspired by a conference in Regina on the Canadian Crown that she attended before she was sworn in, she hosted a conference on "The Crown in the 21st Century" at Government House in January 2016. Scholars from various Commonwealth nations met there to discuss questions such as "To what extent does the Crown fulfil its prime role as a politically neutral institution symbolizing and guaranteeing democratic freedoms? Are the Crown's powers real or nebulous? Are they dwindling or increasing? How do the key players—monarch and vice-regal representatives—function today and how are they perceived?"[384] Conference presenters shared their findings on the role of the Crown in Canada, the United Kingdom, Australia and New Zealand. Former Lieutenant Governor Steven Point chaired a panel on "Indigenous People and the Honour of the Crown," exploring questions about this historically significant relationship and the degree to which the Crown has honoured Indigenous rights and title.

Royal visitors during Guichon's term also brought attention to youth and reconciliation as well as physical and mental health. Prince Andrew, Duke of York, visited Victoria in May 2013 to open the 150th Victoria Highland Games and present the Duke of Edinburgh Awards at Government House. On their trip to BC in September 2014, Prince Edward, Earl of Wessex, and Sophie, Countess of Wessex, flew by helicopter with Guichon to visit the Ditidaht First Nation, where they opened the ninth library organized through Steven Point's "Write to Read Project." In the fall of 2016, Guichon hosted the Duke and Duchess of Cambridge and their children, Prince George and Princess Charlotte, on their first West Coast visit, and an estimated crowd of 25,000 people greeted them at the Legislature. Their itinerary included meeting with refugees at the Immigrant Services Society in Vancouver, visiting the Heiltsuk First Nation and the Great Bear Rainforest, and in Victoria meeting with organizations promoting mental health.

Judith Guichon was in her fifth year as Lieutenant Governor when she was required to perform in the "fire extinguisher" aspect of her constitutional role. This chapter began on April 11, 2017, when Premier Christy Clark asked her to dissolve Parliament, and an election was then set for May 9. The preliminary results announced on election day showed the Liberals with forty-three seats, the NDP forty-one and the Green Party three. The results in two ridings had been very close, but two weeks later when Elections BC had counted the absentee ballots, the seat distribution was unchanged.

Both the Liberals and the NDP now sought the support of the

Left to right: Prince Edward, Earl of Wessex, and Sophie, Countess of Wessex, visited Judith Guichon and Bruno Mailloux at Government House in September 2014.

Image courtesy of Government House of British Columbia.

Green Party, but on May 29, Green Party leader Andrew Weaver announced that his party would support the NDP for the next four years on any budget or confidence motion votes. On the morning of May 31 Weaver and NDP leader John Horgan delivered a written accord and a letter signed by the three Green and all forty-one NDP MLAs to Government House, where it was received by Private Secretary Jerymy Brownridge on behalf of the Lieutenant Governor.

Meanwhile, since Clark was the leader of the largest caucus, the Lieutenant Governor agree to her request for an opportunity to test the confidence of the House, and swore in Clark's new cabinet on June 12. The Legislature was recalled ten days later, but even though the Liberals' throne speech made a number of promises that closely resembled elements of the NDP and Green election platforms, on June 29 the NDP and Green Party MLAs voted together to defeat the Liberals on a vote of confidence on the throne speech. As journalists Justine Hunter and Mike Hager observed the next day in *The Globe and Mail*, it was now the Lieutenant Governor's "unusual task to decide what comes next for British Columbia's government."[385]

In the preceding weeks Guichon had been studying precedents and seeking advice from constitutional lawyers, legal experts, former MLAs and her vice-regal counterparts across Canada and in Britain and Australia to prepare for what lay ahead. Clark could request a dissolution of the Legislature, which would trigger a new election. If so, Guichon would have to decide whether to accept that advice or to exercise her reserve powers and offer NDP Leader John Horgan the chance to form a new government. However, in the lead-up to the meeting between the premier and the Lieutenant Governor at Government House, Clark indicated to the media that she would not ask directly for a dissolution, even though she had a responsibility as premier to advise the Lieutenant Governor. (In fact, Clark revealed later that she *had* asked for a dissolution.) Following their meeting, Guichon met briefly with Horgan. Then, having carefully weighed the options, she chose to exercise her reserve powers, and that evening the Office of the Lieutenant Governor issued a statement:

> As Lieutenant-Governor of British Columbia, and as the representative of Her Majesty the Queen of Canada, I have met with Premier Clark and will accept her resignation. I have asked Mr. Horgan to form a government, he having assured me that

he can form a government which will have the confidence of the Legislative Assembly.[386]

University of Victoria political scientist Michael Prince expressed the mood of much of the province when he commented to the *Times Colonist*, "It's a good day for BC. This is a peaceful transition. We saw peace, order and good government in action today."[387]

Judith Guichon was the second woman to hold the position of Lieutenant Governor in BC so her appointment was not precedent-setting, but her female predecessor, Iona Campagnolo, has the last word on that topic:

> The second woman was far more important than the first woman because in times past the first woman was the last woman. So the second woman means it's been institutionalized; it's no longer an issue.[388]

Guichon was also the second rancher in over a hundred years— the first was Clement Francis Cornwall—to have held the post, and she brought to the position a clear understanding of the challenges facing rural communities and a desire to educate all British Columbians about how the activities of the rural primary sector underpin our economy. Based on her work on the land, Guichon is also committed to sustainability and environmental education, a priority that translated into the Stewards of the Future program that she hopes will encourage young British Columbians to learn about and take responsibility for maintaining a healthy future for BC's diverse natural resources.

XI

Representing the Crown in British Columbia Today

DESPITE THE FACT that the constitutional tasks of Lieutenant Governors in Canada have remained fairly constant, the individuals appointed to this position in BC have interpreted them in diverse ways. While earlier appointees were focused on advancing the interests of the settler society, modern representatives of the Crown have made it a priority to recognize Indigenous culture and history, emphasizing respect and reconciliation.

With support from the Government House Foundation, vice-regal representatives have also initiated far-reaching legacy projects. Over time they have found new ways to reach out to British Columbians, to highlight good works and to engage with youth, the future leaders of the province.

As men and women from a variety of cultural backgrounds are appointed to the position, the office has begun to reflect British Columbia's diverse population. With more funding, the position is no longer limited to the economic elite, and a wider range of citizens have been able to take on this role. With very few exceptions, past Lieutenant Governors were employed in law, politics, transportation and business, and tended to be based in Victoria or Vancouver; to better represent the variety of peoples in communities around the province, future vice-regal representatives may be drawn from other occupational groups and other regions.

More fundamental than their ceremonial and promotional roles, however, Lieutenant Governors, as representatives of the Crown, play an important role in the everyday functioning of Canada's constitutional monarchy and the stability of provincial governments. As the May 2017 BC election and resulting minority government demonstrated, they are on occasion required to make challenging decisions, acting as "constitutional fire extinguishers" in order to safeguard our democratic political system.

Endnotes

Publishing details for books listed below are included in the Select Bibliography.

I. The Evolving Role of BC's Lieutenant Governors

1 MacKinnon. *The Crown in Canada*. 122.
2 McCreery. "The Provincial Crown." 147.

II. The Governors (1849–71)

3 Lord Carnarvon's comment on Despatch to London, Douglas to Labouchere, 2084, CO 305/8. 271; received March 2, 1858, No. 35, Victoria, Vancouver's Island, December 29, 1857.
4 Perry. *On the Edge of Empire*. 111.
5 Smith, Robert L. "Kennedy, Sir Arthur Edward." *Dictionary of Canadian Biography*.
6 Cotton, Peter. *Vice-Regal Mansions of British Columbia*. (Kennedy letter to the *British Colonist*, April 13, 1864.) 31–32.
7 Ormsby. "Frederick Seymour." *BC Studies 22*. 6.
8 Stueck, Wendy. "B.C.'s apology for hanging Tsilhqot'in war chiefs one step in a long healing process," *The Globe and Mail*, October 24, 2014. http://www.theglobe-andmail.com/news/british-columbia/bc-apology-for-hanging-tsilhqotin-war-chiefs-one-step-in-a-long-healing-process/article21307738/.
9 *A Sto:lo Coast Salish Historical Atlas*. (A Sto:lo speech to Governor Seymour, August 1864), 170.
10 *A Sto:lo Coast Salish Historical Atlas*. (A Sto:lo speech to Governor Seymour, 1866), 171.
11 Haworth and Maier. (Letter from Lord Granville to Queen Victoria, June 1869.) 66.

III. Ottawa's Men: From Federal Agents to Industrialists (1871–1914)

12 Saywell, John T. "The lieutenant-governors." *Provincial Political Systems: Comparative Essays*. 22.
13 Ibid. 18.
14 Ibid. 22.
15 Ibid. 23.
16 Fisher, Robin. "Trutch, Sir Joseph William." *Dictionary of Canadian Biography*.
17 Green and Gordon-Findlay. *If These Walls Could Talk*, 18–20.

18 Joseph Trutch, quoted in Paul Tennant, *Aboriginal Peoples and Politics: The Indian Land Question in British Columbia, 1849–1989*. 39.
19 Helmcken. Reminiscences of Dr. John Sebastian Helmcken. 252.
20 Ibid. 255.
21 Ibid. 259.
22 Andrews, G. Smedley. *Sir Joseph William Trutch, K.C.M.G., C.E., L.S., F.R.G.S., 1826–1904: Surveyor, Engineer, Statesman*. 12–13.
23 Fisher, Robin. "Joseph Trutch and Indian Land Policy." In *British Columbia: Historical Readings*, eds. Ward, W. Peter and Robert A.J. McDonald.
24 Helmcken. 256.
25 Andrews. 13.
26 Saywell, John Tupper. "Sir Joseph Trutch: British Columbia's First Lieutenant Governor." 75.
27 Saywell. "Trutch," 78.
28 Loo, Tina. "McCreight, John Foster." *Dictionary of Canadian Biography*. http://www.biographi.ca/en/bio/mccreight_john_foster_14E.html.
29 Saywell. "Trutch," 78–79.
30 Ibid. 80.
31 Ibid. 83.
32 Ibid. 84
33 Belshaw. "Provincial Politics." 139–40.
34 Fisher. "Joseph Trutch and Indian Land Policy." 172.
35 MacPherson, Ian. "Richards, Sir William Buell." *Dictionary of Canadian Biography*.
36 Sutton, Richards Buell. "Looking Back," http://www.rbs.ca/about-looking.html (accessed June 2015.)
37 Brawn. *The Court of Queen's Bench*. Manitoba.172–73.
38 de Kiewiet, C.W. and F.H. Underhill, eds. *Duffer-in-Carnarvon Correspondence, 1874–1878*. 251.
39 de Kiewiet and Underhill. Dufferin to Carnarvon, October 8, 1876. 271.
40 Ibid. 270–71.
41 "The Thunderer Again Refers to British Columbia" from *Times*, September 22, 1876. Reprinted in *British Colonist*, October 27, 1876, 3.

42 Ottawa School of Art, "History of the OSA," http://artottawa.ca/home/about-osa/history-of-the-osa/ (accessed June 16, 2015); Carol Bishop, "The Picture of Oscar Wilde: The Celebrated Aesthete Gazed at the Portrait Frances Richards had Painted of Him. Suddenly, He Had a Brilliant Idea." *The Beaver: Exploring Canada's History*. 34–42.

43 Richards Buell Sutton website and *British Colonist*, June 12, 1894, 5.

44 Harris, Cole. *Making Native Space*. 47.

45 Johnson, Edward Philip. "The Early Years of Ashcroft Manor." 4–6.

46 Ibid. 6–11.

47 Ibid. 12.

48 *Cariboo Sentinel*, August 12, 1865.

49 Johnson. 17–18.

50 Harris. *Making Native Space*. 47.

51 BC Land Title and Survey, List of Surveyors General of BC, https://www.ltsa.ca/cms/list-of-surveyors-general-of-bc (accessed May 18, 2015).

52 Mackie, Richard. "Pearse, Benjamin William." *Dictionary of Canadian Biography*.

53 Report of the Royal Commission on Chinese Immigration, Chapter 3, "Social and Moral Aspects," xlii–xlvii. Based on evidence presented to the Select Committee on Chinese Labour and Immigration, 1879. Available online: https://archive.org/stream/cu31924023463940#page/n167/mode/2up.

54 Stamp, Robert M. *Royal Rebels*. 198.

55 Tennant, Paul. *Aboriginal Peoples and Politics*. 57–58. (Tennant cites BC Legislature Sessional Papers 1887, 257.)

56 Cornwall, Clement F. and Joseph Planta. Papers relating to the Commission appointed to enquire into the condition of the Indians of the North-West Coast (1888). *Report of Commission*, 416. http://dev.bcbib.library.ubc.ca/landing/item/bcbib.163571.

57 Tennant. 59. (Tennant cites North Coast Enquiry, *Papers*, 2.)

58 Ibid. 64. (Tennant cites North Coast Enquiry, *Papers*, 11).

59 "Last Night's Despatches: Proceedings of the Yale Convention," *British Colonist*, September 18, 1868, 3.

60 Morton, James. *The Enterprising Mr. Moody, the Bumptious Captain Stamp*. 132. No footnote to original source provided.

61 Woodward-Reynolds, Kathleen-Marjorie. "A History of the City and District of North Vancouver." 29–30. Quoted from "A Ramble on the Mainland," *Daily British Colonist*, Victoria, April 18, 1876.

62 Woodward-Reynolds. 23–33. Quoted from D.W. Higgins, *Mystic Spring* (Toronto: 1904). 318–33.

63 Ibid. 30.

64 *Colonist*. January 18, 1888.

65 Jackman. *Men at Cary Castle*, 51.

66 Lewis, Zane. H. "Nelson, Hugh." *Dictionary of Canadian Biography*.

67 Ormsby, Margaret. *A Pioneer Gentlewoman in British Columbia: The Recollections of Susan Allison*. 7, 11.

68 Titley, Brian. *The Frontier World of Edgar Dewdney*. 23.

69 Ibid. 28. Quoted from "The Story of My Life: Hon. Edgar Dewdney," *Daily Colonist* (Magazine), August 31, 1913, 10.

70 Titley. 49.

71 Carter, Sarah. *Aboriginal People and Colonizers of Western Canada*. 142.

72 "Last Mountain Lake National Wildlife Area," Environment Canada (http://www.ec.gc.ca/ap-pa/default.asp?lang=En&n=0EEA040C-1) (accessed January 16, 2015).

73 Reynolds, Louise. *Agnes: The Biography of Lady Macdonald*. 144.

74 Titley, Brian. "Dewdney, Edgar." *Dictionary of Canadian Biography*.

75 Ormsby, Margaret. *A Pioneer Gentlewoman*. xli. Letter from Peter O'Reilly to John Trutch, December 1892.

76 Saywell, John T., ed. *Canadian Journal of Lady Aberdeen*. 271. Diary entry for Thursday, August 15, 1894. Victoria, BC.

77 Saywell, ed. *Canadian Journal of Lady Aberdeen*. 147. Diary entry for November 7, 1894.

78 Glenbow Archives Institute, Dewdney Papers, vol. IV, 2671–701, Journal of a Trip to Alaska, 1893. Quoted in Titley, *Frontier World*, 124.

79 "The Jubilee Has Come," *British Colonist*, June 22, 1897, 5.

80 Ormsby, *Pioneer Gentlewoman*, xli. (Letter from Peter O'Reilly.)

81 Jackman. *Men at Cary Castle*. 62.

82 Titley. 139.

83 Jackman. *Men at Cary Castle*. 63.

84 Saywell, John Tupper. "The McInnes Incident in British Columbia." 166.

85 Edmonds, Henry V. "Asylum for the Insane: Report of Commissioners," *Daily Colonist*, January 9, 1884.

86 Jackman, *Men at Cary Castle*, 68.

87 Ibid. 69.

88 Cotton, Peter. *Vice Regal Mansions of British Columbia*. 68.

89 "The Governor Banqueted," *Atlin Claim*, July 22, 1899, 4.

90 *British Colonist*, July 15, 1899, 5.

91 Jackman. 72.

92 Little, J.I. *Patrician Liberal*. 7–20.

93 Ibid. 214.

94 Ibid. 4.

95 Little. 200, 95.

96 Hamelin, "Joly de Lotbinière."

97 Little. 179–89, 196.

98 Little. 220. Quoted from Sir Wilfrid Laurier Fonds, Library and Archives Canada. C788, 59505-7, Laurier to Joly, Ottawa, October 25, 1901.

99 Little. 220–21. Quoted and translated from letters of His Honour Sir Joly de Lotbinière, 1901–06, BC Archives, Mf11A, Henri-Gustave Joly to Edmond, Victoria, March 13, 1902.

100 "Conservative Convention," *Revelstoke Herald*, September 18, 1902, 1.

101 Little. 224.

102 Little. 222. Quoted from letters of His Honour Sir Joly de Lotbinière, 1901–06, BC Archives, Mf11A, Henri-Gustave Joly to Edmond, Victoria, October 12, 1903.

103 Little. 225.

104 Little. 50. Quoted from Susan Crease diary, BC Archives, Crease Family Collection, MS 2879, MfAO 1847, June 15, 1903.

105 Jackman. 82.

106 Belshaw, John Douglas. "The British Collier in British Columbia." 27.

107 Reksten, Terry. *The Dunsmuir Saga*. 164.

108 Ibid. 217.

109 "Vancouver Hoodlums Disgrace Their City—Anti-Asiatic Demonstration Ends in Mobbing of Japanese," *Daily Colonist*, September 8, 1907, 1.

110 Adams, John. *The Ker Family of Victoria, 1859–1976*. 156.

111 Parke, Alice Barrett. *Hobnobbing with a Countess*. 10.

112 Murray, Peter. *Homesteads and Snug Harbours*. 187.

113 *Victoria Daily Times*, August 14, 1900.

114 Morrison, Brad. "Sinking of Iroquois Shocks Residents," *Peninsula News Review*, April 8, 2011, http://www.peninsulanewsreview.com/news/119414604.html; and Murray, *Homesteads and Snug Harbours*, 187.

115 Taylor, G.W. *Automobile Saga of British Columbia*. 102.

116 "Trip North Was Much Enjoyed," *Victoria Daily Colonist*, September 28, 1912, 8.

117 Green and Gordon-Findlay. *If These Walls Could Talk*. 152.

IV. BC's Lieutenant Governors and the First World War

118 "Peoples of BC." *Encyclopedia of British Columbia*. 541–42.

119 Roy, Patricia E. and John Herd Thompson. *Land of Promises*. 102.

120 Ormsby, Margaret A. "Barnard, Francis Jones." *Dictionary of Canadian Biography*.

121 "Authorities have situation in hand," *Daily Colonist* May 11, 1915, 3.

122 Castle, Geoffrey, ed. in *Hatley Park: An Illustrated Anthology*. . 46.

123 Parke, Alice Barrett. *Hobnobbing with a Countess*. Diary entry for September 30, 1897. 189.

124 "Red Cross Works," *Daily Colonist*, August 5, 1917, 17; advertisement for Blue Cross Fund, *Daily Colonist*, August 5, 1917, 5; "Christmas Boxes Sent to Sailors," *Daily Colonist*, November 19, 1918, 8; "Hundreds Dance at Patriotic Bazaar," *Daily Colonist*, November 4, 1917, 19.

125 Saywell, *Office of Lieutenant-Governor*. 215 (fn 75). (From Premiers' Papers, Barnard to Oliver, BC Archives: March 27, 1919.)

126 "Vessel Stuck Fast on Ways," *Daily Colonist*, March 28, 1919, 7.

127 Van Kirk, Sylvia. "Five Founding Families of Victoria." 158.

128 Nellie Hood interview. BC Archives, 1290, 1-1. 2, 4, 5.

129 Ibid., 2-1. 8–10.

130 Ibid., 1-2. 16–17.

131 Ibid., 1-2. 9.

132 Ibid., 1-2. 1.

133 Gordon, Ishbel Maria Marjoribanks. *The Canadian Journal of Lady Aberdeen*. 146.

134 Ibid. 272, 274.

135 Nellie Hood. 1290, 1-2. 16–17.

136 Saywell. *Office of the Lieutenant-Governor*. 142.

137 "Inspects Coolies and Makes Awards," *British Colonist*, January 8, 1920, 12.

138 *British Colonist*, October 22, 1920.

V. Reaching Out to British Columbians in the 1920s

139 Buchan, John. *Lord Minto*. 173.

140 Carter, Miranda. "How to Keep your Crown." *History Today*, Vol. 59, October 10, 2009. 6.

141 Morrison, Brad R. and Christopher J.P. Hanna. "Nichol, Walter Cameron." *Dictionary of Canadian Biography*.

142 "The Lieutenant-Governor." *BC Veterans' Weekly*. BC Archives. Nichol scrapbook. 3.

143 "Ministers Presented to New Governor," *Province*, January 7, 1921. BC Archives. Nichol scrapbook.

144 "Brilliant Scene at Government House," *Colonist*, March 22, 1921. BC Archives. Nichol scrapbook.

145 "First Reception is Brilliant Function," *Colonist*, April 24, 1921. BC Archives. Nichol scrapbook.

146 "Exhibition is Held at Canteen Grounds," *Colonist*, July 27, 1921. BC Archives. Nichol scrapbook.

147 "Thousands Do Honour to Fallen," *Colonist*, October 4, 1921. BC Archives. Nichol scrapbook. 16.

148 "Complimentary Dinner to Lieutenant-Governor" and "The Lieutenant-Governor's Visit," *The Cumberland Islander*, August 20, 1921. BC Archives. Nichol scrapbook.

149 "New Highway is Formally Opened By Two Governors," *Province*, July 3, 1923. BC Archives. Nichol scrapbook.

150 Taylor, C. James. "Historic Sites and Monuments Board." *Oxford Companion to Canadian History*.

151 Clayton, Daniel. *Islands of Truth*. 3–4.

152 "Chief's Canoe Reaches Government House," *Colonist*. September 9, 1924. BC Archives. Nichol scrapbook.

153 "Lieutenant-Governors Meet in Conference," *Daily Colonist*, September 17, 1925, 1.

154 "Victorians Welcome their Excellencies," *Daily Colonist*, August 22,1922. BC Archives. Nichol scrapbook.

155 "Safeguard Youth Lord Byng Urges," *Colonist*, August 23, 1922. BC Archives. Nichol scrapbook.

156 "Miraloma, Residence Ready for the Retiring Lieutenant-Governor." Date and newspaper unknown. BC Archives. Nichol scrapbook.

157 Harris and Phillips. *Letters from Windermere*. xiii.

158 Harris and Phillips. xv.

159 Bradley, Ben. "The David Thompson Memorial Fort." 409.

160 Lothian. *Canada's National Parks*. 60–61.

161 "An Interview with Mrs. Helen (Mackenzie) Piggott." Government House Archives. 3.

162 "Suspend His Honor Like Mohamet's Coffin," *Daily Colonist*, September 24, 1926. 7.

163 "Address by His Honour R. Randolph Bruce, Lieutenant-Governor of British Columbia." *Sir George Simpson, K.B. Centennial Celebration*. Fort St. James, September 17, 1928. 12–14.

164 Klippenstein, F.E. "The Challenge of James Douglas and Carrier Chief Kwah." *Reading Beyond Words*. 187.

165 Dilks, David. *"The Great Dominion." Winston Churchill in Canada*. 111.

VI. Retrenchment and Extravagance in the Great Depression

166 McCreery, Christopher. "The Provincial Crown." *Canada and the Crown: Essays on Constitutional Monarchy*. ed. Jackson and Lagasse. 143. (Lord Bessborough to Sir Clive Wigram, April 18, 1934. Bessborough Papers, West Sussex Record Office.)

167 William Lyon Mackenzie King diaries. Library and Archives Canada. Entry for October 22, 1937.

168 Jackman. *Men at Cary Castle*. 135.

169 Ormsby. *British Columbia*. 446.

170 "Lieutenant-Governors," *Vancouver Province*, September 26, 1932. Tolmie Papers, UBC Archives.

171 *Report of the Committee Appointed by the Government to Investigate the Finances of British Columbia*, Victoria, BC. Charles F. Banfield, 1932; and "The Lieutenant-Governor." Chapter II, Tolmie Papers, UBC Archives. 14–15.

172 Mackie, Richard. "For Empire and Industry." Chapter 1. 1–3.

173 Mackie. *Hamber*. Chapter 12, 1.

174 Ibid. Chapter 13, 8.

175 Brown, Atholl Sutherland. *Buster: Brigadier James Sutherland Brown*. 181.King diaries. Entry for May 30, 1939.

176 King diaries. Entry for May 30, 1939.

177 Letter from Madge (Margaret) B. Molson to Randolph Bruce and Edith Molson, June 18, 1939. Government House Archives.

178 Letter from Madge (Margaret) B. Molson, June 18, 1939.

179 King diaries. Entry for May 30, 1939.

VII. The Lieutenant Governors and the Second World War

180 Harker, D.E. *The Woodwards*.

181 King diaries. Entry for Saturday, February 22, 1941. 4–5.

182 Bothwell and Kilbourn. *C.D. Howe*. 137.

183 Pattullo fonds, BC Archives, MS 0003, vol. 73, file 1. 12–13. (W.C. Woodward to T.D. Pattullo, October 23, 1941.)

184 Cotton. *Vice-Regal Mansions*. 103. (Citing articles in the *Colonist*, May 17, 1943, and March 15 and 16, 1945.)

185 Roy. *Triumph of Citizenship*. (Woodward to Mackenzie King.) 52.

186 Harker. 156.

VIII. The Lieutenant Governors in Postwar British Columbia (1946–60)

187 Adams. *Ker Family of Victoria*. 227–29

188 Jackman. *Cary Castle*. 158. MacGregor, D.A. *They Gave Royal Assent*. 64.

189 Jackman. *Cary Castle*. 157–58.

190 Healy, A.M. *Bulolo*. 31–32.

191 Gwynn-Jones, Terry. "New Guinea's Great Aerial Gold Rush." 100.

192 Idriess, Ion L. *Gold-Dust and Ashes*. 251–52.

193 Banks, Charles. "There is Plenty of Room at the Top," Commencement Address to Colorado School of Mines. *The Mines Magazine*. vol. 30, no. 6 (June 1940). 326.

194 Healy. 31–32.

195 Jackman, *Cary Castle*, 159.

196 Ibid. 160.

197 Ibid.

198 "Indian Chiefs Offer Thanks for Vote," *The Native Voice*, February 1950. 2. https://web.archive.org/web/20140207200524/http://nativevoice.bc.ca/wp-content/uploads/2011/08/5002v04n02.pdf.

199 Mitchell, David. Interview with Clarence Wallace. BC Archives, T3333, 1977-05-31. Tape 3-1. 14.

200 Ibid. Tape 2-1. 2.

201 Ibid. Tape 1-2. 6.

202 Ibid. Tape 1-1. 10–12.

203 Mansbridge, Francis. *Launching History*. 72.

204 Mitchell/Wallace interview. Tape 3-1. 8–10.

205 Ibid. Tape 3-1. 1.

206 Ibid. Tape 3-1. 3–4.

207 Ibid. Tape 3-1. 6–7.

208 Barman, Jean. *West Beyond the West*. 292–93.

209 Mitchell/Wallace interview. Tape 3-2. 1–2.

210 Mitchell, David. *WAC Bennett*. 170.

211 Mitchell/Wallace interview. Tape 3-1, 12.

212 Mitchell. *WAC Bennett*. 197.

213 Ibid.

214 Ross, Ishbel. "The Lifestory of Frank Mackenzie Ross." (1970?) Government House Archives. 12–13.

215 Litt, Paul. *Elusive Destiny: The Political Vocation of John Napier Turner*. 14.

216 Woolliams, Nina G. *Cattle Ranch: The Story of the Douglas Lake Cattle Company*. 208.

217 Ross. "Lifestory," 18; also Neering and Owen, *Government House*, 112.

218 Neering and Owen, *Government House*, 18; Cotton, *Vice Regal Mansions of British Columbia*, 107.

219 Ross, Phyllis G. "History of Government House." Correspondence regarding proposed history, 1959–60. (Mrs. Frank M. Ross to L.G. Wallace, Esq., Deputy Provincial Secretary, Parliament Buildings, Victoria, BC, Re: History of Government House, August 10, 1960. BC Archives, GR 1962, Box 2, file 5.)

220 Ross, Phyllis G. to L.G. Wallace, Esq., August 10, 1960. BC Archives, GR 1962, Box 2, file 5.

221 Litt, Paul. *Elusive Destiny*. 36.

222 Jackman. 175.

IX. Adapting to Social and Political Changes (1960–88)

223 Salomons, Tanisha. "Calder Case." UBC Indigenous Foundations, http://indigenousfoundations.arts.ubc.ca/home/land-rights/calder-case.html.

224 Tidridge, Nathan. *Canada's Constitutional Monarchy.* 95–97.

225 Roy, R.H. *For Most Conspicuous Bravery,* 2.

226 Ibid. 28.

227 Ibid. 50.

228 Ibid. 37.

229 Ibid. 104–5

230 Ibid. 132.

231 Ibid. 172–73

232 Ibid. 212. (Statement by Pearkes to a newspaper reporter.)

233 Roy, 345.

234 Ibid. 347.

235 BC Archives, GR-2809, Wilson Duff Papers, ca. 1950-78, Reel B06047, File 140, Niska "A," "Outline of Lieutenant-Governor's visit to Nass in October 1963." Thanks to Nicholas May for providing this reference.

236 Robertson, Bruce and Maryla Waters. Interview with John Robert Nicholson for the British Columbia Legal History Project, University of Victoria Law Library, SPB Compact Shelving Rm 175, 12.

237 Ibid. 77.

238 Ibid. 47–48.

239 Ibid. 49.

240 Roy, 285.

241 Nicholson interview. 50.

242 Ibid. 71.

243 Ibid. 52.

244 Ibid.

245 Ibid. 50.

246 Ibid. 69.

247 "Pageantry, Discontent in Victoria," "Reality Bothers Legislature," *Ubyssey* (University of British Columbia), January 22, 1971, 1, 16; Climenhaga, Dave. "Poor Gather to Protest," *The Martlet* (University of Victoria), vol. 10, no. 20, January 28, 1971, 3.

248 Nicholson interview. 70–71.

249 Ibid. 75

250 Ibid. 98–99.

251 Watts, Alfred and Maryla Waters. Interview with Walter S. Owen. British Columbia Legal History Project, University of Victoria Law Library, SPB Compact Shelving Room 175.

252 Owen interview. 8–9.

253 Ibid. 10.

254 Ibid. 15.

255 Ibid. 20–21.

256 Ibid. 42–44.

257 Ibid. 31–32.

258 Ibid. 73–74.

259 "Owen to Succeed Nicholson," *Vancouver Sun,* February 13, 1973. Owen Scrapbook.

260 Griffin, Sean. "Walter Owen Named Lt. Gov.—Reward for an Arch Reactionary," *Vancouver Sun,* February 14, 1973. Owen Scrapbook.

261 Mitchell. *WAC Bennett.* 174.

262 Owen interview. 76.

263 Ibid.

264 Robinson, Martha. "Mrs. Walter Owen—Government House to Get an Artist," *Vancouver Sun,* February 15, 1973. Walter Owen Scrapbook.

265 "Owen Proves a Queen's Man," *Vancouver Sun,* February 14, 1973; "New Lt.-Gov. Came Up Hard Way," *Province* (Vancouver), February 14, 1973. Owen Scrapbook.

266 Owen interview, 77.

267 Ibid. 77–78.

268 Ramsay, Bruce. "Vice-Regal Job Is Not an Easy One." [date unknown].

269 Charman, Eric. Memo to the author, June 12, 2016.

270 Eagle, Raymond. *In the Service of the Crown.* 68.

271 Zuehlke, Mark. *On to Victory,* 19–21.

272 Eagle, 253.

273 Ibid. 269.

274 Ibid. 289.

275 Author interview with Michael Roberts, March 5, 2015.

276 Eagle, 284–85.

277 Ibid. 281.

278 Ibid. 283.

279 Henry Pybus Bell-Irving, quoted in Eagle. 310.

280 Roy, Reginald H. Interviews with Robert Gordon Rogers in 1984–85. Government House Archives transcripts. April 10, 1984, and April 19, 1984, 3–4.

281 Rogers interview. April 10, 1984 and April 19, 1984, 5–9.

282 Ibid. 3.

283 Rogers interview. September 6, 1984, 4.

284 Ibid. 3.

285 Ibid. 6.

286 Ibid. 8.

287 Ibid. 12.

288 Rogers interview. September 13, 1984, 10.

289 Rogers interview. November 1, 1984, 1.

290 Ibid. 1–2.

291 Ibid. 11–12.

292 Rogers interview. December 6, 1984, 10.

293 Rogers interview. February 7, 1985, 10.

294 Rogers interview. April 4, 1984, 16.

295 Rogers interview. November 1, 1984, 2.

296 "Vice-Regal Post Ends Politics for BC's Rogers," *The Globe and Mail*, June 27, 1983, 8.

X. Diverse Identities and Priority Projects (1988–2018)

297 McCreery, Christopher. "The Provincial Crown." Jackson and Lagassé, eds. *Canada and the Crown*, 153.

298 Roy, R.H. *David Lam*, 82.

299 Ibid. 69.

300 Ibid. 89.

301 Ibid. 171.

302 Ibid. 177.

303 Ibid. 176.

304 Ibid. 179.

305 Lau/Clayton interview.

306 Roy. 196–97

307 Roberts/Clayton interview.

308 Roy. 203–04.

309 Roberts/Clayton interview.

310 Roy. 224.

311 Roberts/Clayton interview.

312 Lau/Clayton interview.

313 Gardom, Helen/Clayton interview. Quote from Garde Gardom memoirs, unpublished and unpaginated.

314 Meggs, G., and R. Mickleburgh. *The Art of the Impossible*. 23–24.

315 Meggs and Mickleburgh. 65.

316 Barrett, D., and W. Miller. *Barrett: A Passionate Political Life*. 97.

317 Vogel, R. "Garde Basil Gardom." 345.

318 Ibid. 345–46.

319 Campbell, R.A. *Demon Rum or Easy Money*. 165

320 Tennant, P. *Aboriginal Peoples and Politics*. 227–28.

321 Gardom, Garde. "Land Claims: Harmony Must Begin in Ottawa," *Vancouver Sun*, September 9, 1986.

322 Plecas, Robert. *Bill Bennett*. 255–57.

323 Vogel. 346.

324 Gardom, Helen/Clayton interview. Quote from Karen MacDonald comment.

325 Morton, Brian. "Garde Gardom Recalled Fondly as a 'Happy Warrior' with a Terrific Sense of Humour," *Vancouver Sun*, June 19, 2013.

326 "Lieutenant-Governor Garde Gardom Insulted Aboriginal People in His Speech during the BC Cabinet Swearing-in Ceremony Tuesday, the First Nations Summit said Wednesday," *Canadian Press NewsWire/Times Colonist*, March 1, 2000.

327 "An Open Letter to the Honourable Garde Gardom, Lieutenant-governor of British Columbia," *Canada NewsWire*, March 1, 2000, 1.

328 Palmer, Vaughn. "Garde Gardom Mixed Good Humour with Royal Character," *Vancouver Sun*, June 19, 2013.

329 Plecas. *Bill Bennett*, 145.

330 Bondar, Roberta. *Canada: Landscape of Dreams*. 2002.

331 Campagnolo/Clayton interview. 17.

332 MacGregor, Roy. "The Iona Effect," *The Canadian Magazine*, July 23, 1977, 2–6.

333 Frizzell, Alan Stewart, and Anthony Westell. *The Canadian General Election of 1984: Politicians, Parties, Press and Polls*. 21.

334 Campagnolo/Clayton interview.

335 Ibid.

336 Ibid.

337 Ibid.

338 Ibid.

339 "A New Design," Royal BC Museum Learning Portal, A-New-Design.pdf.

340 LeRoy/Clayton interview.

341 Bolton, R.P., and R. Daly. *Xwelíqwiya*, 157.

342 Glavin, Terry. "Point Taken," 28.

343 Point/Clayton interview.

344 Ruenzel/Point interview.

345 Ibid. 1.

346 Mandell, Louise. "The Honourable Steven L. Point, OBC, *Xwĕ lī qwĕl tĕl*," 336.

347 Mandell, 336.

348 Point/Ruenzel interview, 11.

349 Ibid.

350 Mandell, 338.

351 Ruenzel/Point interview, 5.

352 BC Treaty Commission. "A Lay Person's Guide to Delgamuukw." http://www.bctreaty.net/files/pdf_documents/delgamuukw.pdf.

353 http://blogs.ufv.ca/blog/2014/10/gwendolyn-point-next-ufv-chancellor/.

354 Mandell, 339.

355 Ibid.

356 Point/Clayton interview.

357 Bolton and Daly, 207–08.

358 Quoted in Fowlie, "Driven by Literacy."

359 McCue, Duncan. "First Nations in BC Gain Libraries Thanks to Judge, Ex-Officer," CBC News, May 26, 2014. http://www.cbc.ca/news/aboriginal/first-nations-in-b-c-gain-libraries-thanks-to-judge-ex-officer-1.2654846.

360 Point/Clayton interview.

361 McCue. "Libraries."

362 Point/Clayton interview.

363 Lipke, Shelley. "Lieutenant-Governor of BC Claims First Nations Cadet Corps His Own," *Lookout*, vol. 56, no. 11 (March 21,2011). http://www.lookoutnewspaper.com/issues/56/2011-03-21-12.pdf.

364 LeRoy/Clayton interview.

365 Eric Charman, Memorandum, June 12, 2016.

366 LeRoy/Clayton interview.

367 Guichon/Clayton interview.

368 http://www.merrittherald.com/yvonne-tollens-continues-to-advance-agriculture/.

369 Ibid.

370 Guichon/Clayton interview.

371 Ibid.

372 Ibid.

373 Guichon, Judith. "The Gift of Adoption." *Adoptive Families Association of BC*, https://www.bcadoption.com/resources/articles/gift-adoption.

374 Ibid.

375 Guichon/Clayton interview.

376 Ibid.

377 Guichon, Judith. Speech on GH website, October 15, 2015. http://ltgov.bc.ca/news-events/news/speeches/2015/oct/sp_oct1515.html.

378 Guichon, Judith. Speech at "Canadian Submarine Centenary Banquet," August 7, 2014. http://ltgov.bc.ca/news-events/news/speeches/2014/aug/sp_aug7-14.html.

379 Guichon/Clayton interview.

380 Stewards of the Future Toolkit. http://www.ltgov.bc.ca/lg/priority-programs/stewards/PDF1_Stewards_of_the_Future_Complete_Toolkit.pdf, 6.

381 Stewards of the Future Conference Program, June 5–7, 2015, Pearson College UWC. 6–7.

382 Wessel, Emily. "Lieutenant-Governor Comes Home," *The Merritt Herald*, January 7, 2013, 1.

383 Guichon/Clayton interview.

384 Conference Program. "The Crown in the 21st Century: Deference or Drift," 3.

385 Hunter, Justine, and Mike Hager. "Confidence Vote Brings Down BC Liberals," *The Globe and Mail*, June 30, 2017, A1.

386 Office of the Lieutenant Governor. "A Statement from the Lieutenant Governor," June 29, 2017.

387 Kines, Lindsay, quoting Michael Prince. "Lieutenant-governor Invites Horgan to Take Over, Rejects Another Election," *Times Colonist*, June 29, 2017.

388 Campagnolo/Clayton interview.

Select Bibliography

GENERAL SOURCES

Barman, Jean. *West Beyond the West: A History of British Columbia*, Third ed. Toronto: University of Toronto Press, 2007.

Cotton, Peter Neive. *Vice Regal Mansions of British Columbia*. Vancouver: Elgin Publications for the British Columbia Heritage Trust, 1981.

Dictionary of Canadian Biography. http://www.biographi.ca/en/index.php.

Jackman, S.W. *The Men at Cary Castle*. Victoria: Morriss Printing Company Ltd., 1972.

Johnston, Hugh J.M., ed. *The Pacific Province: A History of British Columbia*. Vancouver: Douglas & McIntyre, 1996.

McCreery, Christopher. "The Provincial Crown: The Lieutenant Governor's Expanding Role." In *Canada and the Crown: Essays in Constitutional Monarchy*, edited by D. Michael Jackson and Philippe Lagassé. Montreal & Kingston: McGill-Queen's University Press, 2013, 147.

McGregor, D.A. *They Gave Royal Assent: The Lieutenant-Governors of British Columbia*. Vancouver: Mitchell Press Limited, 1967.

Neering, Rosemary, and Tony Owen. *Government House: The Ceremonial Home of All British Columbians*. Winlaw, BC: Sono Nis Press, 2007.

Ormsby, Margaret A. *British Columbia: A History*. Toronto: Macmillan of Canada, 1971, 1958.

Roy, Patricia E., and John Herd Thompson. *British Columbia: Land of Promises*. Don Mills: Oxford University Press, 2005.

Saywell, John T. "The Lieutenant-Governors." In David J. Bellamy, Jon H. Pammett, and Donald C. Rowat, eds., *Provincial Political Systems: Comparative Essays*. Toronto: Methuen, 1976, 303.

Saywell, John T. *The Office of Lieutenant-Governor: A Study in Canadian Government and Politics*. Toronto: University of Toronto Press, 1957.

THE EVOLVING ROLE OF BRITISH COLUMBIA'S LIEUTENANT GOVERNORS

Cheffins, Hon. Ronald I. "The Royal Prerogative and the Office of Lieutenant Governor." *Canadian Parliamentary Review* (Spring 2000): 14–19.

Donovan, David S. "The Governor General and Lieutenant Governors: Canada's Misunderstood Viceroys." Paper presented at the 2009 Annual Meeting of the Canadian Political Science Association, Ottawa, 27 May 2009.

Hogg, Peter W. *Constitutional Law of Canada*. 1988 Student Edition. Scarborough: Thomson Canada, 1988.

"Lieutenant-Governor." In W. Stewart Wallace, ed., *The Encyclopedia of Canada*, vol. IV. Toronto: University Associates of Canada, 1948, 82–83. Republished in The Quebec History Encyclopedia, http://faculty. marianopolis.edu/c.belanger/quebechistory/encyclopedia/Lieutenant-Governor-CanadianHistory.htm

MacKinnon, Frank. *The Crown in Canada*. Calgary: McClelland and Stewart West, 1976.

Smith, David E. *The Invisible Crown: The First Principle of Canadian Government*. Toronto: University of Toronto Press, 1995.

THE GOVERNORS

Adams, John. *Old Square Toes and His Lady: The Life of James and Amelia Douglas*. Victoria: Horsdal & Schubart, 2001.

Boyd, Robert. *The Coming of the Spirit of Pestilence: Introduced Infectious Diseases and Population Decline among Northwest Coast Indians, 1774–1874*. Seattle: University of Washington Press, 1999.

Budd, Robert. *Voices of British Columbia*. Vancouver: Douglas & McIntyre, 2010.

Elliott, Dave. *Saltwater People*. Saanich, BC: School District No. 63, 1983, 1990.

Fisher, Robin. *Contact and Conflict: Indian-European Relations in British Columbia, 1774–1890*. Vancouver: UBC Press, 1994, 1977.

————."Joseph Trutch and Indian Land Policy." *BC Studies* no. 12 (Winter 1971–72): 3–33.Gough, Barry M. Gunboat Frontier: British Maritime Authority and Northwest Coast Indians, 1846–1890. Vancouver: UBC Press, 1984.

Gough, Barry M. *Gunboat Frontier: British Maritime Authority and Northwest Coast Indians, 1846–1890.* Vancouver: UBC Press, 1984.

Haworth, Kent M., and Charles R. Maier, "'Not a Matter of Regret': Granville's Response to Seymour's Death," *BC Studies*, no. 27 (Autumn 1975): 62–63.

Lutz, John Sutton. *Makúk: A New History of Aboriginal-White Relations*. Vancouver: UBC Press, 2008.

Ormsby, Margaret. "Frederick Seymour, the Forgotten Governor." *BC Studies* 22 (Summer 1974): 3–25.

Perry, Adele. *On the Edge of Empire: Gender, Race, and the Making of British Columbia, 1849–1871*. Toronto: University of Toronto Press, 2001.

OTTAWA'S MEN

Adams, John. *The Ker Family of Victoria, 1859–1976: Pioneer Industrialists in Western Canada*. Vancouver: Holte Publishing, 2007.

Allison, Susan. *A Pioneer Gentlewoman in British Columbia: The Recollections of Susan Allison.* Edited by Margaret A. Ormsby. Vancouver: UBC Press, 1976, 99.

Andrews, G. Smedley. *Sir Joseph William Trutch, K.C.M.G., C.E., L.S., F.R.G.S., 1826–1904: Surveyor, Engineer, Statesman*. Victoria: Published by the British Columbia Lands Service, in cooperation with the Corporation of Land Surveyors of the Province of British Columbia, 1972.

Belshaw, John Douglas. "The British Collier in British Columbia: Another Archetype Reconsidered." *Labour / Le Travail* 34 (Fall 1994): 11–36.

Bishop, Carol. "The Picture of Oscar Wilde: The Celebrated Aesthete Gazed at the Portrait Frances Richards had Painted of Him. Suddenly, He Had a Brilliant Idea." *The Beaver: Exploring Canada's History*, vol. 86, no. 1 (February–March 2006): 34–42.

Brawn, Dale. *The Court of Queen's Bench of Manitoba, 1870–1950: A Biographical History*. Toronto: University of Toronto Press, 2006.

Carter, Sarah. *Aboriginal People and Colonizers of Western Canada to 1900*. Toronto: University of Toronto Press, 1999.

Daschuk, James. *Clearing the Plains: Disease, Politics of Starvation, and the Loss of Aboriginal Life*. Regina: University of Regina Press, 2013.

Ferguson, Gerry. "Control of the Insane in British Columbia, 1849–78: Care, Cure, or Confinement?" In John McLaren, Robert Menzies and Dorothy E. Chunn, eds., *Regulating Lives: Historical Essays on the State, Society, the Individual, and the Law*. Vancouver: UBC Press, 2002, 63–96.

Fisher, Robin. "Joseph Trutch and Indian Land Policy." In W. Peter Ward and Robert A.J. McDonald, eds., *British Columbia: Historical Readings*. Vancouver: Douglas & McIntyre Ltd., 1981, 154–83.

Ford, Lillian. "Coyote Goes Downriver: An Historical Geography of Coyote Migration into the Fraser Valley." MA Thesis, Department of Geography, University of British Columbia, 2000.

Foster, Janet. *Working for Wildlife: The Beginning of Preservation in Canada*, Second Edition. Toronto: University of Toronto Press, 1998 (Second Edition).

Friesen, Gerald. *The Canadian Prairies: A History*. Toronto: University of Toronto Press, 1984.

Green, Valerie, and Lynn Gordon-Findlay. *If These Walls Could Talk: Victoria's Houses from the Past*. Victoria: TouchWood Editions, 2001.

Harris, Cole. *Making Native Space: Colonialism, Resistance, and Reserves in British Columbia*. Vancouver: UBC Press, 2002.

Hearn, George, and David Wilkie, *"The Cordwood Limited": A History of the Victoria & Sidney Railway*. Victoria: British Columbia Railway Association, 1976.

Helmcken, John Sebastian. *Reminiscences of Doctor John Sebastian Helmcken*. Edited by Dorothy Blakey Smith. Vancouver: UBC Press and the Provincial Archives of British Columbia, 1975.

Johnson, Edward Philip. "The Early Years of Ashcroft Manor." *BC Studies*, no. 5 (Summer 1970): 3–23.

Kiewiet, C.W. de, and F.H. Underhill, eds. *Dufferin-Carnarvon Correspondence, 1874–1878*. Toronto: The Champlain Society, 1955.

Laing, F.W. "Early Flour-Mills in British Columbia, Part II—The Upper Country." *British Columbia Historical Quarterly* (July 1941): 191–214.

Little, J.I. *Patrician Liberal: The Public and Private Life of Sir Henri-Gustave Joly de Lotbinière, 1829–1908*. Toronto: University of Toronto Press, 2013.

MacLachlan, Donald F. *The Esquimalt & Nanaimo Railway: The Dunsmuir Years*. Victoria: B.C. Railway Historical Association, 2012.

Morton, James. *The Enterprising Mr. Moody, the Bumptious Captain Stamp: The Lives and Colourful Times of Vancouver's Lumber Pioneers*. North Vancouver: J.J. Douglas Ltd., 1977.

Mouat, Jeremy. "The Politics of Coal: A Study of the Wellington Miners' Strike of 1890–91." *BC Studies*, no. 77, (Spring 1988): 3–29.

Muralt, Darryl E. *V&S: The Victoria and Sidney Railway, 1892–1919*. Victoria: B.C. Railway Historical Association with assistance from the B.C. Heritage Trust, 1992.

Murray, Peter. *Homesteads and Snug Harbours: The Gulf Islands*. Ganges, BC: Horsdal & Schubart, 1991.

Parke, Alice Barrett. *Hobnobbing with a Countess and Other Okanagan Adventures: The Diaries of Alice Barrett Parke, 1891–1900*. Edited by Jo Fraser Jones. Vancouver: UBC Press, 2001.

Reksten, Terry. *The Dunsmuir Saga*. Vancouver: Douglas & McIntyre, 1991.

Reynolds, Louise. *Agnes: The Biography of Lady Macdonald*. Ottawa: Carleton University Press, 1900.

Roy, Patricia E. *A White Man's Province: British Columbia Politicians and Chinese and Japanese Immigrants, 1858–1914*. Vancouver: UBC Press, 1989.

————. *Boundless Optimism: Richard McBride's British Columbia*. Vancouver: UBC Press, 2012.

Ryan-Lloyd, Kate. "Centennial Saga: The Construction of British Columbia's Parliament Buildings." *Canadian Parliamentary Review* (Spring 1998): 23–26.

Saywell, John Tupper. "Sir Joseph Trutch: British Columbia's First Lieutenant Governor." *British Columbia Historical Quarterly*, vol. 19, no. 1–2 (January–April 1955): 71–92.

————. "The McInnes Incident in British Columbia." *British Columbia Historical Quarterly*, vol. 14 (July 1950), 141–66.

Saywell, John T., ed. *Canadian Journal of Lady Aberdeen, 1893–1898*. Toronto: Champlain Society, 1960.

Shave, Harry. "McDougall and the Métis." *Manitoba Pageant*, Spring 1966, vol. 11, no. 3.

Stamp, Robert M. *Royal Rebels: Princess Louise & the Marquis of Lorne*. Toronto & Oxford: Dundurn Press, 1988.

Taylor, G.W. *Automobile Saga of British Columbia*. Victoria: Morriss Publishing, 1984.

Taylor, Robert Ratcliffe. *The Spencer Mansion: A House, a Home, and an Art Gallery*. Victoria: TouchWood Editions, 2012.

Tennant, Paul. *Aboriginal Peoples and Politics*. University of British Columbia Press, 1990.

Titley, Brian. *The Frontier World of Edgar Dewdney*. Vancouver: UBC Press, 1999.

Webber, Jean. *A Rich and Fruitful Land: The History of the Valleys of the Okanagan, Similkameen and Shuswap*. Madeira Park: Harbour Publishing, 1999.

Woodward-Reynolds, Kathleen-Marjorie. "A History of the City and District of North Vancouver." MA Thesis, University of British Columbia, 1943.

LIEUTENANT GOVERNORS AND THE FIRST WORLD WAR

Akrigg, G.P.V., and Helen Akrigg, *British Columbia Chronicle, 1847–1871: Gold and Colonists*. Vancouver: Discovery Press, 1977.

Castle, Geoffrey, ed. *Hatley Park: An Illustrated Anthology*. Colwood, BC: Friends of Hatley Park Society, 1995.

Evans, Greg. "The Beer Brewers." In Nancy Oke, and Robert Griffin, *Feeding the Family: 100 Years of Food & Drink in Victoria*. Victoria: Royal BC Museum, 2011.

Ewert, Henry. *The Story of the BC Electric Railway Company*. Vancouver: Whitecap Books, 1986.

Green, Valerie. *Above Stairs: Social Life in Upper-Class Victoria, 1843–1918*. Victoria: Touchwood Editions, 2011.

Mayer, Elizabeth M. *Stories about People of German Language Background in Victoria, BC*. Victoria: E.M. Mayer, 1986.

Minaker, Dennis. *The Gorge of Summers Gone: A History of Victoria's Inland Waterway*. Victoria: Dennis Minaker, 1998, rev. 2005.

Morton, Desmond. *Fight or Pay: Soldiers' Families in the Great War*. Vancouver: UBC Press, 2004.

Van Kirk, Sylvia. "Tracing the Fortunes of Five Founding Families of Victoria." *BC Studies*, no. 115/116 (Autumn/Winter 1997/98): 149–80.

Wood, James A. "Social Club or Martial Pursuit? The BC Militia before the First World War." *BC Studies*, no. 173 (Spring 2012): 41–68.

REACHING OUT TO BRITISH COLUMBIANS IN THE 1920s

Bradley, Ben. "The David Thompson Memorial Fort: An Early Outpost of Historically Themed Tourism in Western Canada." *Histoire sociale / Social History*, vol. XLIX, no. 99 (June 2016): 409–29.

Buchan, John. *Lord Minto: A Memoir*. London, Thomas Nelson and Sons, 1924.

Carter, Miranda. "How to Keep Your Crown." *History Today*, Vol. 59, 10 October, 2009, 6.

Clayton, Daniel. *Islands of Truth: The Imperial Fashioning of Vancouver Island*. Vancouver: UBC Press, 2000.

Dawson, Michael. *Selling British Columbia: Tourism and Consumer Culture, 1890–1970*. Vancouver: UBC Press, 2004.

Dilks, David. *"The Great Dominion": Winston Churchill in Canada, 1900–1954*. Toronto: Thomas Allen Publishers, 2005.

Fulton, Gordon. "Roads of Remembrance." *Manitoba History*, no. 31 (Spring 1996), http://www.mhs.mb.ca/docs/mb_history/31/roadsofremembrance.shtml.

Harris, R. Cole, and Elizabeth Phillips, eds. *Letters from Windermere, 1912–1914*. Vancouver: UBC Press, 1984.

Klippenstein, Frieda Esau, "The Challenge of James Douglas and Carrier Chief Kwah." In Jennifer S.H. Brown, and Elizabeth Vibert, eds., *Reading Beyond Words: Contexts for Native History*, Second Edition. Peterborough, ON: Broadview Press, 2003: 163–92.

Lothian, W.F. *A Brief History of Canada's National Parks*. Ottawa: Parks Canada, 1987.

Reimer, Chad. *Writing British Columbia History, 1784–1958*. Vancouver: UBC Press, 2009.

Weir, Winnifred A. "Robert Randolph Bruce, 1861–1942." *B.C. Historical News* (Summer 1997): 8–10.

GREAT DEPRESSION

Bradley, Ben. "'A Questionable Basis for Establishing a Major Park': Politics, Roads, and the Failure of a National Park in British Columbia's Big Bend Country." In Claire Elizabeth Campbell, ed., *A Century of Parks Canada, 1911–2011*. Calgary: University of Calgary Press, 2011, 79–102.

Brown, Atholl Sutherland. *Buster: A Canadian Patriot and Imperialist—The Life and Times of Brigadier James Sutherland Brown*. Victoria: Trafford Publishing, 2004.

Mackie, Richard. "For Empire and Industry: Eric Hamber and British Columbia." Biography submitted to The Hamber Foundation, Vancouver, BC, March 1987. Manuscript filed with Hamber family papers at the City of Vancouver Archives.

Minnekhada Park Association. *The History of Minnekhada Farm*. 2005, 9. http://www.minnekhada.ca/documents/Minnekhada%20history.pdf.

Schreiner, John. *The Refiners: A Century of BC Sugar*. Vancouver: Douglas & McIntyre, 1989.

LIEUTENANT GOVERNORS AND THE SECOND WORLD WAR

Bothwell, Robert, and William Kilbourn. *C.D. Howe: A Biography*. Toronto: McClelland and Stewart, 1979.

Harker, Douglas E. *The Woodwards: The Story of a Distinguished British Columbia Family, 1850–1975*. Vancouver: Mitchell Press Limited, 1976.

Roy, Patricia E. *Triumph of Citizenship: The Japanese and Chinese in Canada, 1941–1967*. Vancouver: UBC Press, 2007.

LIEUTENANT GOVERNORS IN POSTWAR BRITISH COLUMBIA (1946–60)

"Former B.C. Lieutenant-Governor Leaves $1 Million to University." *Ubyssey*, 1 December 1961, 1.

Gwynn-Jones, Terry. "New Guinea's Great Aerial Gold Rush." *Air and Space Magazine*, August–September, vol. 1, issue 3 (1986), 100.

Healy, A.M. *Bulolo: A History of the Development of the Bulolo Region, New Guinea*. Canberra: New Guinea Research Unit, The Australian National University, 1967.

Idriess, Ion L. *Gold-Dust and Ashes: The Romantic Story of the New Guinea Goldfields*. Sydney and London: Angus and Robertson Ltd., 1945.

Kennedy, Dorothy Sinclair. "Phyllis Ross, L.L.D., C.B.E., O.C." *British Columbia Historical News*, vol. 21, no. 4 (Fall 1988): 19.

Litt, Paul. *Elusive Destiny: The Political Vocation of John Napier Turner*. Vancouver: UBC Press, 2011.

Mansbridge, Francis. *Launching History: The Saga of Burrard Dry Dock*. Madeira Park: Harbour Publishing, 2002.

Mitchell, David J. *W.A.C.: Bennett and the Rise of British Columbia*. Vancouver: Douglas & McIntyre, 1983.

"Phyllis Gregory Ross (1903–1988)." Senate Tributes, http://www.library.ubc.ca/archives/tributes/tribr.html.

Reimers, Mia. "BC at its Most Sparkling, Colourful Best": Post-war Province Building through Centennial Celebrations." PhD dissertation, University of Victoria, 2007.

Willetts, Claudia. "Princess Margaret Celebrates British Columbia's Centenary, 1958." Canadian Royal Heritage Trust. http://crht.ca/princess-margaret-celebrates-british-columbias-centenary-1958/.

Woolliams, Nina G. *Cattle Ranch: The Story of the Douglas Lake Cattle Company*. Vancouver: Douglas & McIntyre, 1979.

ADAPTING TO SOCIAL AND POLITICAL CHANGES (1960–88)

"Brigadier 'Budge' Bell-Irving." *The Telegraph* (London), 23 October 2002.

Dufour, Pat. "Brisking with the Rogers." *Times Colonist*, 19–20 August 1984, C1.

Eagle, Raymond. *In the Service of the Crown: The Story of Budge and Nancy Bell-Irving*. Ottawa: The Golden Dog Press, 1998.

Elizabeth Jane Rogers obituary, *Times Colonist*, 28 June 2011.

Gutstein, Donald. *Vancouver Ltd*. Toronto: J. Lorimer, 1975.

Hogrefe, Gunter. "End of an Era—Ocean Falls: 1971 to 1980." Chapter 12 in Bruce Ramsey, *Rain People: The Story of Ocean Falls*. Second Ed. Kamloops, BC: Wells Gray Tours Ltd., 1997.

Hunter, Justine. "Widow of B.C.'s 20th Lieutenant-Governor dies at 93." The *Vancouver Sun*, 30 August 1995, B5.

Litwin, Grania. "Flower Ladies Keep House in Bloom." *Times Colonist*, 9 December 2004: B5.

Nicholson, John Robert. Transcript of Tape. British Columbia Legal History Project. Interviewers: Bruce Robertson with Maryla Waters, 1979. University of Victoria Law Library.

Owen, Walter S. Transcript of Tape. British Columbia Legal History Project. Interviewers: Judge Alfred Watts and Maryla Waters, 1978. University of Victoria Law Library.

Robert Gordon Rogers obituary. *Times Colonist*, 27 May 2010.

Roy, Reginald H. *For Most Conspicuous Bravery: A Biography of Major-General George R. Pearkes, V.C., through Two World Wars*. UBC Press, Vancouver, 1977.

———. Interviews with Robert Gordon Rogers in 1984–85. Government House Archives transcripts.

Scrapbook of Walter Stewart Owen's term as Lieutenant Governor of B.C., 1973–1978. Walter Owen fonds, Law Society of British Columbia Legal Archives, Vancouver, BC.

Tidridge, Nathan. *Canada's Constitutional Monarchy*. Toronto: Dundurn Press, 2011.

Zuehlke, Mark. *On to Victory: The Canadian Liberation of the Netherlands, March 23–May 5, 1945*. Vancouver: Douglas & McIntyre, 2010.

DIVERSE IDENTITIES AND PRIORITY PROJECTS (1988–2018)

Barrett, Dave, and William Miller. *Barrett: A Passionate Political Life*. Vancouver: Douglas & McIntyre, 1995.

Bolton, Rena Point, and Richard Daly. *Xweliqwiya: The Life of a Stó:lo Matriarch*. Vancouver: UBC Press, 2013.

Campbell, Robert A. *Demon Rum or Easy Money: Government Control of Liquor in British Columbia from Prohibition to Privatization*. Ottawa: Carleton University Press, 1991.

"Cattle Breeder Led by Example." *Merritt Herald*, Merritt, BC, 26 November 2010, 10.

Charman, Eric. Memorandum, 12 June 2016.

Clayton, Jenny. Interview with David Lam's daughter Doreen Lau, 23 April 2015.

———. Interview with former Private Secretary Herbert LeRoy, Victoria, BC, 30 June 2015.

———. Interview with former Private Secretary Michael Roberts, Victoria, BC, 5 March 2015.

———. Interview with Helen Gardom, Vancouver, BC, 23 April 2015.

———. Interview with Iona Campagnolo, Comox, BC, 18 April 2015.

———. Interview with Judith Guichon at Government House, Victoria, BC, 9 December 2015.

———. Interview with Steven Point, Abbotsford, BC, 11 September 2015.

Cowan, Robert, and Joan Cowan. *Enderby: An Illustrated History*. Enderby, BC: Enderby and District Museum Society, 2005.

Cran, Gregory. *Negotiating Buck Naked: Doukhobors, Public Policy, and Conflict Resolution*. Vancouver: UBC Press, 2006.

Donnelly, Peter, and Bruce Kidd. "Two Solitudes: Grass-Roots Sport and High-Performance Sport in Canada." In Richard Baily, and Margaret Talbot, eds., *Elite Sport and Sport-For-All: Bridging the Two Cultures?* London: Routledge, 2015.

Fletcher, Tom. "Former Lt. Gov. Lam dies." *Parksville-Qualicum News*, 29 November 2010, 15.

Fowlie, Jonathan. "Lieutenant-Governor Steven Point is Driven by Literacy." *Vancouver Sun*, 25 September 2010.

Garde Gardom obituary. *Vancouver Sun*, 29 June 2013.

Glavin, Terry. "Point Taken." vanmag.com, September 2008, 28.

Hadley, C.J. "The Wild Life of Allan Savory." *Rangelands*, vol. 22, no. 1 (Feb 2000).

Hallsor, Bruce. "Crown Meets Test in Wake of British Columbia Election." *Canadian Monarchist News*, (Autumn 2017): 6–7.

Hume, Jim, and Nic Hume. "The Essential Iona . . ." *Times Colonist*, 17 June 2007, D1.

Jackson, Emily. "4-H Livestock Auction to Honour Former Lt.-Gov. Garde Gardom." *Vancouver Sun*, 22 August 2010.

Johnson, Joe. "Exit Interview: B.C. Lt.-Gov. Steven Point Speaks at the End of His Term." *The Ubyssey*, 7 November 2012.

"Lieutenant Governor Trials Sea Legs." *Lookout*, 9 June 2014, 11.

Litwin, Grania. "House Beautiful: A Serenely Regal Residence." *Times Colonist*, 3 July 2014.

Ludwig, Michaela. "Meet British Columbia's Dinosaurs." *British Columbia Magazine*, 3 July 2015.

Mandell, Louise, Q.C. "On the Front Cover: The Honourable Steven L. Point, OBC, Xwĕ lī qwĕl tĕl." *The Advocate*, vol. 66, part 3, May 2008: 335–42.

Meggs, Geoff, and Rod Mickleburgh. *The Art of the Impossible: Dave Barrett and the NPD in Power, 1972–1975*. Madeira Park, BC: Harbour Publishing, 2012, 23–24.

Patillo, Roger. *The Canadian Rockies: Pioneers, Legends and True Tales*. Victoria, BC: Trafford Publishing, 2005, 206.

Parry, Malcolm. "Town Talk: Garde Gardom's Warmth Will Be Missed." *Vancouver Sun*, 21 June 2013.

Plecas, Bob. *Bill Bennett: A Mandarin's View*. Vancouver: Douglas & McIntyre, 2006.

Roy, Patricia. "British Columbia." *Canadian Annual Review of Politics and Public Affairs* (1975).

Roy, Reginald. *David Lam: A Biography*. Vancouver: Douglas & McIntyre, 1996.

Ruenzel, Lydia. Interview with Steven Point, Museum of Anthropology, 4 March 2013.

Vogel, Richard. "On the Front Cover: Garde Basil Gardom." *The Advocate*, vol. 51, part 3, May 1993.

Walker, Susan. "In Victoria, the Rebirth of a Totem Pole." *Canadian Art*, 28 September 2012.

Woo, Andrea. "Judith Guichon, the Lieutenant-Governor who decided BC's political fate." *The Globe and Mail*, 29 June 2017.

Acknowledgements

Funding for this book was provided by Government House, where Jerymy Brownridge, James Hammond, Chantelle Fortin and Thandi Williams provided essential support. The volunteer Archives Group—Caroline Duncan, Elaine Currie, Teresa Haggart, Carmel Linka, Robin Patterson and Catherine Spencer—have given me useful advice and assistance with sources.

Many thanks to individuals who have shared their insights and personal accounts by participating in interviews, including Judith Guichon, Steven Point, Iona Campagnolo, Helen Gardom, Karen MacDonald, Brione Gardom, Doreen Lau, Michael Roberts, Herbert LeRoy and Eric Charman.

Archivists, access specialists and librarians have assisted the research process at the BC Archives, the Law Society of British Columbia, the University of Victoria Library and Archives, the City of Vancouver Archives, the University of British Columbia Archives and the Greater Victoria Public Library.

Presentations by constitutional experts and historians at a conference hosted by the Honourable Judith Guichon in January 2016, "The Crown in the 21st Century", helped place this book in a broader context.

This book builds on the work of many fine historians who have written about individual Lieutenant Governors and the vice-regal office generally. Many thanks to scholars, friends and family for their advice, information and assistance, including Lorne Hammond, Richard Mackie, Mona Brash, Gillian Thompson, Jack Little, Nicholas May, Melissa Lem, Heather Dickinson, Amanda Bullen Densmore, Brandy Fedoruk, Stephanie Clayton, Ben Bradley, Chris Hanna, Delphine Castles and others. In particular, I am grateful to Gary Mitchell and Patricia Roy for valuable feedback on drafts of this book, to Betty Keller and Patricia Wolfe for their careful editing, and to Rebecca Pruitt MacKenney for supporting this book through to completion.

My parents, Margaret and Jim Clayton, have supported this project every step of the way. To my husband, Christian Lieb, thank you for encouraging me to write this book and for many stimulating discussions on the topic.

Index